DATE

ALSO AVAILABLE FROM
EATING FRESH PUBLICATIONS

Cooking Fresh from the Bay Area
The Bay Area's Best Recipes for Eating
Local, Organic Produce at Its Seasonal Best

Cooking Fresh from the Mid-Atlantic
Tantalizing Recipes, Celebrated Chefs and Conversations
on the Essential Nature of Small-scale Farming

the Grassfed gourmet cookbook

Healthy Cooking and Good Living with Pasture-Raised Foods

Shannon Hayes

FOREWORD BY BRUCE AIDELLS

EATING FRESH PUBLICATIONS

About EATING FRESH[SM]

Eating Fresh seeks to connect consumers to local agriculture and to demonstrate the taste, health, and community benefits of eating local, seasonal, organic food. Through regional cookbooks and by other means, Eating Fresh works to help build local food systems and to spark a national campaign for transforming the way we shop for, cook, and think about food.

EATING FRESH
PUBLICATIONS

16 Seminary Avenue • Hopewell, NJ 08525
609-466-1700 • www.eatingfresh.com

The Grassfed Gourmet

Published by Eating Fresh[SM] Publications
Copyright ©2004 by Shannon Hayes

Classic Pulled Pork reprinted with permission from *The Best Recipe: Grilling & Barbecue* book by the editors of *Cook's Illustrated* magazine. For a trial issue of Cook's call 800-526-8442. Selected articles, recipes, subscription information, and cook books are available online at www.cooksillustrated.com

Author photograph: Teri Currie
Inside photographs: Bob Hooper
Recipe editor: Gerry Gould
Copy editor: Teddy Diggs
All recipes in this book have been tested for home preparation.

Printed in the United States on recycled paper.

First Edition

ISBN: 0-9673670-2-6
Library of Congress Control Number: 2004109123

Distributed by Ten Speed Press • PO Box 7123, Berkeley, CA, 94710 • www.tenspeed.com

For my parents, Jim and Adele Hayes,
who brought me into this way of life.
Thank you for teaching, sharing, accepting,
and for being wonderful people.
I'm a lucky girl.

CONTENTS

Foreword by Bruce Aidells ix

Acknowledgments xi

Introduction: From Farmer to Foodie xiii

Chapter One: Grass-Fed 101 1

Chapter Two: Beef, Bison, Venison, and Veal 11

Chapter Three: Lamb and Goat 83

Chapter Four: Pork 133

Chapter Five: Poultry and Rabbits 171

Chapter Six: Dairy and Desserts 219

Chapter Seven: Finding and Working with Your Farmer 237

Rubs and Resources 253

Index 263

FOREWORD

Not only do I write cookbooks about meat and sausage-making, I am also an avid collector of cookbooks. I measure a successful first cookbook by its ability to provide me with new information that can make my cooking better or increase my knowledge on a subject. And if there are at least two recipes in the cookbook that I would make on more than one occasion, I consider the book a good investment.

Shannon Hayes's *The Grassfed Gourmet Cookbook* not only meets this criteria but has exceeded it. First, my knowledge of the benefits of pasture-raised meats has been expanded, and second, this book has way more than two recipes I plan to make again and again. The Moroccan Spiced Pork Loin with Pear-Raisin Chutney has already become a household favorite. And I don't need any excuses, like warm sunny weather, to get out my grill to make Armenian Lamb Shish Kabobs or the Classic Pulled Pork with Homemade Barbecue Sauce. Finally, even a warm day won't stop me from braising up a pot of Garlic-Tomato Short Ribs.

But *The Grassfed Gourmet Cookbook* is not just about the recipes; it's about the advantages and attributes of eating foods from animals raised on pasture. For me, there are several criteria by which I rank the eating experience. First is taste. No matter how good a food is for my health or well-being, I'm not going to eat it more than once if it doesn't deliver good taste. I have found that animals that have been raised in conditions and environments reflecting their natural habitat and that have been allowed to grow and mature as they do in nature provide meats that taste good and are pleasing to eat. Added to this is my second criterion: the meat I'm eating should be healthier both for me and for the animal. In the case of grass-fed animals, this means that the animal was raised on pasture and not in an artificial or forced environment.

That said, the cooking methods used for pasture-raised meats differ from those used for mass-produced meats. Tender cuts of grass-fed beef or game are often quite lean and therefore must be cooked gently. Other cuts, such as steaks and chops, cook more quickly, and their cooking times need to be adjusted accordingly. In The Grassfed Gourmet Cookbook Shannon Hayes provides a wealth of information to guide you through this process and to ensure that these healthier meats taste their best.

I'm a person who wants choice, and I often find that foods produced on a large scale limit those choices. Producing food for the mass market often requires using mass feeding strategies and choosing only those animal breeds that are best suited for high volume. Unfortunately, the animals chosen for mass production are not often the ones that produce the best-tasting meat. Once you enter the world of grass-fed meats, you'll find farmers who understand that the diversity and variety found in many of the nearly forgotten heritage breeds lead to better flavor and quality.

Those of us who care more about the quality and flavor of meat are generally willing to pay the extra cost for animals raised on small farms by knowledgeable farmers who employ environmentally sound and humane practices. Raising heritage breeds costs more, which is likely what caused them to lose favor in the mass market. Fortunately, however, as long as we consumers are willing to support the reintroduction of heritage breeds and the rearing of animals on pasture, not only will the small-scale farms that produce these animals survive, but other farms may enter the field as well.

I can assure you that the more you know about pasture-raised foods, the more you'll want to make them a part of your life. *The Grassfed Gourmet Cookbook* is a required companion for all of us who wish to enjoy these foods and support a better way of farming and eating.

Bruce Aidells
Oakland, California
September, 2004

ACKNOWLEDGMENTS

Bountiful acknowledgments are in order to every person who made this book possible. I've had a wonderful time working on this project, especially because of the resounding support received from so many people.

First, thanks to Jim and Adele Hayes, my parents, who in addition to providing encouragement, generously supplied most of the meat for the testing. By including me in their business, they allowed me to learn firsthand about grass farming. I am especially thankful to them for the many hours they spent patiently answering my questions. They are tremendous assets to the sustainable agriculture community.

Thanks to all the farmers who contributed recipes to this endeavor. There are too many to name here, but they can be found in the back of the book. They have all been wonderful correspondents, making this a very enjoyable (and tasty) project.

Next, thanks to my recipe testers, who bravely came forward in a time of need and did fabulous work: Kelly Beers, Carol Clement and John Harrison (Heather Ridge Farm), Adele Hayes and Bob Hooper (Sap Bush Hollow Farm), Amy Kenyon (Skate Creek Farm), Cornelia McGiver, Judy Pangman (Sweet Tree Farm), Dawn Reis, and Jennifer Small (Flying Pigs Farm). I don't think all the money in the world could have hired a more competent and talented group of test chefs.

Special thanks to Tom, Clara, and Alexandra Clack, who, on learning of my distaste for "renal cuisine," took it upon themselves to perfect (and test, several times over) the perfect kidney recipe.

Thanks to Mary Ellen Driscoll, of *Fine Cooking* and Freebird Farm, who so patiently assisted me with meat tasting; and thanks to Denny Shaw, Cornell University's meat scientist, for spending so much lab time helping me to conduct experiments and answering my questions.

Thanks to all the farmers who welcomed Bob and me into their homes, who spent countless hours touring us about and allowing us to record their voices: Diane Roeder, of Sojourner Sheep; Alan Zuschlag, of Touchstone Farm; Forrest, Nancy, and Betsy Pritchard, of Smith Meadows; Melvin and Suvilla Fisher, of the Organic Grass Farm; Jim and Ginger Quick, of Honey Creek Farm; Kay and Steve Castner, of Kaehler's Mill Farm; Pam, Jim, Kate, Luke, Emerson, and Alta Millar, of Zu Zu's Petals; and Jen Small and Mike Yezzi, of Flying Pigs Farm. We left each home with a deeper respect for the land, a profound appreciation for the way these farmers live their lives, and best of all, new friendships.

Thanks to my friend Carl Krumhardt, who took such good care of us during our long farm-touring road trip. When we were most tired, he gave us soft pillows, home-cooked food, and a good night's rest… and an address where our replacement tent poles could be delivered! Carl inspired us with his amazing photographs, filling us with the energy and spirit we needed to continue.

Thanks to Bruce Aidells, the author of *The Complete Meat Cookbook,* for teaching me, through his writing, to cook meat masterfully and for taking the time to offer me guidance and insight as I pursued my own project. His work is a boon to the sustainable farming community, and many small farmers are grateful for all that Bruce does.

Thanks to Jo Robinson, the author of countless books, but most important *Why Grassfed Is Best*. If it weren't for Jo reaching out and offering her ideas and encouragement, none of this would ever have happened. Her writing and research have been an amazing help to grass farmers across the country, and we are indebted to her.

Finally, thanks to my dear, sweet, patient husband, Bob. He has been my premier recipe tester, my best source of encouragement, and a tireless editor and companion. Bob, no matter what I do in life, you make it all wonderful just by being there. I love you.

From Farmer to Foodie

It was a Monday evening in late fall, a time when all the best restaurants in central New York State are usually closed. Our farm, Sap Bush Hollow, along with several other regional organic, pasture-based farms—farms that choose to raise animals on grass rather than in feedlots—had been asked to donate products for a gala event being held that night. The area's best chefs were gathering at one of the swankiest restaurants in the capital city to prepare a dinner using ingredients grown and raised locally. After dinner, a panel of farmers and chefs was organized to discuss ways in which our professions could work more closely together in support of great food and great farming. The event was one of the first of its kind in the region. My parents, my husband, and I—all four of us farmers—were honored to be there and happy to have our food featured at a gourmet event.

As farmers, we live in a world connected to—*but decidedly apart from*—the culinary world, the world of celebrated chefs and four-star restaurants. This isn't to say I haven't been off the farm. I'm educated, I've traveled extensively, and I've eaten at my share of fine restaurants, but farming is a world of its own, tied more to the ebb and flow of nature than to the pulse of changing food trends. At the cocktail hour, after a few awkward attempts to engage in conversation with professional epicureans, my family and I gravitated toward the company of other farmers. In our corner, we swapped stories about the growing season, as well as notes about lambing percentages and tips on direct marketing. Soon, hungry and running low on conversation, my family and I edged toward the dining room. I'll never forget the moment when the double doors were finally opened. There we stood, like four Cinderellas, mesmerized by the opulent décor of the dining room, the endless trains of food carts, and the breathtaking presentation of the dishes.

I took my seat in front of a plate beautifully arranged with several different kinds of meat resting under vivid patterns of multicolored sauces. I have tremendous appreciation for the skills of talented chefs, particularly those who have mastered the art of pairing meats or fish with sauces. As a pasture-based farmer, however, I've learned that the flavors of grass-fed meats are unlike those of the corn- or grain-fed meats that are more common in American cuisine. In fact, those of us familiar with grass-fed meats have become accustomed to subtler seasonings, and we often prefer to forgo heavy sauces, which disguise the meat's distinct flavor. This evening in particular, I felt that the flavors and textures of the meats were inconsistent with the accompanying sauces. I wondered if the chefs had become so accustomed to the flavors and textures of grain- and corn-fed meats that they were unaware of the unique characteristics of meats from animals raised on pasture. This was the first of many surprises that evening.

My family's business is growing and raising food, but that night I learned that what goes on in the restaurant world is as foreign to me as what goes on in the banking business. Although partnering farmers and chefs at a dinner and discussion may sound like an invitation to a love-fest, what ensued more closely resembled divorce court. Soon into the farmer-chef panel discussion, it became clear that both groups felt misunderstood. The farmers complained that the chefs don't fully appreciate the quality of the food they grow and raise. The chefs complained that the farmers don't understand the indomitable forces of the consumer marketplace. According to the chefs, that marketplace would eat only chicken breasts and lamb loin chops. As a farmer, I'm keenly aware that there's a whole lot more of the animal attached to those parts. And I know I can't raise chicken breasts and lamb loin chops alone. I left that night depressed—and awakened to how separated the worlds of good farming and good food had become.

My family had begun raising animals on pasture years before, but that evening proved to be a critical moment in my food and farming education. In the weeks that followed, I came to understand that if my family was going to be direct-marketing clean, healthy, pasture-raised meats—and successfully differentiating ourselves from mass-produced, grain-fed, grocery-store meat—we needed to know about more than simply raising livestock. We needed to understand the art of cooking. And we needed to make sure that our customers had terrific experiences with the foods we sold.

So began a luscious journey that transformed me from an uninspired diner—one who ate only a minimal amount of meat in a half-hearted attempt to maintain some protein in my diet—to a hard-core carnivore. For a girl brought up around livestock, I knew surprisingly little about the packages we sold from our freezer. My education began with cookbooks and textbooks and charts depicting every conceivable cut of meat and where on the animal they came from. I learned about the extraordinary nutritional value of grass-raised animal products, and I learned about the unique flavors and textures that separate grass-fed meats from their conventionally raised counterparts. I wouldn't let customers walk out our door without first finding out what they planned to do with their purchases. Each morning, I'd walk to the freezer, close my eyes, and grab a package. No matter what the cut, I had to learn what to do with it by dinnertime.

Initially, my success rate was dismal. Then, slowly, I began to "get it." The change started with that first juicy steak, then the spectacular ham, and then the savory, slow-cooked spareribs. I became our farm's best customer. I was cooking meat nearly every night of the week.

Sound unhealthy? It shouldn't. Grass-fed meats are more nutritious than the conventionally raised meats you find in the grocery store (including organic meats that are not pasture-raised). They contain the proper ratio of omega-3 and omega-6 fatty acids. They're lower in fat and calories than conventional meats, and they're higher in conjugated linoleic acid (the cancer-fighting fat) and vitamins. Soon, I dropped a few pounds. Both my husband and I noticed that our hair and skin were looking healthier. We rarely got sick. Certainly it wasn't the meat alone. My interest in the benefits of pasture-raised foods had led me to a wide variety of locally grown and raised foods. I was shopping at farmers' markets and incorporating many more fresh fruits and vegetables into my diet. My lifestyle—as well as my relationship to food—was changing. And it wasn't just the health issues that were driving this change; it was the realization of how delicious these foods are and how simple it is to shop for and prepare them. Still, I do credit the grass-fed meats and dairy products with the dramatic changes in how I looked and how I felt.

I wasn't alone in my enthusiasm for grass-fed foods. Restaurateur and chef Alice Waters began talking about them. Writer Michael Pollan began discussing them. A feature article that appeared in the Atlantic Monthly in May 2003 effused that the search for grass-fed meat was "worth it." Inspired by evidence of the nutritional value of grass-fed meat, Jo Robinson, the author of When Your Body Gets the Blues, The Omega Diet, and Pasture Perfect, launched Eatwild.com, a Web site devoted to collecting and compiling information and research results on the benefits of pasture-raised foods (to date, Eatwild.com has had more than half a million visitors and now averages between 1,000 and 2,500 visitors a day). Finally, the infinitely pragmatic Tim Bowser, executive director of FoodRoutes Network, an organization that promotes local food systems, summarized the entire landscape of health, environmental, and social benefits of raising animals on pasture with the comment: "I don't believe in panaceas, but grass-based farming comes pretty close."

It has been seven years since that dinner, and relationships between farmers and chefs have changed, ushering in a new generation of professionals who are rediscovering their roots and who, like their grandparents and the master chefs of history alike, are making the connection between great food and great farming. Famous chefs are televised at farmers' markets, racing from stall to stall, smelling and tasting, and celebrating fresh ingredients and locally grown and raised foods. The number of farmers' markets is growing at record rates, as are memberships in community supported agriculture (CSA) farms. Consumers are beginning to see farmers for who they are: skilled professionals whose hard work in the fields, dedication to the business, and commitment to stewarding the land are making the case that small-scale agriculture isn't only a culinary boon but also a social and economic imperative. Together, farmers and chefs are showing us the joys—and yes, the simplicity—of eating with the seasons and of choosing organic and locally grown and raised foods.

More recently, chefs and home cooks across the United States are working with grass-fed and pasture-raised meats and dairy products. Those of us who love to cook, who are watching our weight, who care about animal welfare and the environment, or who are dealing with health issues are taking seriously the practical reasons for choosing grass-fed meats and dairy. And to the delight of small family farmers everywhere, with some help—and a healthy dose of courage—we're beginning to move beyond chicken breasts and lamb loins; we're learning to prepare and enjoy cuts of meat that our grandparents and great-grandparents regularly ate, including shoulder chops, shanks, and chuck roasts.

My journey was not the making of a career epicurean. I didn't set out to become a gourmet cook. I'm just a local farm girl who loves a good hunk of meat—admittedly, and quite possibly, to the point of obsession. Today, I think and dream about meat. I fantasize about fresh hams and cracklings and Italian sausages. I've been known to wax poetic about herb-roasted chickens and crispy goose skin and pot roasts and shish kabobs and pan-seared steaks. In recent years, our product line at Sap Bush Hollow has expanded to include grass-fed beef, pork, geese, turkeys, lamb, and chickens. Given the opportunity, I will sing the praises of all of them.

This book is a tribute to those mouth-watering cuts of meat from animals that have roamed and grazed on lush green grass. Grass-fed meats and dairy products are different from—and infinitely better than—the conventionally raised foods found in grocery stores. In the coming pages I'll describe the true differences between grass-fed and conventionally raised foods, and I'll explain how they affect cooking and preparation techniques. I'll provide simple approaches for preparing foods that require very little in terms of flavor additives and sauces. Within these pages, you'll find many of my favorite recipes, as well as those from grass-based farmers from across the United States and Canada.

It may be a while before you find grass-fed meats in your local grocery store (you may, however, have an easier time finding grass-fed dairy products in stores). Entering the world of grass-fed meats and other farm-fresh foods requires a new kind of shopping. Often, it means coming to know the farmer personally, whether at your local farmers' market, at a roadside stand, or on his or her back porch. This can be intimidating at first, but the result is well worth the effort. Many of us have grown accustomed to conducting business without hearing another person's voice or looking someone in the eye. This book deals with that problem head-on. You'll learn about the culture of livestock farming. You'll learn how to evaluate a farm, whether you're standing on the soil or talking with the producer on the phone. You'll learn how to be a welcome customer and how to get the most out of your visit to a farm. Most important, you'll discover how truly rewarding it is to connect with your community and your region through farming.

You'll also learn that sometimes, purchasing grass-fed meat requires a different sort of buying arrangement. Although many farmers sell retail cuts, which means that you can buy a pound of hamburger or two steaks (just as you would at the grocery store), other farmers require that you buy animals as wholes, halves, or quarters. You may never have purchased an animal in this way, but soon you'll know how to use the different cuts of meat, and you'll welcome the impact your new buying habits have on your menus, your meals, and your budget. And without fail, the meat recipes in this book are designed to help you cook just about every cut imaginable.

Not everyone lives in a community surrounded by green pastures and grazing livestock or even with a nearby farmers' market. If this is you, this book will help you find grass-fed meat, either by way of the directory of farmers or by way of the many listed Web sites that contain comprehensive databases of producers of grass-fed meats and dairy products.

I have selected and arranged recipes to suit a variety of needs and tastes. Some are geared toward harried families looking for nutritious meals that can be prepared on a tight schedule. Others are geared toward budget-conscious cooks who are committed to healthy cooking. Others are what I call showcase recipes—real showstoppers that could mean a sudden surge in your popularity as friends vie for dinner invitations. Some require only minimum preparation time. Finally, still others are likely to please kids.

One of the greatest joys of cooking and serving grass-fed meats and dairy products is knowing that they come from farmers who have made conscious choices about stewarding the land in environmentally responsible ways, raising livestock in a humane fashion, and living their own lives in accordance with their values. Here, you'll meet many of those farmers and have access to their favorite recipes. It's my hope that as you read their stories and savor their favorite dishes, you'll come to realize the magnitude of your decision to support them and their colleagues by making grass-fed meats and dairy products your first choice.

CHAPTER ONE

GRASS-FED 101

Congratulations! If you've picked up this book, you're about to enter a world of culinary splendor. Grass-fed meats and dairy products not only are a healthful source of protein but also are, in my opinion, the most delicious source.

For most of us, the idea of grass-fed meats and dairy products is intuitive. After all, when we picture healthy livestock, where do we see them? Out grazing in emerald-green fields, of course. When we read to our children their first books about farm animals, the sheep are pictured playing with lambs on flower-covered hillsides. Baby calves are running with their mothers in meadows. The animals are not shown standing in a feedlot, ankle-deep in excrement, and feeding on a grain-based diet laced with chemicals, antibiotics, and hormones. The bad news is that factory-produced livestock are now a major source of food in this country. The good news is that it doesn't have to be this way. We can feed our families food that comes from animals that do indeed graze in lush, green pastures and that enjoy humane treatment throughout their lives.

Animals raised on pasture eat what they are naturally inclined to eat in the wild. Wild herbivores never stand in the same spot; they continually move on to fresh grass. Today, farmers can manage pastures, keeping fields in a continual state of growth. Pasture-raised animals stay on a given section of pasture for only a brief period of time—usually anywhere from one to four days—and are then moved to fresh, green forage. There are, of course, exceptions. Omnivorous livestock, such as pigs and chickens, can't live on grass alone: they need to have their diets supplemented with grain. Grain and hay also serve to carry livestock through droughts and winter months, although even in those cases, supplemental feed is used sparingly. By comparison, although cows and beef stock that end up in large-scale factory farms may begin their lives eating grass at pasture, once they're old enough for production they are confined to cramped stockyards, paddocks, climate-controlled "factories," or feedlots for the remainder of their lives and are fed a diet made up primarily of grain and supplements.

So, how do you know how your food was raised and what the animal was fed? Deciphering the myriad labels that appear on meats and dairy products is a challenge. With labels such as *organic, range-fed, free-range, all natural,* and *grass-fed,* the health-conscious consumer can easily feel defeated or confused. The following information should help unravel the mysteries of today's labeling system as it applies to meat:

- *Free range.* The *free-range* label may—but may not necessarily—indicate that the animal was put outside or in a barnyard sometime during its lifetime. However, this label does not guarantee that the animal was raised on a diet of grass in a carefully managed pasture.

- *Natural.* According to the U.S. Food Safety and Inspection Service, the label *natural* can be applied to any product that does not contain "artificial ingredients, coloring ingredients, or chemical preservatives; and the product and its ingredients are not more than minimally processed." In other words, minimally processed foods, such as fresh meat and poultry, automatically qualify to be labeled *natural,* regardless of what the animals were fed or whether or not they were treated with antibiotics or hormones.

- *Organic.* The *organic* label is an assurance that the meat you're buying was raised without the use of synthetic products and that the livestock feeds were not sprayed with synthetic pesticides or fertilizers. It also means that the animals were not treated with unnecessary antibiotics, hormones, or genetically modified organisms of any kind. Be aware, however, that even though organic standards, at the time of writing, do contain some pasture requirements, this is not a guarantee that the meat came from livestock with a predominantly pasture-based, all-natural diet. Hence, there is no assurance that organic meats will have the same nutritional benefits as grass-fed meats. Although some organic producers may opt to raise their livestock on grass, animals can subsist primarily on a grain-based diet (so long as the grains are also organic) and still earn the federal organic label.

- *Grass-fed.* If you want the benefits of grass-raised meats, then look for information indicating that the livestock were raised in this fashion. Key words might be *grass-raised, pastured, range-fed, Argentine style,* or *New Zealand style.* Talk to shop owners to find out what they know about the growers, or better yet, take the time to find growers in your area and visit them personally. The surest way to guarantee that your meat comes from animals raised in the healthiest manner possible is to see them grazing on lush green pastures. In addition to recipes, the chapters in this book contain information on how to find a farmer in your area, tips for ensuring that the farmer is raising the livestock properly, and a directory of grass-based farm listings.

What are the advantages of eating meat from animals raised on grass? Take your pick. Grass-fed meats come with a rich assortment of health, environmental, social, and economic benefits:

- *Health benefits.* Jo Robinson, in her landmark book *Why Grassfed Is Best!,* uncovers the growing body of research supporting the notable health benefits of grass-fed meats. In addition to being lower in fat and calories than grain-fed meats, grass-fed meats are rich in "good fats"—notably, omega-3 fatty acids, which are linked to blood pressure reduction, healthy brain function, and the slowed growth of many types of cancer. In addition, grass-fed meats and dairy products are a rich source of conjugated linoleic acids, or CLAs, another "good fat," which, according to Robinson, "may be one of our most potent defenses against cancer." Beyond that, these meats are known to contain antioxidant vitamins and are much less likely to carry the virulent strain of *E. coli* 0157:H7. A 1998 study in *Science* magazine reported an *E. coli* count of 6,300,000 cells per gram of meat in grain-fed animals versus 20,000 cells per gram in grass-fed meat.[1] Furthermore, there is reason to believe that the *E. coli* found in grass-fed meat is much less likely to survive our first line of defense—our stomach acids. Although *E. coli* is typically unable to survive ruminant stomach acids, a cow whose diet is unnaturally high in grains generally has a higher level of acidity in its digestive tract. Thus, any *E. coli* that develops easily acclimates to the acid environment and can therefore survive human stomach acids. The very few *E. coli* cells found in grass-fed cattle have not become acclimated to an acid environment and so are less likely to survive in our own systems.[2]

- *Environmental benefits.* The pasturing of animals encourages biodiversity, improves soil fertility, and eliminates the waste-management problems associated with confinement-feeding operations. Feeding animals on grass reduces greenhouse gases in the air due to a process called carbon sequestration, wherein the grasses and legumes found in well-managed pastures are able to draw excess carbon dioxide from the air and return it to the soil as carbon. Most important, buying pasture-raised products from a farmer in your area helps keep the farm in business. The more commercially viable your local and regional farms are, the more likely it is that they will continue as farms and that the land will not be turned into housing subdivisions, shopping malls, and parking lots. If you live in an area that is rapidly losing open space, consider that there are few better uses of wide-open spaces than small-scale family farms. They enhance the landscape, provide a local food source, and make good use of the land they occupy.

- *Social benefits.* Purchasing grass-fed meats and dairy products has a dramatic impact on animal as well as human welfare. Animals raised on lush, green pasture experience significantly less stress over the course of their lives than their factory-raised counterparts. They're not overcrowded, they're able to get exercise, and they can act on their natural instincts—moving to shade in the heat of the day, eating when they're hungry, or even playing with each other. Because pastured animals frequently move to new grass, they enjoy clean and spacious environments and are less likely than are confined animals to become ill or to contract an array of diseases. In addition, farmers working on grass-based operations enjoy a healthier work environment than those who work on large-scale factory farms. They are less likely to suffer from respiratory problems resulting from the dust, ammonia, and dangerously high levels of carbon dioxide so common in confinement facilities.[3]

- *Economic benefits.* Although grass-based farms are more labor-intensive, farm inputs, such as fossil fuels, are kept to a minimum, thus significantly reducing farmers' expenses. Furthermore, farmers are able to get a fair price for their product when they sell to informed, socially responsible consumers who are willing to pay the true cost of their food rather than relying on artificial price supports for the grain used to produce conventionally raised meat. This means that farm families can enjoy a fair return for their labor. Small-scale family farms—such as many pasture-based farms—that are locally owned and operated contribute in numerous ways to a community. They hire local workers, contract with local service providers, purchase local goods, and participate in local activities. Unlike most other types of businesses, farms are unlikely to pull up roots and move somewhere else. They are invested in the community.

Your decision to purchase grass-fed foods is an important one. The production of grass-fed meats and dairy products helps heal our environment, it ensures the welfare of the livestock, and it enables farmers to realize better working conditions and a fair income. And grass-fed meats are healthier. But the benefits don't stop there. Grass-fed meats and dairy products taste better than their conventionally raised counterparts. Grass-fed pork and lamb have a particularly rich and savory flavor. Grass-fed beef tends to be lean and juicy, with a rich, robust flavor. Pasture-raised chickens have a firm texture and the type of flavor that older generations remember from their youth. Once you've experienced these superior foods, you'll never want to purchase conventionally raised meat or dairy products again.

So now that you know why pasture-raised meats are a better choice, you'll need to learn a few things about cooking them. Grass-fed meats cannot always be prepared in the same way as conventionally raised meats. They're lower in fat and more flavorful. Cooked improperly, grass-fed meats can be tough. Overseasoned, grass-fed meats can lose their unique taste. But don't worry: you don't need to be a four-star—or even a three-star—chef to enjoy the benefits of pasture-raised foods. You simply need to learn a few basic cooking principles. The recipes in this book will guide you through the process of preparing and cooking grass-fed meats. Once you understand the basic principles, you can adapt any of your favorite recipes to accommodate whatever grass-fed meats you buy.

There are four basic principles for cooking grass-fed meats:

1. Put away your timer, get a good meat thermometer, and be prepared to use it.

2. Turn down the heat.

3. Learn when to use dry-heat cooking methods and when to use moist-heat methods.

4. Ease up on the seasonings and sauces.

1. *Put away your timer, get a good meat thermometer, and be prepared to use it.* Grass-fed meats are significantly lower in fat than the meats you're likely to find on grocery store shelves. Since fat works as an insulator, it changes the way your meat cooks. Lean roasts will cook in the oven faster than roasts that are higher in fat. Also, there is likely to be much more variation in the size and thickness of the cuts of grass-fed meats than you may be accustomed to. "Finished animals"—those that have properly filled out with fat and muscle and are ready to go to market—can vary tremendously in size. Some animals are finished at a low weight; some are larger. One rib-eye steak might weigh ten ounces, but the same cut from another animal could weigh six ounces. Reduced fat and variable size both mean that cooking times for the meat will vary. Although I have provided you with some estimated times for the recipes in this book, the only way to know that the meat is done to your liking is to use a high-quality meat thermometer.

   I'm fond of the digital thermometers found in most kitchen stores. These come with a slender probe attached by a wire to a digital readout that sits outside the oven. Before cooking the meat, place the probe deep into the cut, away from the bone and away from the bottom of the pan; do not take the probe out and reinsert it into several different places. Placing the probe properly and leaving it in place keeps the juices inside the meat, where they belong. It also means that you can leave the oven door closed while checking the temperature of the meat, thereby regulating the temperature of the oven and saving energy. The table on page 9 gives the ideal internal temperatures for the various meats.

2. *Turn down the heat*. I've said it several times now, and I will say it several more times throughout the book. In general, grass-fed meat is lower in insulating fat. If the heat is too high when grass-fed meat is cooked, the moisture and the fat will exit quickly, which will toughen the protein. Until you're thoroughly familiar with cooking grass-fed meats, it's best to set the flame a little lower when you're grilling or frying, and to set the oven temperature lower, than is customary.

3. *Learn when to use dry-heat cooking methods and when to use moist-heat methods*. This is a tip that works for *all* meats—both conventional and grass-fed. When cooking meat, there are two methods. The first is the dry-heat method. This is the process whereby fats and water are pulled from the meat, thus firming it up until it reaches the desired doneness. Dry-heat methods include pan-frying, broiling, roasting, barbecuing, grilling, stir-frying, and sautéing. Dry-heat cooking methods are appropriate for tender cuts of meat—loin cuts, for example—those that come from the animal muscles that do the least work. When you press down on an uncooked lamb loin chop, it's soft and squishy. The job of the cooking process is to remove the water and fat until that lamb chop toughens just enough to make it firm but juicy. Doing so requires a dry-heat method.

Moist-heat methods are used for tougher cuts of meat and include braising, stewing, crock-pot cooking, and boiling. Tougher cuts typically come from the animal parts that do a lot of work, such as the shoulders. When muscles do a lot of work, they develop a connective tissue protein called collagen, which is what makes the meat tough. When a cut of meat contains collagen, your job as the chef is to break down the collagen, thus making the meat tender. When you press down on a corned beef brisket, it's tough. Boiling that meat breaks down the collagen, thereby tenderizing the meat.

Some cuts that work with moist-heat methods also work with a dry-heat method I call *super-slow roasting*. In this technique, tougher cuts of meat—such as shoulder chops of lamb and pork, beef chuck roasts, steaks, top rounds, and eye of rounds—are put in the oven at 170°F and allowed to roast for several hours. The resulting meat is extremely flavorful and juicy, because the juice does not escape at such a low temperature. A preliminary study I conducted with Denny Shaw, a Cornell University meat scientist, found that meats cooked using this method held their temperature much longer when they came out of the oven. This technique also reduces the likelihood that the meat will be overdone. Meats roasted several hours at very low temperatures will stay rosy and pink longer.

Most home cooks have not had the opportunity to work in a butcher shop and learn where each cut of meat comes from on the animal. To help you better understand different cuts of meat, each chapter of this book contains charts listing the most common cuts, followed by the appropriate cooking method. As you venture beyond the recipes here, keep the charts nearby to help guide you in preparing grass-fed meats.

4. *Ease up on the seasonings and sauces.* The most common mistake made by chefs and home cooks is not trusting that prime cuts of grass-fed meat have sufficient flavor to stand on their own. As a nation, we've become accustomed to the flavor and texture of conventionally raised, factory-farmed meats. We assume we need to give the meat flavor through the use of seasonings and sauces. This may be true of the meats sold in grocery stores or served at most restaurants. But animals raised on pasture produce meats that have a distinctive flavor. Grass-fed meats should be seasoned delicately so as not to mask or compromise their true flavor. Although cuts best suited for moist-heat cooking methods are stronger in flavor—and thereby better able to handle heavy seasonings—this isn't always the best way to enjoy prime cuts. When you first begin cooking grass-fed meats, try using simple herb rubs or just salt and pepper so that you can experience the true flavor of the meat; in other words, learn how the meats are *supposed* to taste. Once you become accustomed to the diverse range of flavors of grass-fed meats, you can venture into recipes involving seasonings and sauces. But again, I encourage you to first experience and appreciate the true flavors of these meats.

The remaining chapters in this book are organized into the following categories: beef, bison, venison, and veal; lamb and goat; pork; poultry and dairy. The introduction to each section contains some basic cooking principles and some suggestions for evaluating farms that grow the particular kind of meat; the recipes, many of which come from pasture-based farmers throughout North America, follow each section introduction. I have identified which recipes are good when cooking on a budget, which might work well for children, which are best when cooking in a hurry, which require minimum preparation time, and which are suitable for when you want to create an elegant, "showcase" feast.

So, go forth bravely into the exciting new world of grass-fed meats—and be sure to bring your appetite!

As you explore the world of grass-fed meat, you will discover that most farmers market their meats flash-frozen in butcher paper, plastic wrap, or Cryovac packages. Do not allow this meat to thaw until you are ready to cook it. The safest way to thaw frozen meat is to either (1) set the meat on a platter or in a bowl and place it in the refrigerator for two to four days (depending on the size of the cut) before you use it; or (2) wrap it in a plastic bag and submerse it in cold water. Although it is possible to thaw meat in a microwave, I strongly urge you to avoid this practice whenever possible. Typically, microwave-thawed meat will contain portions that are still frozen and portions that are fully cooked, making it impossible to prepare a dish that is cooked consistently throughout.

Ensuring that your dinner is safe to eat is easy, provided you follow a few simple practices. Do not prepare raw foods (such as the salad that you might be serving with your meal) on the same surfaces or with the same utensils that you use to prepare your meats. This will ensure that your raw foods will not be exposed to *E. coli* or other bacterial contaminants.

Also, always be sure to cook your meats properly. The best way to do this is to purchase a meat thermometer and follow the temperature recommendations provided below. Note that although I make certain temperature recommendations based on what I feel ensures maximum taste and juiciness, the USDA gives recommended temperatures that are significantly higher, taking extra precautions to ensure that any bacterial contaminants (and any lingering flavor, in my opinion) are killed. I feel that knowing the source of your meat and how it was produced (on grass, of course!) is the best way to ensure that it is free of contaminants, and so I am willing to take a few risks in order to enjoy a great steak. Whether you follow my internal temperature guidelines or the USDA's is entirely your decision.

Ground meat is much more likely to be a hazard if not fully cooked because *E. coli* contaminants lie on the outside surface of the muscle tissue. During the grinding process, external tissues are mixed with internal tissues, increasing the likelihood of *E. coli* contamination. This is why steaks and roasts may be eaten rare, but hamburger should always be cooked so that the center of the burger is no redder than light pink. The USDA recommends an internal temperature of 160°F for ground meat. However, if your hamburgers rest at 155°F for 15 seconds, or are held at 150°F for 1 minute, this will also kill any lingering bacteria. [4]

TABLE 1

RECOMMENDED INTERNAL TEMPERATURES FOR COOKED MEAT

The following table provides the ideal internal temperatures at which to remove the meat from the oven. Meat requires an additional resting period of about 5 to 10 minutes for chops and steaks and 15 to 30 minutes (depending on size) for roasts. During that time, the internal temperature of the meat will climb about 5 degrees for steaks and chops and 10 to 15 degrees for roasts.

Each type of meat comes with two recommendations. The first is the suggested range— the temperatures that true meat lovers are likely to use when cooking the meat. The second is the USDA-recommended temperature range, which I feel is too high to ensure maximum flavor and juiciness. But the ultimate decision on this matter lies with the cook.

MEAT	SUGGESTED INTERNAL TEMPERATURES	USDA RECOMMENDED INTERNAL TEMPERATURES
Beef, Bison, and Venison	120°–165°F	140°–170°F
Veal	125°–155°F	150°–170°F
Lamb and Goat	120°–145°F	140°–170°F
Pork	145°–165°F	170°F
Chicken	160°–165°F	180°F
Turkey (unstuffed)*	160°–165°F	180°F
Goose	170°F	180°F
Duck	160°–170°F	180°F
Rabbit	160°F	160°F

* If you cook the stuffing inside a turkey, the internal temperature of that stuffing must reach 165°F in order to be considered safe.

CHAPTER TWO

Beef, Bison, Venison, and Veal

Beef

Nowhere has the grass-fed movement caused greater ripples than in the beef industry. This is partly because beef holds favored status among meat lovers in the United States. But it is also because the beef industry represents some of the more monumental changes that have taken place in the nation's farming system in the past fifty years.

The dominant belief in this country is that the highest-quality beef is corn-fed beef. The truth, however, is that cows are meant to eat grass, not corn. For a steer to stay alive on corn, a ration must be blended to include various protein supplements, as well as a constant regimen of antibiotics. In a typical feedlot, a cow's diet is roughly 95 percent grain. A diet this high in grain results in a lower ph in the cow's rumen (the first chamber of the animal's stomach). The antibiotics are necessary primarily to prevent liver infections. This isn't the case with organic corn-fed beef. A diet for organic corn-fed cattle would include significantly less grain—no more than 60 percent of the overall diet—and the roughage would be at least 40 percent, thus reducing the likelihood of lowered ph in the rumen.

So how did we come to feed our beef cows a predominantly grain-based diet? The answer involves both public policy following World War II and public demand for cheap food. When the war ended, chemical companies, in need of new markets, focused their attention on U.S. agriculture. During this time, petrochemical fertilizers were widely adopted, and the country saw a surplus of corn. With the help of federal subsidies, corn could be sold to the beef industry for less than the cost to produce it. As a result, today's beef cattle typically spend the first half to two-thirds of their lives on pasture or rangeland, after which they're moved into massive, crowded feedlots. Here, their new grain-based diet is supplemented with antibiotics and growth hormones, causing them to fatten faster and cheaper than they would on grass. It's not unusual for calves to receive hormone implants when they're born, and often antibiotics are added to a mineral mix that is offered to calves while they're on pasture. As a result of these policies, subsidies, and farming practices, beef, which was once regarded as something of a luxury, is relatively inexpensive. In fact, most Americans today can afford to eat beef several times a week.

The fact that many people believe the "best" beef is corn-fed has a lot to do with good public relations. Today, most Americans have become accustomed to the flavor of grain-fed beef, which has more fat, a coarser texture, and a less-intense flavor. But most people born before World War II would probably find the flavor of grass-fed beef reminiscent of the meat they ate as children and young adults.

To better understand the flavor differences, I put together a small (and admittedly biased) tasting panel composed of Maryellen Driscoll, editor-at-large for *Fine Cooking* and also a farmer, my husband, and me. We prepared both conventional grain-fed and grass-fed pot roasts and New York strip steaks and set about sampling them. Since all of us normally eat grass-fed meat, we naturally preferred the taste of grass-fed to grain-fed. But there were some legitimately discernible differences, aside from simple flavor preferences.

In the pot roasts, the grass-fed chuck roast had much more striation, or "grain" in the muscling, compared to the store-bought roast. After five hours in the braising liquid, the grain-fed chuck was fatty but not juicy. In contrast, the grass-fed meat was exceptionally juicy but had very little fat. The grass-fed roast left a clean taste in the mouth, was aromatic, and absorbed the flavors of the cooking liquids. By comparison, the grain-fed meat carried none of the flavor of the braising sauce and left a fatty coating in the mouth. The grain-fed meat did not have a bad flavor per se; rather, in our estimation, it simply had no distinct flavor at all.

Our findings were similar for the steaks. We closed our eyes and sampled bites from each steak. We all agreed that although they were equally tender, the grass-fed steak had a more pronounced grain and the grain-fed was slightly pulpier. The biggest difference was in the flavor. With the grain-fed steaks, it was difficult to tell what type of meats we were tasting. Conversely, with the grass-fed meat, the beef flavor was immediately apparent. The natural flavors were much more assertive.

I conducted a second set of preliminary experiments with Cornell University's meat scientist Denny Shaw. We compared three conventionally raised, certified-Angus, wet-aged, top-round roasts with three Angus-cross dry-aged grass-fed top-round roasts. Again, the grass-fed beef won out. Subjectively, we found the grass-fed beef to be juicier and more tender than its conventionally raised counterpart. It also had a genuinely beefier flavor. Then, for an objective analysis, we pulled several core samples from each of the roasts and took a tenderness measurement on a Warner/Bratzler scale (the industry standard). Half of the roasts were cooked using a standard dry-heat roast at 310°F, and half were cooked using the super-slow and low method at 180°F. In each of these methods, the grass-fed meat received the more favorable, tenderness scores. The average score for the grain-fed beef was 6.27, and the average score for the grass-fed beef was 5.20. When performing a Warner/Bratzler test, the lower the score, the more tender the meat.

Despite these highly favorable reviews, epicureans across the country are not necessarily in agreement. Although many do agree that grass-fed beef has a cleaner taste and doesn't coat the mouth, it's still subject to criticism. An article in the *New York Times* summed up the sentiments of most grass-fed critics by noting that in spite of the environmental and health benefits, grass-fed meat in general "is wildly inconsistent, often tough and stringy, with an off taste."[1]

Whereas factory-farming conditions make it easy to produce consistent grain-fed meat, there are tremendous variations in the grass-fed industry—particularly in the grass-fed beef industry. This is due partly to the diversity of beef production. The flavor of grass-fed beef will vary based on the breed of cow, the region where it was raised, and the age at which it was harvested. If we're going to move out of the industrial agricultural paradigm, then we should welcome these variations in flavor. However, although there might be variation in *flavor,* there are three ways that pasture farmers can control for the *quality* of the beef. As a consumer, you should understand these quality-control factors to help you choose a farm from which to buy grass-fed beef.

FACTORS FOR CONTROLLING BEEF QUALITY

There are three elements to consider when choosing a farm to provide pastured beef: (1) genetics, (2) grass quality, and (3) the harvest process. Even if you don't hold a Ph.D. in animal science, it's relatively easy to determine if a farmer is taking these factors into account.

HOW CAN I KNOW IF MY GROUND BEEF IS SAFE TO EAT?

On July 19, 2002, at the height of barbecue season, the USDA announced a recall of 19 million pounds of ground beef that may have been contaminated with the *E. coli* pathogen. Contaminated meat caused twenty-eight people in seven states to fall ill. Seven people were hospitalized. This was the second-largest meat recall in history, behind the 25 million pounds recalled in 1997.

Food-borne illness is a serious concern in this country. The National Center for Disease Control estimates that annually, four thousand Americans die and five million suffer from illness as a result of eating contaminated meat and poultry. In 1993, the new and highly virulent *E. coli* strain 0157:H7 was discovered after an outbreak at the Jack in the Box restaurant chain, resulting in hundreds of illnesses and four deaths.

Historically, our stomach acids destroyed *E. coli*, a common bacterial contaminant. However, this new strain, 0157:H7, has proven resistant to these acids. Many believe that this new, more virulent strain developed in feedlots where conventionally raised cattle are sent before slaughter. In feedlots, where cattle diets are almost entirely grain, the pH of the cows' rumen (the first chamber in a cow's stomach) drops, becoming acidic. Scientists speculate that 0157:H7, which is resistant to the digestive acids in human stomachs, developed in the high-acid environment of the beef cows' rumen.

Ground beef is more likely to be contaminated than other cuts, because *E. coli* contamination lies on the exterior part of the muscle tissues. In steaks and roasts, this is the part of the meat that has direct contact with heat; thus, if the meat is cooked properly, any *E. coli* contamination will be killed immediately. When the meat is ground, those exterior parts of the muscle are mixed in with the interior parts. So whereas *E. coli* bacteria are found only on the outside portion of a steak, it can be mixed throughout a hamburger. If a burger is rare on the inside, there is a possibility that the *E. coli* bacteria were not killed during the cooking process.

How do you protect yourself? If you're eating grass-fed meat from a source you trust, you're taking the most important step. Animals finished on grass, animals whose rumens are thus not likely to be so acidic, are believed to be less likely to carry 0157:H7, the virulent strain of *E. coli*. Also, because small farmers have their meat processed in small batches (usually one beef animal is processed at a time), their meat is less likely to be contaminated by tainted meats from unknown sources. Still, grass-fed meats should be cooked properly: cook your burgers to an internal temperature of 160°F. Finally, be careful when working in the kitchen. Don't prepare foods that you plan to eat raw—such as tomatoes or salads—using the same utensils and cutting surfaces used for meats.

If you follow these simple precautions, chances are you'll be fine. So go ahead and enjoy that burger!

Sources: F. Diez-Gonzalez et al., "Grain-feeding and the Dissemination of Acid-resistant Escherichia Coli from Cattle," *Science* 281 (1998): 1666; J. B. Russell, F. Diez-Gonzalez, and G. N. Jarvis, "Potential Effect of Cattle Diets on the Transmission of Pathogenic Escherichia Coli to Humans," *Microbes Infect* 2, no. 1 (2000): 45–53.

Genetics

Although genetics may sound like a mysterious subject, the role of genetics in quality beef production is quite simple. Selective breeding has produced animals with a genetic make-up that enables more fat to get into the meat tissues earlier. The incorporation of fat into the meat tissues is called *marbling*. When an animal has adequate marbling in the meat, it's considered *finished,* which means that it's ready for harvest.

Grass-based farmers want beef stock that will marble quickly so that the animal can be completely finished on grass during the growing season. Supplementing an animal's diet with grain in order to finish it causes a reduction in the CLAs and omega-3s. The problem in today's modern beef industry is that most steers have been bred to have extremely large frames that fatten quickly on corn but that require a long time on grass before they're ready for harvest.

Therefore, many grass farmers prefer to work with smaller-framed animals, which are more likely to fill out properly during the growing season. This is why a number of the heritage breeds are so valuable to the grass-fed meat industry. Grass farmers are turning to older, less common breeds—such as Devons, Galloways, and Highlands—because they're more suited to finishing on grass than are the large-framed, conventionally popular Charolais, Simmental, or large-framed Angus (as opposed to the old-style, smaller-framed Angus).

Still, many grass farmers are able to produce quality beef without incurring the expense of heritage breed animals. There is a great deal of genetic variation among even the most common breeds, and a farmer with a good eye can find a small-framed Angus-cross calf without any trouble.

Even if the farmer does have large-framed cattle, this does not necessarily indicate that the meat quality will be poor. It simply means that the farmer must be patient and allow the animal the time it needs to be properly finished. Whereas feedlot cattle are often finished before they are two years old, grass-fed cattle may be processed as early as eighteen months or as old as four years. The variation in age is due to the variation in the types of cattle. Those with smaller frames will finish faster than those with larger frames. If your farmer makes sure that the animals are harvested properly and have access to good-quality grass, then the variation in age will not affect the quality of the meat. If an animal is older, there will be more collagen interactions in the muscles. Thus, when using moist-heat methods, the meat may require more cooking time than the recipe suggests. So if your pot roast is not tender after the recommended cooking time, simply cook it a little bit longer. It will be every bit as delicious.

How to know if your farmer is accounting for genetics:

- Ask farmers how they selected the cattle they're raising. The answer should include details on how well the animals finish on grass. If a farmer is raising a breed you've never heard of, try looking it up on the Breeds of Livestock Web site at the Oklahoma State University Department of Animal Science (http://www.ansi.okstate.edu/breeds). This site contains a comprehensive description of livestock breeds and will note if the type of cattle mentioned performs well on grass.

- Ask when the cattle will be ready for slaughter. A conscientious farmer will send cattle to slaughter when they have adequate finish. Thus, some animals will probably be ready sooner or later than others.

Grass Quality

Any farmer who has worked the ground for a long time can speak about changes the land has seen over the years: where old barns once stood, who grew what crops and where, how the farmhouse has changed, the shifting course and flow of the streams, and how the technology has evolved. Many will even tell you about the changing sound of their pastures. That's because one of the surest ways farmers can monitor the environmental health of their land is simply to "listen" to it. When a pasture is grazed properly, its sound will change over time. Farmers will often go out into their fields, sit quietly for a minute or two, and count the number of different bird songs, frog calls, and insect buzzes they hear. Healthy pastures support an increase in biodiversity—a wider variety of plant and wildlife species.

Good pasture management requires diligent stewardship. A farmer cannot simply open the barn gate and allow the animals to roam freely for the spring and summer. The impact on the soil and grass from grazing needs to be constantly monitored and the livestock need to be steadily moved through, allowing the pastures to rest and recover. This method of using many small pastures in rotation not only is easier on the ground but also typically maintains a crisscross of tree lines, brushy hedgerows, or even thick woodlots, all of which provide rich habitat for insects, the birds that eat them, and the mammals that in turn hunt the birds. And even though ground-nesting grassland birds, such as meadowlarks, bob-o-links, and savannah sparrows, *are* disturbed by passing herds, they fare far better when pastures are periodically grazed instead of mowed or trammeled to dust. Finally, since animals are kept moving to new grass, water is brought to them and they are rarely, if ever, allowed direct access to streams, ponds, or other sensitive water edges. On a more global scale, good pasture management makes environmental sense from the standpoint of reducing the use of fossil fuel; grazing ruminants (sheep, goats, and cattle) don't require grain to be processed and shipped, nutrient loads (animal waste) are naturally dispersed, and the farmer doesn't need to constantly run heavy machinery in order to manage the land.

Another grass consideration involves livestock weight gain. For the meat of beef animals to be tender, they must gain weight at a rate of one to two pounds per day before they're processed. (In feedlots, a typical gain is three pounds per day). If the rate of gain is less, the meat will be tough. Whereas feedlots can achieve rapid weight gain by feeding fattening corn to livestock, the grass farmer must make this happen with pastures alone. That means the cattle must be dining on grasses that not only are as delicious as possible but also contain the maximum amount of energy. Pastures must be grazed only when they are in their leafy, vegetative state. The grass should be about 6 to 10 inches tall when the animals are introduced to it. If the grass is higher than that, then it has probably gone to seed. Once this happens, the energy has gone into the lignin (the woodier plant tissue), and the cattle can no longer digest it efficiently. More important, the grass is significantly less palatable. When pastures are overgrown, the animals will eat only enough to survive—they will not eat to gain weight.

The other concern is when the grasses in a pasture are too short and the cattle are unable to get a good mouthful. In my father's words: "Cows are union workers. They will only graze eight hours a day." Thus, if the grass is easy to get—taller than six inches—then each time the livestock open their mouths, they're getting more food, and they will grow faster. If the grass is too short, they will again eat only enough to survive, and when the whistle blows at the end of the eighth hour, they will retreat to the shade for the remainder of the day.

How to know if your farmer is accounting for grass quality:

• Ask to see the pastures where the animals are grazing. If it's the first day the animals are on the field, the grasses should be between 6 and 10 inches. If they're shorter, it's possible that the farmer is getting ready to move the cattle to a new pasture (cattle should not be grazing on grasses less than 3 inches in height). The farmer will probably tell you this. If the grass is too tall, be aware that the rate of gain might not be appropriate to ensure tender meat.

The Harvest Process

I know of no grass farmers who entered into the vocation to earn a lot of money. Most of them work with livestock because they like animals. Thus, the harvest, or slaughter of the animals, is one of their greatest concerns. They've worked very hard to make sure their livestock have had a wonderful quality of life. When it's time for that life to end, the conscientious farmer wants the experience to be as calm and painless as possible. This is for the animal's benefit as well as the farmer's peace of mind. But it is also a way to make sure the meat is as tender and delicious as possible. Animals that are stressed at slaughter will secrete surplus adrenaline and lactic acid, causing the meat to be tough and to have an off-flavor. Pasture-based farmers take a number of precautions to keep this from happening:

- *Minimizing the distance to the slaughterhouse.* Pasture-based farmers try to work with slaughterhouses that are as close as possible to the farm to minimize travel stress. Unfortunately, with the demise of small, independent slaughterhouses across the country, it's not uncommon for farmers to have to truck their animals long distances.

- *Maintaining calm.* Animals are loaded onto the truck quietly in order to keep them calm. Some farmers actually keep a "lead cow" that's accustomed to traveling. She will board the truck first, and the others will follow her calmly. Other farmers will even go to such lengths as periodically loading the beef animals over the growing season so that they get used to the truck, or screening the truck drivers and refusing to work with anyone who has difficulty remaining calm and quiet during the loading process. Some farmers will have their animals trucked to the slaughter facility the night before so that the cattle will have time to calm down in their new surroundings. Others will try to schedule their livestock to be processed first thing in the morning, before there is any other activity.

- *Arranging for on-site slaughter.* If you're purchasing a whole animal, some farmers will actually arrange for a quick slaughter to take place right on the farm. Many would prefer that all slaughters happen this way, but there are a number of legal barriers.

- *Ensuring good slaughterhouse conditions.* Today's slaughterhouses have undergone tremendous changes to minimize the stress that animals endure during the harvest. Research has been done to determine the most comforting and calming mechanisms for moving livestock, the appropriate positions for the kill, and the best methods for ensuring that the animal is killed quickly and painlessly.

How to know if your farmer is making sure that the animal is harvested properly:

- Watch your farmer with the animals. If she or he is treating them well while they're living, the farmer is probably going to make sure they're properly cared for at the harvest.

- Ask about how the animals are killed. One of the problems of our modern food system is that consumers are out of touch with what happens to their food before they buy it at the grocery store. The death of an animal in order to sustain life is a natural process. Taking the time to express your concerns and asking questions about how the slaughter is handled helps guarantee that good practices are always utilized and that your meat is as tender and flavorful as possible.

ℬISON

Although this chapter includes bison, or buffalo, only one recipe is dedicated exclusively to this type of meat. This is because the recipes that you use for beef will work for bison, provided you remember a few caveats:

- Unlike beef, bison meat does not marble. And grass-fed bison is somewhat firmer and tighter than feedlot bison. Thus, when cooking roasts, make sure that you strictly adhere to the low-temperature rule. While some of the beef recipes mentioned in this book (such as the standing rib recipe) tell you to cook the meat at 300°F, never exceed 225°F when roasting bison.

- Bison meat is much darker in color than beef, but you can cook it to the same temperatures (after a resting period, the thermometer should read 120°F for rare, 125°F for medium rare, 135° to 140°F for medium, 145° to 150°F for well done). Because of the color, when you slice into it, you may think that it's more rare than you'd like. Until you become accustomed to the variation in color, trust your thermometer. Mary Graese, of Northstar Bison in Wisconsin, also reminds her customers that because there is no marbling in the meat, bison will cook even faster than grass-fed beef. So that instant-read thermometer will be all-important as you cook your bison.

- Finally, bison does not taste like beef. It's significantly richer, with a nutty finish and a full-bodied flavor. Consider cutting back on some of the seasonings mentioned in the recipes so that you can experience the unique taste.

Venison

The grass-fed beef recipes will work equally well with venison. The cooking temperatures are the same, but like bison, venison does not marble. Hence, when you roast the meat, do not exceed 225°F, and consider adding liquid to the pan or placing a bit of fat on the meat to add moisture (this technique is described in the Slow-Roasted Venison in Raisin Sauce recipe). If you're preparing tender cuts, such as loin or rib chops or a tenderloin, it's appropriate to use high temperatures. However, the meat will cook very quickly, so take care not to overcook it. Like bison, venison is also darker in color. Martha Goodsell, of Fallow Hollow Deer Farm in New York, describes the cooked meat as "kidney bean red."

The use of the term *venison* in this book refers to deer, elk, moose, or antelope (pronghorn). Those animals may have been shot in the wild, or they may have been farm-raised. Goodsell, who raises fallow deer on her farm, points out that the flavor will vary considerably between domesticated and wild venison. Venison shot in the wild will often have reached sexual maturity, whereas farm-raised venison will likely be harvested before this time. Also, Martha points out, their diets vary. Farm-raised venison, particularly the fallow deer she raises, are grazers, subsisting on grasses, whereas venison living in the wild are browsers, eating whatever they can find, including apples, pine needles, leaves, or acorns, as well as grass. All of these things will affect the flavor of the meat.

Suggested cutting instructions for venison are included in the last chapter, but because of the variability in size—due to whichever age and species you are working with—the instructions might require some adjustments when you're working with your farmer or processor.

Veal

Those people who gave up their beloved veal out of concerns for animals being raised in tight confinement can rejoice to know that grass-based farms offer a tasty alternative. Grass-fed veal calves lead a decidedly different life than conventionally raised veal calves. When they're born, grass-fed calves are moved out to pastures, where they dine on their mothers' milk and fresh pasture. The meat from these calves will be slightly pinker than the ghost-white meat of conventionally raised animals. It will also have significantly more flavor and texture.

Because the meat is so young and tender, feel free to use your favorite veal recipes. They'll work beautifully with grass-fed veal, although in some cases, when using moist-heat methods, you might need to cook the meat longer.

WHAT DO YOU MEAN MY MEAT IS AGED?

Although the idea that "fresh is best" might work for seafood and produce, meat, especially beef, needs to be aged in order to guarantee optimum flavor and tenderness. There are two methods of aging used in the beef industry today: wet-aging and dry-aging.

Dry-aging, or the process of storing the beef carcass in a humidity-controlled cooler just above 32°F for two to three weeks, used to be standard practice. However, this method was replaced in the 1960s by a process called *wet-aging,* in which fresh meat is immediately cut into primals— the first large sectional cuts that the carcass is divided into, such as the chuck, the ribs, the short loin, the sirloin, and the round—and then vacuum-packed in plastic bags. This technique quickly became the industry-preferred method, since it was more convenient and less expensive than dry-aging. With the switch to wet-aging, slaughterhouses no longer needed to store large, unwieldy beef carcasses, and there was significantly less shrinkage in the meat (in dry-aging, up to 10 percent of the carcass weight may be lost, reducing the profits on meat sales). The process was also less time-consuming.

An article in the *Journal of Food Science* cites several studies, conducted over the past forty years, that show dry-aged meat is more tender and flavorful.[1] Still, more than 90 percent of the nation's beef supply is wet-aged. In spite of this standard industry practice, many pastured-beef producers have taken extra pains to make sure that their meat is dry-aged, ensuring that the beef is as delicious and as tender as possible.

1. R. E. Campbell et al., "Dry Aging Effects on Palatability of Beef Longissimus Muscle," *Journal of Food Science* 66, no. 2 (2001): 196–99.

Listening to the Land

Honey Creek Farm, Jim and Ginger Quick, Green Lake, Wisconsin

A signature characteristic of the alternative farming movement has been a radical shift in farmers' relationships with the land. Following the World War II era, agriculture became synonymous with domination of land and nature. People were to control the landscapes, the animals, and even the climate. But the first lesson a sustainable farmer gleans is that the land should be allowed to speak for itself. The land partners with you in your livelihood; in order to be successful, you must learn to listen to the land.

If personalities could be attributed to the land, the acreage of Honey Creek Farm in Green Lake, Wisconsin, might best be described as wise. Honey Creek Farm has been home to Ginger Quick since her parents purchased it in 1948, when she was just an infant. Her father paid less than five thousand dollars for the property, and in turn, it provided him with a livelihood to raise his family. Ginger says that her dad, Ben, kept dairy cows and grew corn, hay, wheat, peas, sweet corn, and hogs. He worked through the Dust Bowl and was concerned, long ahead of his time, about the environmental damage that could result from farming. He was thus one of the first farmers in Green Lake to practice erosion control.

Ben was known throughout the community for his radical views, so it came as no surprise that when the dairy industry changed, he refused to change with it. Ginger explains: "I remember when the agricultural agents and the chemical companies started pushing the farms around here to get bigger. They kept saying: 'You've got to have a bulk tank. You've got to make your barn bigger. You've got to milk more cows. You've got to rent more land.' My dad didn't have a lot of faith in agricultural agents and chemical companies. He said, 'No, I'm not going into debt.' And he kept small."

When the milk companies refused to buy milk from farmers still using milk cans (as opposed to the new bulk tanks), Ben opted to retire rather than increase farm expenses. Ginger's husband, Jim, recalls how those changes in the dairy industry affected the rest of the farmers in Green Lake. "It used to be that twenty milking cows would support a family and pay for the children to go on to school. But today, a family can't live as well milking even 150 cows." Ben's decision to retire without expanding allowed him to live out his life happily on his land, leaving his family with no debt or burdens.

When Jim and Ginger took over the farm in 1982, they continued to farm as Ben had taught them; they raised row crops and hogs, and they finished steers on grain. But in the tradition of his father-in-law, Jim remained attuned to the fields he worked, particularly as he plowed them up each spring. "The smell of freshly turned soil is one of the sweetest things in life," he says, "but the thought of what I was destroying was equally disturbing. The plow would destroy the soil structure. It turns everything upside down. And then there would be imbalances in the nutrients, because the structure had been ruined." Jim wanted to change his farming practices, but he didn't know what to do next. "I felt that if I could leave the land to structure itself, then that was the way I should do it. I didn't like imposing my will on the land. I guess I like to consider the soil a living thing. It deserves our respect, just like the animals we raise."

Jim was concerned with more than just the soil of Honey Creek. He was unhappy with how his animals were marketed, which was often through a local sale barn, where they were usually purchased by a large meat packing corporation. "I had a real hard time selling any of my animals to go over the scale and down to a large meat packer for slaughter," Jim recalls. "At these huge plants, these animals come off the semis, and they never quit running until they're frozen in a package. And there's no recognition for the life that's being taken."

Jim found a solution to his concerns when he attended a grazing conference in the early 1990s and learned, much to his surprise, that people were raising and finishing livestock on pasture. "Ginger and I were products of the post–World War II agricultural boom. We thought if we were going to produce good-quality beef, it had to be corn-fattened. I didn't know that up until that war, almost all the beef in this country were grass-fed."

Thus, Honey Creek Farm and its stewards underwent another round of changes to safeguard the soils and to improve the quality of life for the livestock produced. Jim and Ginger sold their plow, moved the cows and steers out to pasture, got a flock of chickens, and began direct-marketing grass-fed meats. Ginger remembers the dramatic difference she and Jim saw in their land. "Over where the cornfields used to be, it would feel hard to walk over it by the end of the summer. And now, it's spongy. There's *life* under there. And it is such a beautiful thing."

Jim and Ginger still face a significant challenge with their new farm enterprise. Grazing has reduced their expenses, improved the land, and provided a better quality of life for their animals, but to keep their livestock from being trucked from three to five hundred miles to a large meat packer, they had to find a local, direct market. Jim recalls the biggest obstacle he faced as he transitioned his farm to a purely pasture-based operation: "My biggest fear was that my products wouldn't be accepted. That there would be resistance to grass-fed meat." He worried that he would not be able to overcome that resistance. Laughing, Ginger adds that Jim didn't have enough confidence in the quality of his work.

"He plays down his product," she claims. Jim chuckles and concurs. "It's true. I have a hard time giving the products of my labor their fair due. I need to improve on that."

Things improved a few years ago, when Jim and Ginger got creative with their marketing. "We knew we needed to do more to sell the meat," says Ginger, "because we were ending up with steers that needed to be butchered, and they weren't sold yet." Jim says that in 2001, they found the solution in Ginger's garden. Ginger tells the story: "Last summer, I grew so many peppers, I didn't know what to do with them. So I took them to the farmers' market in Ripon. And I happened to take some of Jim's business cards, and a sign telling people that we also had fresh pasture-raised beef and chickens. So I took some orders that day, and the next week, Jim came back with me. We really enjoyed it."

Today, Ginger grows nineteen varieties of peppers for the farmers market, along with garlic, leeks, and tomatoes. She explains how they chose their crops. "We specialized in vegetables that you would use to season beef. Think of a good taco. You've got your beef, tomatoes, garlic, peppers, onions..." Jim jumps in and says that having a beautiful market stall filled with fresh vegetables has made a big difference in his marketing success. "It opens the door for us to talk to people, and for people to talk to us. If you just set up a little stand with your literature, with just the meat, people might pass you by. But if we can sell them peppers or garlic or leeks, then eventually, as they come back, at some point they'll be interested in the meat we have to offer."

Jim is relieved to finally be able to sell his meat directly to the people who will be eating it and to therefore be able to do all the processing on a small scale. "I have no problem eating my animals," he remarks, "But I like there to be recognition for the life that was there, and that I'm taking for a purpose. I feel they deserve that much. It's part of a natural cycle, that you take life to sustain life. I feel like, when I butcher a chicken, or take my steers to Dave at Pine River Processing, the animals are killed one at a time. Even if nothing is said, there's a one-on-one relationship. You approach the animal, and you take its life. It's not done on an assembly line by mechanical means. You look at the animal, and there's recognition. It's not a product. It is a living thing."

A stroll around Honey Creek Farm is a testament to the reverence for the life it supports. The soils, even after a late summer drought, are soft and yielding beneath the grasses. The chickens and cows graze contentedly, the garden and its bounty of peppers are welcoming. This is wise land: it has chosen its stewards well, and they vigilantly partner with the land. Ginger puts these feelings into words when she looks around, and her eyes grow teary. "I love this place," she says, "but I don't own this place. This place owns me."

ℛECIPES

STANDING RIB ROAST 27

SLOW-ROASTED VENISON IN RAISIN SAUCE 28

FLASH-ROASTED BEEF 29

SUPER-SLOW-ROASTED BEEF 30

VEAL SALTIMBOCCA 32

VEAL CHOPS 33

POLISH STUFFED BEEF ROLL 34

GRILLED FLANK, SKIRT, OR HANGER STEAKS 36

GARLIC-HERB STEAKS IN A BOURBON PAN SAUCE 37

CLASSIC GRILLED STEAKS 38

SUPER-SLOW-ROASTED ROSEMARY-CRUSTED CHUCK STEAK 39

BULGOGI 40

BISON SIRLOIN STEAK 41

BACKWOODS MEAT PIE 42

VENISON VEGETABLE HASH 43

VENISON BAKED IN SOUR CREAM 45

FREEMAN HOMESTEAD MOUSSAKA 46

SLOW-COOKER CHILI 47

BURGERS 48

BEST-EVER BEEF BURGERS 49

FETA AND HERB STUFFED BURGERS 49

FIESTA BEEF CASSEROLE 50

MEATBALLS IN PINEAPPLE SAUCE 51

MEXICAN CORNBREAD 52

FLAMBEAU ROAST 53

CALIFORNIA POT ROAST 54

BEEF TONGUE 55

TONGUE WITH CAPERS AND BÉCHAMEL SAUCE 56

VEAL POT ROAST 58

LINDA'S SAUERBRATEN 60

LUISELLA'S BOILED BEEF 62

STUFFED BREAST OF VEAL 64

GRILLED VEAL SHORT RIBS 66

TERIYAKI SHORT RIBS 67

GARLIC-TOMATO SHORT RIBS 68

BOEUF À LA BOURGUIGNONE (BEEF BURGUNDY) 70

OLD-FASHIONED BEEF STEW 71

BRAISED BEEF WITH RICH GRAVY AND RICE 72

CHILI BREW BEEF STEW WITH FLOATING BISCUITS 74

OSSO BUCO 76

BEEF STOCK 78

FRENCH ONION SOUP 80

All recipes without attribution are from Shannon Hayes, Sap Bush Hollow Farm, West Fulton, New York.

Standing Rib Roast

There is nothing more appropriate for a formal dinner than a standing rib roast, and thankfully, few things are easier to prepare.

SHOWCASE • MINIMUM PREPARATION

TYPICALLY, A STANDING ROAST SERVES TWO PEOPLE PER RIB. THUS, A 3-BONE ROAST SERVES SIX, A 4-BONE ROAST SERVES ABOUT EIGHT PEOPLE, AND A 5-BONE ROAST SERVES TEN. HOWEVER, FINISHED GRASS-FED BEEF FROM DIFFERENT BREEDS PRODUCES ROASTS OF VARYING SIZES. USE YOUR OWN JUDGMENT WHEN EVALUATING A ROAST, FIGURING ON ROUGHLY 1 POUND PER PERSON (INCLUDING BONE WEIGHT).

> Basic Herb Rub (see page 253)
>
> 1 standing rib roast

Rub Basic Herb Rub into the meat, particularly into the spaces between the meat and bones. Cover with plastic wrap, and allow to sit at room temperature for 2 hours.

Preheat oven to 300°F.

Place the roast, fat side up, in a large roasting pan. Insert a meat thermometer into the large end, away from the bone. Cook a 4-pound roast for about 2 hours, or until the meat thermometer registers 115° to 120°F for rare, 125° to 130°F for medium, or 135° to 140°F for well done.

Remove the roast from the oven, tent loosely with foil, and let rest for 20 minutes before carving and serving. During this time, the meat will continue cooking (the internal temperature will increase about 10°F). A finished rare roast should be about 125°F, medium at least 135°F, and well-done 140° to 145°F.

Slow-Roasted Venison in Raisin Sauce

The bacon in this recipe helps keep the meat moist and imparts a smoky flavor to the venison; the fruitiness of the raisin sauce accentuates the venison's rich game taste.

SHOWCASE • ON A BUDGET

SERVES 6

For the raisin sauce:

2 tablespoons unsalted butter

1 small onion, finely diced

1 apple, peeled, cored, and diced

2 cups raisins

⅓ cup honey

2 cups fresh orange juice

¼ cup fresh lemon juice

2 tablespoons orange zest

For the roast:

Oregano-Salt Rub (see page 255)

1 venison roast, about 3 pounds

4 slices thick-cut bacon

Preheat oven to 250°F.

To make the raisin sauce: Heat the butter in a medium-size saucepan. Add the onion and apple, and sauté over medium heat until soft. Add the raisins, and sauté 1 minute longer. Stir in the honey and the orange and lemon juices. Bring the mixture to a boil, then lower the heat to simmer. Cook until the sauce is reduced by one-third. Add the zest, and simmer, uncovered, 10 minutes longer.

Using a potato masher, squash half of the fruit to blend it with the liquid. Remove ¾ cup of the sauce to use for basting the roast. Reserve the rest to serve alongside the cooked meat.

Rub the Oregano-Salt Rub into the meat. Lay the strips of bacon on top of the roast, blanketing it as completely as possible. Set the meat on a rack in a roasting pan. Roast for 30 minutes at 250°F, basting at least twice with the raisin sauce. Turn the heat down to 170°F, insert a meat thermometer, and cook until the internal temperature of the meat reaches 130° to 135°F, about 3 to 4 hours. Baste every 30 minutes with the raisin sauce.

Remove the roast from the oven, and tent loosely with foil. Allow the meat to rest for 5 to 10 minutes before carving. Spoon any pan juices on top of the sliced venison and bacon, and pass the reserved raisin sauce separately.

Flash-Roasted Beef

Use this recipe to show off your tender beef roasts such as the tri-tip. Also known as a triangle roast, tri-tip is lean, tender, and flavorful. Make sure your roast is completely defrosted before using this method; otherwise, it will probably be too rare for your liking.

SHOWCASE • IN A HURRY • MINIMUM PREPARATION

SERVINGS VARY, DEPENDING ON THE SIZE OF THE ROAST. WITH A BONELESS ROAST, FIGURE ½ POUND PER PERSON.

> Salt and freshly ground black pepper or an herb rub (Garlic-Herb Rub, page 254; Cumin-Cinnamon Rub, page 254; or Garlic-Rosemary Rub, page 255)
> 1 tenderloin roast or 1 tri-tip roast

Rub liberal amounts of salt and pepper or an herb rub into the meat, cover loosely with plastic wrap, and let rest at room temperature for 2 hours.

Preheat oven to 450°F.

Set the meat on a rack in a shallow roasting pan lined with foil. Roast for 20 minutes. Continue cooking until the meat reaches 120°F for rare, 125°F for medium-rare, or 130°F for medium.

Remove the roast from the oven, tent loosely with foil, and let rest for 10 minutes before carving and serving. The temperature should increase another 5°F while the roast is resting.

Super-Slow-Roasted Beef

Nothing beats super-slow roasting for turning even the toughest cuts of meat into wonderful roasts. No matter how lean your roast may be, this technique ensures a beautiful cut of beef that is juicy, pink in the center, and absolutely delicious. And the best part is that overcooking the beef is just about impossible. The meat insulates itself: super-slow roasting dries the outside of the roast and locks in the moisture, enabling the meat to cook in its own juice. The flavor will be extra beefy, but be patient. Super-slow roasting takes a long time.

ON A BUDGET • MINIMUM PREPARATION

SERVINGS VARY, DEPENDING ON THE SIZE OF THE ROAST. WITH A BONELESS ROAST, FIGURE ½ POUND PER PERSON.

> 1 beef roast, such as London broil; top, bottom or eye of the round, or sirloin
>
> Herb rub (Garlic-Herb Rub, page 254 or Cumin-Cinnamon Rub, page 254)

Rub the roast with the herb rub of your choice, wrap loosely in plastic, and allow to sit at room temperature for 2 hours.

Preheat oven to 250°F.

Place the meat in a small roasting pan, insert a meat thermometer, and cook for 30 minutes. Turn the oven heat *as low as you can* (most modern ovens do not go below 170°F, but if yours will accurately go as low as 150° or 160°F, so much the better). Continue cooking the meat until the thermometer registers 120° to 125°F. Because these tend to be lean cuts, I recommend that you do not cook them any further than medium-rare. As a guide, figure on 1 hour and 10 minutes per pound of meat at 170°F.

Remove the roast from the oven, tent loosely with foil, and let rest for 5 to 10 minutes. Carve into very thin slices to serve.

GALLOWAYS ON GRASS

Steve and Kay Castner, Kaehler's Mill Farm, Cedarburg, Wisconsin

Saving heritage-breed livestock is a worthy pursuit for a multitude of reasons. Heritage breeds are living artifacts of human history. They increase biosecurity by guaranteeing genetic diversity among the species. But many grass farmers have more pragmatic reasons for safeguarding the genetic legacy of these animals. Several heritage-breed animals were selectively bred to perform well on pasture, whereas many of the modern dominant breeds were developed to perform only in feedlot situations.

This was the reason that Steve and Kay Castner, of Kaehler's Mill Farm in Cedarburg, Wisconsin, chose to raise Galloway beef on their fields. Galloways are an ancient breed of cattle from Scotland, and they are presently on the American Livestock Breed Conservancy's watch list. They're characterized by a double-hair coat, which makes them the bane of the conventional cattle feedlot industry but a boon to grass farmers. With no barns at Kaehler's Mill Farm, Galloways were the perfect breed to endure Wisconsin's harsh winters. Their coarse outer coat protects them from the elements, and their second, softer layer of hair helps keep them warm throughout the winter without having to gain an extra layer of fat.

According to Kay, the Galloways and Galloway crossbreds that she and Steve raise are first-rate foragers. They fatten beautifully on grass, requiring no grain to have adequate finish to go to the butcher. Both purebred Galloways and Galloway crossbreds are widely recognized for producing superior-quality meat that is juicy, tender, and flavorful.

But those aren't the only reasons why Kay and Steve selected Galloways for their herd. Since they breed cows as well as market grass-finished beef, Kay says they wanted cows with good mothering instincts, something that has been bred out of many of the factory-farm livestock breeds. "They're good mothers," says Kay about the Galloways. "We don't pull calves [assist with delivery], ever."

What are the drawbacks of Galloways? Kay responds without hesitation: "You get too attached to them." A tour through her herd confirms how docile these animals are as Fergus the bull allows Kay to walk up and nuzzle him and as each of the cows comes forward to nibble alfalfa cubes from her hand before she and her Border collie, Jen, move them to fresh pasture.

Veal Saltimbocca

Nancy Pritchard, Smith Meadows, Virginia

Maple-smoked ham from pigs raised on grass is a delight, but if the grass farmer nearest you offers only traditionally smoked hams, try one. It'll work too.

SHOWCASE • IN A HURRY

SERVES 3 TO 4

6 veal cutlets	½ teaspoon freshly ground coriander
6 thin slices maple-smoked ham	2 tablespoons olive oil
6 thin slices Swiss cheese	4 large sprigs of fresh rosemary
½ cup all-purpose flour	1 cup dry white wine
1 teaspoon coarse salt	
¼ teaspoon freshly ground black pepper	

Pound the veal cutlets with a small meat hammer until they are a little more than ⅛-inch thick. Cut the cutlets into strips approximately 2½ by 5½ inches.

Slice the ham and cheese so that you have as many strips as you have veal strips. Lay the veal on a cutting board, and place a slice of ham and a slice of cheese on each cutlet. Roll the stacks tightly and skewer each with a toothpick to hold it together.

Mix the flour, salt, and ground spices on a flat plate. Roll each skewered cutlet in the spiced flour until evenly dusted.

Heat the olive oil and two rosemary sprigs over medium-high heat in a large skillet. Carefully place the skewered cutlets into the pan. Gently roll them in the pan until the veal looks done—5 minutes or less. Add ½ cup of the white wine, and simmer the rolls for another 2 minutes. Remove the cutlets to a warmed platter garnished with the remaining rosemary. Deglaze the skillet with the rest of the white wine.

Pour the sauce over the cutlets and serve hot.

Veal Chops

Amy Kenyon, Skate Creek Farm, New York

The intriguing part of this recipe is its simplicity. The minimalist approach, in Amy Kenyon's words, "allows the flavor and tenderness of veal to speak for itself."

SHOWCASE • IN A HURRY • MINIMUM PREPARATION

SERVES 2

> 1 clove garlic, minced
>
> 3 tablespoons olive oil
>
> 2 veal loin or rib chops
>
> Salt and freshly ground black pepper to taste

Mix the garlic and olive oil together, and brush onto the veal chops. Sprinkle each chop with salt and pepper. Grill or broil under high heat for 4 to 5 minutes per side.

WHAT TO DO WITH LEFTOVER BEEF?

In our tiny household, from time to time we want nothing more than to cook up a nice beef roast. The trouble is, we're often faced with what to do with the leftovers. Although any meat cooked in liquid—such as in the Osso Bucco, Teriyaki or Garlic Tomato Short Ribs, Tongue, California Pot Roast, or Chili recipes—can be gently rewarmed the next day (and will often taste even better), beef dishes cooked using dry-heat methods need to be treated a little differently.

Don't try to reheat a cut of steak or roast beef—it will only cook further and turn gray and tough. Instead, slice it thinly for a roast beef sandwich, pair it with sharp cheddar cheese and ranch dressing on a salad, warm it *briefly* in a frying pan for use in burritos or fajitas, or use it to make a taco salad.

Polish Stuffed Beef Roll

Jack Knorek, Oak Moon Farm, Michigan

Here's a traditional way to use a very inexpensive cut of meat. If you're looking for a high-protein dish, this is it! It can be served hot as a main dish or cold as an appetizer or on sandwiches. Be sure to boil two eggs before you begin.

SHOWCASE

SERVES 6 TO 8

For the stuffing:

3 eggs, uncooked

½ cup milk

1 cup breadcrumbs

2 eggs, hard-boiled, roughly chopped

1 pound ground beef

¼ chopped fresh parsley

¼ teaspoon dried marjoram

¼ teaspoon garlic powder

½ teaspoon salt

½ teaspoon freshly ground black pepper

For the beef rolls:

2 beef steaks, top or bottom round, 1 pound each

Salt and freshly ground black pepper to taste

6 cups beef broth, or 6 cups water + 6 beef bouillon cubes, or

   6 cups good-quality, low-sodium canned beef broth

Cheesecloth and butcher twine

3 tablespoons butter

To make the stuffing: Lightly beat 2 of the uncooked eggs. Combine milk, breadcrumbs, beaten eggs, hard-boiled eggs, ground beef, parsley, marjoram, garlic powder, salt, and pepper; mix gently and well, being careful not to overmix.

To make the beef rolls: Place each round steak between two sheets of plastic wrap; using a wooden meat mallet, pound each steak into a rectangle about 12 inches long, 8 inches wide, and $\frac{1}{4}$ inch thick. Remove the plastic wrap, and place the steaks on a platter. Sprinkle one side with salt and pepper, and with the seasoned side in, roll each steak tightly; set aside.

In a large pot, bring the beef broth to a boil (or bring water to a boil and add the bouillon cubes); reduce to simmer.

Unroll the steaks; beat the remaining egg with a fork, and brush the egg over the inner side of each steak. Spread half the stuffing evenly (to within 1 inch of the edges) on the steaks. Roll each steak tightly, wrap with cheesecloth, and tie with butcher twine, wrapping the string several times along the length of the rolls.

Place the rolls in the broth, and simmer, covered, for 1 hour. Remove them from the broth; cut twine, and unwrap cheesecloth. (The broth may be used as a base for gravy.)

In a large skillet, melt the butter, and sauté the rolls until brown.

To serve warm, slice the beef rolls, and serve with gravy. To serve cold, remove the rolls from the skillet, cool, and refrigerate. Serve as an appetizer or as a sandwich filling on thick, crusty bread.

Grilled Flank, Skirt, or Hanger Steaks

Flank, skirt, and hanger steaks have become quite fashionable in recent years, due largely to their appeal for bistro-style and Tex-Mex cooking. They come from the chest and side of the beef and are long, thin, and rather tough. However, cooked until just rare, they become one of the beefiest, most flavorful cuts to be found. Their cumbersome size can make them unwieldy for the stovetop, so they are best seared quickly over a very hot grill.

IN A HURRY • MINIMUM PREPARATION

SERVES 4 TO 6

> Garlic, Salt, and Pepper Rub (page 255) or
>
> Cumin-Cinnamon Rub (page 254)
>
> 2 flank, skirt, or hanger steaks

Start the grill, lower the lid, and heat until the coals are very hot.

Select one of the spice rubs above. Rub the mixture into both sides of the steak.

Place the meat over the fire, and with the lid open, grill over high heat for about 5 minutes or until the underside is brown and seared. Flip the steak over, and grill an additional 2 to 3 minutes or until it reaches your preferred level of doneness (remember that the steaks will continue to cook once you take them from the grill, so it is best to remove them just before they are done to your liking).

Remove the meat from the fire, tent loosely with foil, and let rest for 3 to 5 minutes.

To maximize tenderness, slice the steaks very thinly against the grain for serving.

Garlic-Herb Steaks in a Bourbon Pan Sauce

I take my steaks very seriously, and as far as I'm concerned, this is the best (and possibly the only) way to prepare them. Much to my husband's delight, I also view these steaks as quintessential camping fare; they cook up just as beautifully over a backpacking stove as they do in our kitchen.

SHOWCASE • IN A HURRY • MINIMUM PREPARATION

SERVES 2

2 steaks, 1 inch thick (T-bone, porterhouse, top blade, filet mignon, New York strip, or rib eye steaks will all work)

3 tablespoons Garlic-Herb Rub (see page 254)

2 tablespoons olive oil

2 tablespoons butter

⅓ cup bourbon

Generously coat each of the steaks with the Garlic-Herb Rub. Set them aside, and bring the meat to room temperature, about 30 minutes to 1 hour

Heat the skillet over a medium-high flame. Add the olive oil and butter. Once the butter has melted and begins to spatter lightly, add the steaks. Cook for about 5 to 6 minutes per side for medium-rare, or until they achieve the desired level of doneness (the internal temperature should be between 120° and 130°F).

Remove the steaks from the pan and tent with foil.

Turn the heat to low, add the bourbon, and simmer 2 minutes longer, stirring constantly and scraping up any browned bits. Set the steaks on warmed plates, top with the bourbon pan sauce, and serve.

Classic Grilled Steaks

No summer would be complete without a barbecue dinner of grilled steaks and fresh salad from the garden. Below are basic, no-fail techniques for ensuring your place as the neighborhood grill maestro.

SHOWCASE • IN A HURRY • MINIMUM PREPARATION

SERVES 2 (RECIPE IS EASILY DOUBLED)

> 2 steaks, preferably 1½ inches thick (T-bone, porterhouse, New York strip, top blade, rib eye, or rib steaks will all work)
>
> Coarse salt and freshly ground black pepper or
> herb rub (Garlic-Herb Rub, page 254; Cumin-Cinnamon Rub, page 254; or Garlic-Rosemary Rub, page 255)

Sprinkle the steaks liberally with salt and pepper or season with one of the herb or spice rubs suggested above.

Bring the steaks to room temperature while you prepare your grill. Heat the grill so that one-half is hot and the other half is just warm.

Lay the steaks on the hot half of the grill, and sear until well-browned, about 2 to 3 minutes. Turn, sear until well-browned, and move them to the warm side of the grill. Grill them 5 to 10 minutes longer, or until they've reached the desired doneness (120°F for rare, 135°F for medium). To gauge the temperature, insert a meat thermometer into the *side* of the meat rather than the top, being sure not to get close to any bones.

When the steaks have reached the right temperature, remove from the grill, tent with foil, and let rest for 3 to 5 minutes before serving.

Super-Slow-Roasted Rosemary-Crusted Chuck Steak

Chuck steaks cooked using this long, slow method will be flavorful and amazingly delicious—especially when served with a dish of melted butter for dipping! Because it comes from the animal part that does a lot of work, the chuck has loads of flavor. Although the meat will not be as tender as a filet or New York strip steak, this slow-roasting technique helps to significantly tenderize an ordinarily tough cut.

If you are unsure about your oven's accuracy at such a low temperature, verify it with an oven thermometer.

ON A BUDGET • MINIMUM PREPARATION

SERVES 3 TO 6, DEPENDING ON THE SIZE OF THE CUT

> Garlic-Rosemary Rub (see page 255)
>
> 1 chuck steak or chuck roast, 2 ½ to 5 ½ pounds

Preheat oven to 250°F.

Rub Garlic-Rosemary Rub into the chuck. Cover loosely with plastic wrap, and let rest at room temperature for 30 to 60 minutes. Roast the meat in a shallow pan for 30 minutes, then lower the oven temperature to 170°F. Continue to roast for 4 to 6 hours (depending on the weight—the larger the cut, the longer the roasting time), or until an internal meat thermometer registers 120° to 125°F. To ensure tenderness, do not cook beyond 125°F.

Allow the meat to rest, tented loosely with foil, for 5 to 10 minutes before slicing and serving.

Bulgogi

Jack Knorek, Oak Moon Farm, Michigan

When I lived in Asia, my friends and I would hunt down Korean restaurants to get our bulgogi fix. Here's one of the best recipes I've seen for this delicious Korean dish. It is typically served with sticky rice and kimchi, an assortment of fermented vegetables. Unless you live near an Asian food market, kimchi will probably be hard to come by. Subsequently, a nice side dish would be lightly steamed fresh spinach tossed with sesame oil and toasted sesame seeds. Korean red pepper flakes can be found in Asian food markets and in the Asian food section of supermarkets. If you can't find them, try substituting hot Spanish chili powder or dicing a dried chili pepper (remove the seeds and the white membrane first).

Some farms sell thinly sliced round steaks as minute steaks, sandwich steaks, or shaved steaks. If your local farmer does not offer these, you can make your own by thinly slicing a partially frozen round steak or round roast. To adapt this recipe for a child's palate, omit the red pepper flakes.

IN A HURRY • MINIMUM PREPARATION • ON A BUDGET • KID-FRIENDLY

SERVES 2 TO 3

¼ cup soy sauce

2 tablespoons sesame oil

2 tablespoons sugar

1 tablespoon salt

1 bunch green onions, chopped into 1-inch pieces

6 cloves garlic, chopped

2 tablespoons Mirin (sweet Japanese cooking wine) or sherry

2 tablespoons Korean red pepper flakes

1 pound thinly sliced round steak (top, bottom, or eye)

1 tablespoon peanut or vegetable oil

Mix the soy sauce, sesame oil, sugar, salt, green onions, garlic, wine, and red pepper flakes. Add the beef; marinate for at least 30 minutes (or overnight) in the refrigerator.

Bring to room temperature. Stir-fry the meat over medium-high heat in the peanut oil until the meat is nicely browned, but be careful not to overcook. Depending on the size and shape of your pan, you may have to cook the meat in batches. The meat should not need to cook for more than 1 minute.

Bison Sirloin Steak

Mary Graese, Northstar Bison, Wisconsin

Mary submitted this recipe, assuring me that it's a foolproof way to enjoy a wonderful bison steak... she was right! Although the steaks take 2 hours to cook, you need spend only a few minutes in the kitchen. This is a great dish to prepare if you are entertaining.

SHOWCASE • MINIMUM PREPARATION

SERVES 4

3 tablespoons fresh basil or 1 tablespoon dried basil

1 tablespoon coarse salt

$1\frac{1}{2}$ teaspoons freshly ground black pepper

2 bison sirloin steaks, $1\frac{1}{2}$-inches thick, about 1 pound each

2 to 3 tablespoons olive oil

Preheat oven to 170°F.

Combine the basil, salt, and pepper in a small bowl. Cut each of the steaks into 8-ounce portions, and trim away any sinew. Brush the steaks on both sides with olive oil, then rub the spice mixture into the meat. Cover loosely with plastic wrap, and let rest at room temperature for 30 to 60 minutes.

Heat a frying pan over high heat, and sear the steaks for 2 to 3 minutes on each side. Place the meat on a shallow baking sheet, and roast, uncovered, for 2 hours for medium-rare. If you are unable to serve the steaks immediately, they will hold in the 170°F oven for at least another hour and still be pink in the center.

Backwoods Meat Pie

Here's a simple recipe suited for preparing at a rustic camp as well as at home.

ON A BUDGET • KID-FRIENDLY

SERVES 4

2 pounds venison steak,
cut into 1½-inch cubes

½ pound smoked ham,
diced into small cubes

¼ pound butter (one stick)

½ cup all-purpose flour

2 teaspoons salt

1 teaspoon freshly ground
black pepper

2 tablespoons olive oil

1 onion, finely diced

2 cups beef stock

2 teaspoons dried parsley

2 teaspoons dried rosemary

1 bay leaf

3 carrots, cut into bite-size pieces

6 medium unpeeled potatoes, quartered

3 tablespoons freshly grated
Parmesan cheese

1 clove garlic, crushed

2 eggs, beaten

Bring venison and ham to room temperature.

Heat 2 tablespoons of the butter in a large skillet. Combine the flour, salt, and pepper in a shallow bowl. Dredge the venison and ham cubes in the flour mixture, and brown in the skillet.

Remove the meat; add the olive oil and onion to the pan, and sauté 2 minutes.

Return the meat to the pan. Add the stock, and bring to a boil, then lower the heat to simmer, scraping up any browned bits. Add the parsley, rosemary, and bay leaf; simmer until the venison is tender, about 1½ hours. Add the carrots, and cook 15 minutes longer. If you start to run out of liquid, add just enough stock or water to cover the meat.

Meanwhile, preheat the oven to 350°F.

Boil the potatoes until they are tender. Mash them with the remaining butter, Parmesan cheese, and crushed garlic. Allow them to cool slightly, and whip in the eggs. Mixture should be smooth and fluffy.

Using ¾ of the potatoes, line *only* the sides (not the bottom) of a deep, 3- to 4-quart nonreactive ovenproof pan with a 1½-inch-thick layer of potatoes. Place the dish in the oven, and bake for 10 minutes, or until the potatoes have set.

Pour the venison stew into the casserole, top with the remaining mashed potatoes, and bake 20 to 30 minutes longer, or until the top of the potatoes turns light gold.

Venison Vegetable Hash

This is a quick and easy supper made with a few fresh summer vegetables from the garden and some leftover meat. If you don't have venison on hand, beef or pork will work just as well.

ON A BUDGET • IN A HURRY • MINIMUM PREPARATION

SERVES 2 TO 4

> 1 medium onion, finely diced
>
> 1 bell pepper, finely diced
>
> 2 tablespoons unsalted butter
>
> 2 medium tomatoes, seeds removed, finely chopped
>
> 2 tablespoons celery, roughly diced
>
> 2 tablespoons fresh parsley, finely minced
>
> 1 cup beef stock or water
>
> 3 cups diced cooked venison, beef, or pork
>
> 4 tablespoons fresh breadcrumbs
>
> Salt and freshly ground black pepper to taste

In a large skillet, sauté the onion and pepper in the butter over medium-low heat until the onion is translucent. Add the tomatoes, celery, and parsley, and sauté 2 minutes longer. Add the stock (or water), and simmer, uncovered, for 5 minutes. Add the meat, and continue to cook until heated through. Stir in the breadcrumbs to thicken the mixture, season to taste with salt and pepper, and serve immediately with crusty bread.

WHAT IS CHRONIC WASTING DISEASE?

Although chronic wasting disease (CWD) has been documented in the United States since at least the 1960s, the increased media attention of late may cause many to wonder if eating venison is safe.

According to the United States Department of Agriculture (USDA) Department of Animal and Plant Health Inspection Service (APHIS), CWD is a fatal neurological disease that affects wild and captive elk, white-tailed deer, mule deer, and captive black-tailed deer. It is part of a family of diseases called the transmissible spongiform encephalopathies, which includes Creutzfeldt–Jakob disease in humans, bovine spongiform encephalopathy in cows (or mad cow disease), and scrapie in sheep.

CWD is a serious concern for wildlife managers and venison farmers. Scientists do not know what causes it, nor do they know how it is spread. Thus, it could seriously alter herd populations and may deter hunting for fear that the disease could pose human health risks.

At this point, the disease has been identified in Colorado, Wyoming, Nebraska, Illinois, New Mexico, South Dakota, Wisconsin, Montana, Minnesota, Utah, Oklahoma, Kansas, Saskatchewan, and Alberta. However, only a small number of the herd populations have actually been infected, and public health officials discourage any exposure to CWD-infected meat. Most state wildlife agencies are working hard to institute surveillance and protection programs for CWD. In some states, venison farmers are participating in captive herd certification programs, and information is available from the Chronic Wasting Disease Alliance (http://www.cwd-info.org/) regarding preventive measures hunters should take, including the following:

- Do not shoot, handle, or eat any animal that is behaving abnormally (particularly animals that stumble, tremble, lack coordination, seem listless, salivate excessively, drink and urinate to excess, have an odd posture, or have drooping ears). Be sure to report any such animals to local wildlife authorities.

- Wear rubber gloves when field-dressing all venison.

- Bone out meat from the animal. Avoid sawing through the bone, as well as cutting through the brain or spinal cord.

- Avoid handling the brain and spinal tissues.

- Do not eat the brain, spinal cord, eyes, spleen, tonsils, or lymph nodes of the animal.

- If you have your venison commercially processed, insist that your meat be processed separately and not mixed with meat from other animals.

Venison Baked in Sour Cream

Here's another recipe that makes a delicious dinner out of only a few ingredients.

ON A BUDGET • MINIMUM PREPARATION • KID-FRIENDLY

SERVES 4

> 2 pounds venison or beef round steak, cut into 1½-inch cubes
>
> 1 cup sour cream
>
> 1 cup milk
>
> 4 tablespoons unsalted butter
>
> Salt and freshly ground black pepper to taste
>
> 1 small onion, finely diced
>
> 3 tablespoons all-purpose flour
>
> ½ pound fresh mushrooms, coarsely diced
>
> 4 cups cooked blend of wild and brown rice

Preheat oven to 325°F.

Bring the venison, sour cream, and milk to room temperature.

Heat the butter in a large, deep skillet over medium-high heat.

Sprinkle the venison liberally with salt and pepper, add to the skillet, and sauté until nicely browned. Remove the meat to a covered casserole.

Loosen the browned bits in the pan, add the diced onion, and cook until translucent. Lower the heat, sprinkle the flour over the remaining fat, onions, and browned bits, and mix. When well blended, stir in the sour cream, milk, and mushrooms. Simmer for 5 minutes, stirring constantly while scraping up any browned bits. Season to taste with salt and pepper.

Pour the sauce over the venison, cover, and bake for 1 to 1½ hours, or until the meat is tender. Serve over wild rice blend.

Freeman Homestead Moussaka

Rae Ellen Freeman, Freeman Homestead, New York

Rae Ellen makes this recipe using her own homemade ricotta cheese, although a good-quality store brand will work. If you don't have ground venison on hand, this is also a tasty and nutritious way to use your ground lamb, beef, goat, bison, or beefalo. Kids will likely enjoy it, and it is a terrific one-dish supper.

IN A HURRY • ON A BUDGET • KID-FRIENDLY

SERVES 4

2 cups cooked green beans

2 tablespoons olive oil

1 medium onion, finely diced

2 cloves garlic, chopped

1½ pounds ground venison

Salt and freshly ground
   black pepper to taste

1 8-ounce can tomato sauce

1 teaspoon freshly ground cinnamon

3 eggs, slightly beaten

1½ cups ricotta cheese

2 teaspoons freshly ground nutmeg

½ cup freshly grated Parmesan cheese

Preheat oven to 350°F.

Coat the inside of a deep casserole or 9-x-12-inch baking pan with butter. Add the beans.

In a medium-size skillet, heat the olive oil; add the onion, and sauté until translucent. Add the garlic. Sauté for 1 minute, then add the venison, and sauté until brown. Sprinkle lightly with salt and pepper. Stir in the tomato sauce and cinnamon. Spoon over the beans.

Blend the eggs, ricotta cheese, and nutmeg; spread over the meat; top with the grated Parmesan, and bake for 30 minutes.

Remove from oven, and serve.

Slow-Cooker Chili

The secret to chili is how you select and use your chili peppers. If dried ancho and chipotle peppers are not available in your local market, just substitute, bearing these points in mind: dried chiles have a richer, fruitier flavor than fresh; smaller chiles are hotter than larger ones; the seeds and white veins generally contain all the heat but no chili flavor; and finally, if you like great chili flavor but are less enamored with the spice, add one whole chili pepper to the pot, but remove it before serving. The recipe below is for a medium-hot chili.

ON A BUDGET · MINIMUM PREPARATION

SERVES 6

For the chili:

1 pound dried dark red kidney beans

2 tablespoons fresh lemon juice

1 pound ground beef

2 tablespoons olive oil

1 dried ancho chili pepper, seeds and
   white membrane removed, chopped

1 dried whole chipotle pepper

1 medium onion, coarsely chopped

1 28-ounce can crushed tomatoes

2 cloves garlic, chopped

2 tablespoons chili powder

1 teaspoon freshly ground cumin

1 teaspoon dried oregano

1 teaspoon salt

1 teaspoon freshly ground
   black pepper

For the topping:

1 cup shredded Monterey Jack
   or cheddar cheese

1 cup sour cream

Cover beans with warm water, stir in lemon juice, cover, and soak in a warm place for 18 to 24 hours. Drain, rinse, and place in a slow cooker.

In a skillet over medium-low heat, brown the ground beef in olive oil. Combine the meat and remaining chili ingredients in the slow cooker, and cook on high for 4 to 5 hours or on low for 8 to 10 hours, until the beans are tender. Depending on how your cooker works, you may need to add an extra ½ cup of water during the cooking time to prevent the chili from drying out. Remove the whole chipotle pepper.

Serve the chili topped with shredded cheese and a generous dollop of sour cream.

Burgers

Grass-fed beef makes fabulous classic hamburgers using only ground beef and salt and freshly ground black pepper, but here are a few other ways to prepare them. Regardless of which method you choose, be sure to check the handy tips below for the ultimate hamburger.

TIPS FOR COOKING THE ULTIMATE HAMBURGER

Loren A. Olson, M.D., Malabar Farm, Iowa

Loren Olson takes the business of burgers seriously, elevating their production to high science and an art form. Below are a few of his tips, plus a few extra considerations to guarantee the perfect burger. For safety, ground beef should be kept refrigerated until just before cooking and the burgers should be cooked to a minimum internal temperature of 160°F.

1. The ideal patty is 6 ounces of raw meat (ideally, ground chuck), shaped into a 4½-inch circle, ¾-inch thick on the edges and ½-inch thick in the center. To do this, simply form the burger, then gently press in the center on one side to form a small depression. These patties will cook evenly, and they will not end up puffy and round.

2. If you're grilling your burger, be sure that the grill is hot and that the grate is clean. This should help ensure that the burgers won't stick, but it is OK to brush on a little oil before cooking as a preventive measure.

3. Burgers should be grilled or fried over medium-high heat for a nice crusty exterior and a juicy interior. According to Loren, you can tell if your grill is hot enough if you can hold your hand 5 inches above the grill rack for 3 to 5 seconds, but no longer.

4. Leave the grill uncovered while the burgers cook.

5. Six-ounce burgers do not require much cooking time—2 minutes and 30 seconds on the first side and 3 minutes after flipping will yield a medium burger.

6. Don't press on the burgers with your spatula while you are cooking—you'll squeeze out the juices.

7. To toast buns, split them open, and lay the halves, cut-side down, on the grill rack for the last 45 to 60 seconds of the cooking time.

8. If you like cheeseburgers, try shredding the cheese and mixing it in with the ground beef *before* you make the patties. The cheese will be more evenly distributed, and you won't risk overcooking your burger while you're trying to melt a slice of cheese on top after your burger is done.

Best-Ever Beef Burgers

Tina Sawchuck, Muriel Creek Cattle Company, Alberta, Canada

IN A HURRY • ON A BUDGET

MAKES 4 HAMBURGERS

1½ pounds ground beef, preferably 80% lean (20% fat)

1 egg, lightly beaten

2 teaspoons oyster sauce

2 teaspoons Worcestershire sauce

1 teaspoon dried, minced onion

½ teaspoon garlic powder

½ teaspoon salt

¼ teaspoon freshly ground black pepper

¼ cup fresh breadcrumbs

Place the ground beef in a mixing bowl. Whisk together the egg, oyster sauce, Worcestershire sauce, minced onion, garlic powder, salt, and pepper. Pour over the ground beef; add the bread crumbs. Using your hands, lightly mix all the ingredients together. Cook according to the instructions on page 48.

Feta and Herb Stuffed Burgers

Kacey and Kelly Peterson, River Run Farm, Oregon

IN A HURRY • ON A BUDGET

SERVES 3

⅓ cup crumbled feta cheese

1 heaping tablespoon fresh oregano, minced

2 tablespoons fresh spinach, chopped

1 pound ground beef

Salt and freshly ground black pepper to taste

Mix feta, oregano, and spinach in a small bowl; set aside. Divide the ground beef into three equal portions, and form into burgers. Place ⅓ of the feta mixture in the middle of each patty, and re-form into a patty, making sure you cover the stuffing with meat. Sprinkle with salt and pepper, and cook as directed on page 48.

Fiesta Beef Casserole

Tom and Dale Lasater, Lasater Grasslands Beef, Colorado

The Lasater family has been ranching cattle since 1882. This recipe from the current operators, Tom and Dale, is an easy dish to bring to potluck suppers and a good way to make a little ground beef go a long way.

IN A HURRY • ON A BUDGET • KID-FRIENDLY

SERVES 6

> 2 tablespoons olive oil
>
> 1½ to 2 pounds ground beef
>
> Salt and freshly ground black pepper to taste
>
> 1 tablespoon chili powder
>
> 12 ounces chunky salsa
>
> 1 cup corn, fresh or frozen
>
> ¾ cup mayonnaise or sour cream
>
> 2 cups crushed tortilla chips
>
> 2 cups shredded sharp cheddar or jack cheese
>
> 1 head lettuce, coarsely chopped
>
> 3 tomatoes, seeded, coarsely chopped

Preheat oven to 350°F.

Coat a large, heated skillet with olive oil. Add the ground beef, sprinkle with salt, pepper, and chili powder; cook until the meat browns.

Remove beef to a large bowl, and add the salsa, corn, and mayonnaise or sour cream. Spread one-half of the meat mixture on the bottom of a 2-quart casserole. Top with one cup of the tortilla chips, followed by one cup of the cheese. Repeat the layers. Bake for 20 minutes.

Serve on a bed of chopped lettuce, and top with tomatoes.

Meatballs in Pineapple Sauce

Aleta Casciaro, H. and Seth Williams, Earth Cycle Farm and Troedel Place, Washington

This is a delightful recipe for an appetizer or for a potluck gathering.

ON A BUDGET • IN A HURRY • KID-FRIENDLY

SERVES 10 AS AN APPETIZER

For the meatballs:

½ cup dry breadcrumbs

2 tablespoons finely chopped onions

½ teaspoon salt

½ teaspoon Worcestershire sauce

1 egg, lightly beaten

1 pound ground beef

2 tablespoons olive oil

Mix all the ingredients, except the olive oil, in a large bowl. Shape into 1½-inch balls. Sauté meatballs in the olive oil over medium heat, turning occasionally, for about 15 to 20 minutes, until browned. Pour off the fat, remove the meatballs from the skillet, and set aside.

For the pineapple sauce:

½ cup packed light brown sugar

1 tablespoon cornstarch

1 13¼-ounce can of chunk pineapple, in natural, unsweetened juice

⅓ cup apple cider vinegar

1 tablespoon soy sauce

1 small green bell pepper, coarsely chopped

Mix together the brown sugar and cornstarch, and add to the skillet used for the meatballs. Pour in the pineapple and juice, and add the vinegar, soy sauce, and chopped pepper. Over medium heat, bring to a boil, stirring constantly. Reduce heat immediately, add the meatballs, and simmer 10 minutes longer.

Mexican Cornbread

Joyce Hetrick, Heifer Creek Highlands, Arkansas

This recipe is fun to make and it helps a little meat go a long way.

ON A BUDGET • IN A HURRY • KID-FRIENDLY

SERVES 4 TO 6

½ cup plus 2 tablespoons olive oil

1 large onion, finely chopped

1 pound ground beef

Salt and freshly ground
    black pepper to taste

1 cup yellow or white cornmeal
    (not self-rising) + 1 to 2 tablespoons

½ teaspoon baking soda

¾ teaspoon salt

¾ teaspoon freshly ground cumin

1 ½ teaspoons chili powder

1 teaspoon garlic powder

1 cup milk

2 eggs, beaten

1 cup corn (fresh, frozen, or canned
    and drained)

½ pound sharp cheddar cheese, grated

2 or 3 jalapeño peppers,
    finely chopped (optional)

Preheat oven to 350°F.

Heat 2 tablespoons of the olive oil in a medium-size frying pan. Add the onion and sauté until translucent. Add the ground beef, sprinkle lightly with salt and pepper, and cook until browned. Pour off any accumulated fat.

Combine 1 cup of the cornmeal, the baking soda, salt, and spices in a large bowl. In a separate bowl, whisk together the milk, the remaining ½ cup of the olive oil, eggs, and corn. Stir the liquids into the cornmeal mixture, mixing by hand just until smooth; do not overmix. Set aside.

Grease a large iron skillet, and warm over very low heat. Sprinkle a thin layer of cornmeal on the bottom, brown slightly, and then pour in half the batter. Gently spread the meat and onion mixture on top; add the cheese and jalapeños. Pour the remaining batter on top.

Bake for 40 to 50 minutes, until golden brown; a toothpick inserted in the center should come out clean.

Flambeau Roast

Jon and Wendy Taggart, Burgundy Pasture Beef, Texas

Here's a delicious way to enjoy some of the otherwise tougher cuts of beef. This recipe calls for significantly less liquid than a traditional pot roast, so the resulting broth is rich and flavorful.

SHOWCASE • ON A BUDGET

SERVES 4 TO 6

> 2 teaspoons coarse salt
>
> 1 teaspoon freshly ground black pepper
>
> 2 ½ to 3 pounds roast, either chuck, rump, or heel of the round
>
> 2 tablespoons olive oil
>
> 1 onion, coarsely chopped
>
> 2 cloves garlic, coarsely chopped
>
> 1 shallot, finely chopped
>
> ½ to ⅔ cup good brandy
>
> Fresh herb bouquet of thyme, rosemary, and a bay leaf (or 1 dried bay leaf and 1 teaspoon each of dried thyme and rosemary)

Preheat oven to 225°F.

Rub the salt and pepper into the roast. Heat olive oil in a Dutch oven, and brown the roast on all sides. When browning is almost complete, add the onion, garlic, and chopped shallot. Continue cooking until the onions are translucent.

Remove the roast from the heat. Add the brandy, and immediately light the roast with a match. Allow the fire to burn out on its own, then add the herbs. Cover, and place back on medium heat until the meat begins to sizzle.

Roast the meat, covered, in oven until tender (about 2 to 3 hours). Slice. Spoon the sauce over the meat when serving.

California Pot Roast

Nancy Oswald, Oswald Cattle Company, Colorado

This recipe is so easy that your kids could, with a little help, put it together before they leave for school and finish it up when they get home. School-age children are never too young to participate in your kitchen doings.

ON A BUDGET • MINIMUM PREPARATION • KID-FRIENDLY

SERVES 6

1 4-to-5-pound chuck, rump,
   or round roast

1 tablespoon salt

2 teaspoons freshly ground black pepper

3 tablespoons olive oil

½ cup water

2 cups tomato sauce, fresh or canned

1 onion, coarsely chopped

2 cloves garlic, minced

2 tablespoons dark brown sugar

½ teaspoon dry mustard

¼ cup fresh lemon juice

¼ cup apple cider vinegar

¼ cup ketchup

1 tablespoon Worcestershire sauce

Rub the chuck roast with the salt and pepper.

Heat the olive oil in a large skillet over medium-high heat, and brown the roast, about 3 minutes per side.

Place the meat in a slow cooker with the water, tomato sauce, onion, and garlic. Cook on low heat all day, for about 5 to 6 hours.

About 1¼ hours before you are ready to eat, combine the brown sugar, dry mustard, lemon juice, vinegar, ketchup, and Worcestershire sauce. Pour over the meat, and continue cooking another hour until fork-tender.

Remove the meat, slice, and place on a warm platter. Meanwhile, let the sauce thicken by simmering on the stove for a few minutes; pour over sliced roast and serve.

Beef Tongue

Jim Quick, Honey Creek Farm, Wisconsin

Jim Quick says this is his all-time favorite cut of beef because it is always tender, moist, and flavorful. If you like the idea of pot roasts but find them too dry, you'll love tongue. If you've never tried it, go on... be adventurous.

SHOWCASE • ON A BUDGET • MINIMUM PREPARATION

SERVES 4

1 tablespoon paprika

2 teaspoons chili powder

1 tablespoon kosher (coarse) salt

1½ teaspoons freshly ground black pepper

1 teaspoon sugar

1 beef tongue

2 onions, sliced thin

2 cloves garlic, coarsely chopped

1 cup beer or water

Combine the paprika, chili powder, salt, pepper, and sugar in a small bowl. Rub liberally on the beef tongue.

Place the onions and garlic in a slow cooker, add the tongue, and pour in the beer or water. Cook on the lowest heat setting for 5 to 6 hours, until the meat is tender.

When you are about ready to eat, remove the tongue to a platter, and allow it to cool for a few minutes. Peel off the skin, being careful not to burn your fingers.

Cut into ¼-inch-thick slices. Arrange the slices on warmed plates, and top with the onion and garlic juices from the pot.

If you have leftovers, tongue makes an excellent sandwich meat, eaten cold with a little mustard and some good bread.

Tongue with Capers and Béchamel Sauce

Marc Fournier, Sap Bush Hollow Farm, New York

My mother has to be the world's fussiest eater. She is one of those people who does not willingly dine outside their comfort range—in her case, meat roasts and potatoes. Imagine her horror when Marc Fournier, our French friend from the Pyrenees, insisted that he prepare beef tongue for her. Much to her surprise—and mine—she fell in love with this dish, and you will too. Be sure you begin by soaking the tongue overnight.

SHOWCASE • ON A BUDGET

SERVES 4 AS A MEAL, OR 6 TO 8 AS AN APPETIZER

1 beef tongue

2 quarts water

1 tablespoon cider vinegar

2 whole cloves

1 small onion, whole

3 bay leaves

2 carrots, coarsely chopped

2 teaspoons sea salt

½ teaspoon freshly ground black pepper

4 tablespoons capers, rinsed and drained

Put the tongue in a large pot with the water and vinegar. If necessary, add more water to make sure it is completely covered. Soak for a minimum of 12 hours.

Three hours before you are ready to serve, insert the cloves into the onion, and add it to the pot along with the bay leaves, carrots, salt, and pepper. Over medium-high heat, bring to a boil, reduce to a simmer, cover, and simmer for 2 to 3 hours, until the tongue is fork-tender.

Remove the tongue from the pot, reserving the broth. Allow the tongue to cool slightly. Meanwhile, make the béchamel sauce using the broth.

For the béchamel sauce:

2½ tablespoons unsalted butter

2½ tablespoons all-purpose flour

2 cups cooking broth from the tongue

½ teaspoon salt

¼ teaspoon freshly ground white pepper

Melt the butter in a 2½-quart saucepan. Using a wooden spoon, blend in the flour to make a paste. Stir over medium heat until the butter and flour begin to foam—about 1½ to 2 minutes. Turn the heat off, and wait for the bubbling to cease.

Add 1½ cups of the broth, and whisk to blend thoroughly. Turn the heat back on to medium-low, and continue to whisk gently (making sure no bits of flour stick to the pot) until the sauce begins to boil. Cook for 2 to 3 minutes, stirring constantly and slowly adding more broth if it gets too thick. The sauce should be thick enough to coat a spoon. Remove from heat. Add salt and pepper to taste.

Proceed with peeling and slicing the tongue, but stop periodically to whisk the béchamel sauce to prevent skin from forming over the surface.

Trim off any bones or fat attached to the tongue. Using a sharp knife, slice down the center, piercing only the top layer of skin. Peel the skin away with your fingers, and cut the meat into ¼ -inch slices. Arrange on warmed plates, spoon the béchamel sauce on top, and garnish with capers.

Veal Pot Roast

Pam Moore, Sunnyside Farm, New York

Pam Moore adapted this recipe from Sally Fallon's version of traditional pot roast. Sally Fallon writes: "In the German-speaking areas of Europe, housewives marinated beef or game several days in buttermilk before cooking it. The results are extremely tender and flavorful." Testing this recipe, we found the taste subtle and delicate, not heavy and over-bearing. When you plan to make this roast, begin marinating the roast at least three days—or even up to eight—before you cook it.

ON A BUDGET • MINIMUM PREPARATION

SERVES 4 TO 6

2 pounds veal London broil, arm, or chuck roast (or substitute a beef roast)

3 to 4 cups buttermilk (see note)

2 tablespoons unsalted butter

2 tablespoons extra virgin olive oil

1 onion, cut into wedges

2 cups stock (meat, poultry, or vegetable)

½ cup dry red wine

1 teaspoon fresh thyme, or ½ teaspoon dried

1 pound boiling potatoes, cut into small chunks

½ pound carrots, scraped and cut into ¾-inch rounds

2 tablespoons all-purpose flour

½ cup ice water

Sea salt and freshly ground black pepper to taste

Pierce the roast several times with a sharp knife and marinate in the buttermilk in the refrigerator for several days, turning occasionally. However, if you have enough buttermilk to cover the roast completely, turning it will be unnecessary.

Preheat oven to 300°F.

Remove the roast from the buttermilk, and pat dry. Heat the butter and olive oil in a heavy, large skillet. Add the onion and then the roast. Cook over medium heat until the meat browns, about 5 to 7 minutes per side. Remove the meat, and pour off any excess fat.

Add the stock, wine, and thyme; bring to a boil, scraping up any browned bits. Cook for about 3 minutes.

Place the roast in a casserole dish, add the stock mixture, cover, and bake for 3 to 5 hours, or until fork-tender. About 1½ hours before you are ready to eat, add the potatoes and carrots.

Take the casserole from the oven, remove the meat and vegetables, set them aside, and keep warm. Pour the stock from casserole into a skillet and bring to a boil. Slowly whisk the flour into the ice water and, when smooth, add to the skillet. Continue to cook over medium heat, stirring frequently, until the sauce thickens and is slightly reduced. Season the sauce to taste with salt and pepper. Pour the sauce over the meat, and serve.

Note: If you don't have buttermilk handy, bring 1 quart whole milk to room temperature, and mix in 4 tablespoons of white vinegar, fresh lemon juice, or Kombucha tea. Allow the mixture to rest for 5 to 10 minutes before using.

Linda's Sauerbraten

Sara Cameron, Cameron Ranch, Wyoming

Sara Cameron and her husband, Pete, operate a cattle and sheep ranch in central Wyoming. This sauerbraten (German for sour roast), coupled with red cabbage and potato pancakes, is a family favorite. To fully enjoy it, begin marinating the meat at least 2 days before you plan to cook it.

SHOWCASE • ON A BUDGET • MINIMUM PREPARATION

SERVES 8

3½ to 4 pounds rump or sirloin tip roast

1 cup water

1 cup red wine vinegar

1 large onion, thinly sliced

1 lemon, unpeeled, thinly sliced

10 whole cloves

4 bay leaves

6 peppercorns

2 tablespoons salt

2 tablespoons sugar

12 gingersnaps, crushed

Place the roast in a deep ceramic or glass bowl. Combine the water, vinegar, onion, lemon, cloves, bay leaves, peppercorns, salt, and sugar; pour over the meat. If the liquid doesn't cover the meat, add equal parts of water and vinegar until it is completely submersed. Cover and refrigerate for 2 to 4 days—the longer it marinates, the more intense the flavors. Turn the meat occasionally while it is marinating.

When you're ready to cook it, place the roast in a slow cooker. Pour in 1 cup of the marinade, cover, and cook on low for 6 to 8 hours, until the meat is fork-tender. Remove the meat, and keep warm.

To make gingerbread gravy:

Strain the liquid, and return it to the cooker. Stir in the crushed gingersnaps, cover, and cook on high for 10 to 15 minutes.

Slice the meat and top with the gravy. Serve with red cabbage (see page 121) and potato pancakes.

For the potato pancakes:

SERVES 4 (CAN EASILY BE DOUBLED)

> 3 large baking potatoes
>
> 5 tablespoons finely chopped onion
>
> 1 teaspoon salt
>
> ½ teaspoon freshly ground black pepper
>
> 2 eggs, beaten
>
> 3 tablespoons fine dry breadcrumbs, crushed crackers, or wheat germ
>
> 2 tablespoons olive oil
>
> 3 tablespoons unsalted butter

Peel the potatoes and grate into a medium-size bowl. Wrap in several layers of cheesecloth, and squeeze out as much water as you can. Return the grated potatoes to the bowl, and stir in the chopped onion, salt, pepper, eggs, and breadcrumbs. If the mixture seems watery, add more crumbs.

Heat the oil and butter in a heavy skillet. Drop the batter into the oil in heaping spoonfuls. Fry until brown on both sides. Serve with plain yogurt and applesauce.

Luisella's Boiled Beef

Luisella Masserini and Riccardo Gorini, Mother Nature's Beef, Manitoba, Canada

Luisella Masserini developed this recipe as a reduced-fat alternative to a traditional Italian dish, "Bollito in Salsa Verde." Although it takes all day to prepare, it does not require a lot of time standing in the kitchen.

ON A BUDGET

SERVES 8

> $4\frac{1}{2}$ pounds brisket
>
> 1 bulb garlic, cloves peeled and left whole
>
> 2 stalks celery, coarsely chopped
>
> 3 carrots, scraped, coarsely chopped
>
> 2 onions, cut in eighths
>
> 1 sprig fresh rosemary, or 1 teaspoon dried rosemary
>
> 3 bay leaves
>
> 1 sprig fresh sage, or 1 teaspoon dried sage
>
> 1 teaspoon salt
>
> 2 cups chopped fresh parsley, or $\frac{1}{2}$ cup dried
>
> 2 tablespoons capers, rinsed and drained
>
> 2 tablespoons Dijon mustard
>
> $\frac{1}{3}$ cup olive oil
>
> $\frac{1}{3}$ cup balsamic vinegar
>
> 1 small sweet red onion, quartered

Place the brisket in a large pot with the garlic, celery, carrots, onions, rosemary, bay leaves, sage, and salt. Cover with water, bring to a boil, and reduce the heat until the broth is boiling lightly. Continue at a gentle boil, covered, for 2 to $2\frac{1}{2}$ hours, until tender. Turn the heat off, and rest the meat in the broth at least 20 minutes. Remove the meat, cover with aluminum foil, and cool at room temperature for 2 hours.

Package and freeze the remaining broth for another use (Riccardo Gorini notes that this broth is perfect for making risotto alla parmigiana, which can be found in most Italian cookbooks).

To make the sauce, blend together the parsley, capers, mustard, olive oil, vinegar, and onion in a food processor.

Cut the brisket into thin slices. Spread a light amount of sauce in the bottom of a medium-size serving dish. Set one layer of meat on top. Add more sauce, and continue layering meat and sauce until they are both used up. If necessary, the sauce can be thinned by adding equal amounts of olive oil and balsamic vinegar.

Place in the freezer for 4 hours. Remove and serve cold or slightly warmed with warmed fresh flatbread.

MY POT ROAST ISN'T TENDER!

You followed the recipe faithfully, and your pot roast isn't tender. What happened? Did the farmer sell you bad meat? Did I provide you with a bum recipe?

Hopefully, neither of us is at fault. You're not to blame either. Meat that is braised is usually one of "the tougher cuts," which are taken from the front of the animal or from the round or shanks. These are the parts that do the most work and therefore have a lot of collagen, or connective tissue. The purpose of cooking them in liquid is to break down that collagen, tenderizing the meat.

The trick with grass-fed meat, however, is that not all animals are going to have the same amount of collagen in their muscles. Older animals, in particular, will have more chemically mature collagen, which does not break down as easily as the collagen in young animals. This meat will require more cooking time in the liquid.

So don't be mad; just be patient. Simply allow your pot roast to braise for a little while longer.

Stuffed Breast of Veal

For a real treat, ask your local veal producer to have a boneless breast of veal prepared for you by a favorite butcher. Make sure you request that the butcher cut a pocket in the meat for you as well. If this is not possible, buy the breast and cut the pocket yourself—slice it from the large end toward the point—and remove the small rib bones after the meat is cooked. Do this by breaking them away from the joints and then pulling them free from the meat. You could also serve it with the bones in: simply carve around the bones and tell your guests to look for them.

SHOWCASE

SERVES 6

For the stuffing:

3 tablespoons unsalted butter

6 tablespoons olive oil

1 large onion, finely diced

1 bunch fresh spinach
   (about 10 ounces), finely chopped

¾ pound bulk pork sausage (breakfast
   or sweet Italian sausage work best)

1 cup cooked rice

2 teaspoons dried thyme

½ teaspoon salt

¼ teaspoon freshly ground
   black pepper

¼ teaspoon freshly ground nutmeg

2 eggs, slightly beaten

1 cup finely chopped walnuts

1 breast of veal

For the braise:

Salt and freshly ground black pepper

1½ cups dry white wine

2 cloves garlic

4 sprigs parsley

1 bay leaf

1 sprig thyme

1 onion, pierced with 2 whole cloves

1 cup veal or chicken stock

1 large tomato, seeded, diced

2 pounds veal or beef bones

1 cup pitted black olives

¼ cup chopped fresh parsley

Begin by making the stuffing. Heat the butter and 3 tablespoons of the olive oil in a large, heavy skillet. Add the onion, and sauté over medium heat until translucent. Add the chopped spinach, and sauté 3 minutes longer, or until the spinach wilts. Remove the mixture to a large bowl.

Add the sausage to the skillet, and cook until browned. Pour the sausage and any pan drippings into the spinach and onion mixture. Thoroughly mix in the rice, thyme, salt, pepper, nutmeg, eggs, and walnuts. Allow the mixture to cool slightly.

Once the stuffing is cool enough to handle, stuff it into the breast of veal. Do not overfill the veal pocket. If there is extra stuffing left over, use it to stuff bell peppers, or heat it later and serve it separately with dinner. Secure the stuffing in the pocket by sewing the pocket shut with a trussing needle and string or by threading it closed with a metal skewer.

Preheat the oven to 300°F.

Heat the remaining 3 tablespoons of olive oil over medium-high heat in the skillet. Sprinkle the breast of veal lightly with salt and pepper, and brown on both sides. Transfer the veal to a casserole or braising pan. Add ½ cup of the white wine to the skillet, and simmer 2 to 3 minutes, scraping up any browned bits. Pour the pan juices on top of the veal.

Set the garlic, parsley sprigs, bay leaf, and thyme on a square of cheesecloth; tie it tightly into a bundle with butcher twine, and place it in the roasting pan. Quarter the clove-pierced onion, and add it to the pan with the stock, the remaining 1 cup of wine, and the diced tomato. Arrange the veal bones around the side.

Cover tightly (if you don't have a cover, foil will work), and roast for 1½ hours. Uncover the pan, turn the veal, and add more wine or some water if the cooking liquid has evaporated (the vegetables should be covered). Cover the pan once more, and cook for another 1 to 2 hours, until the veal is fork-tender. Remove the cover, and roast 1 hour longer, or until the veal is golden brown. Remove it to a large platter, and tent it with foil.

Set the braising pan over medium heat on your stovetop, and bring the liquid to a simmer. Strain the sauce by removing the vegetables, bones, and cheesecloth. Add the olives and fresh chopped parsley, and simmer for 3 to 5 minutes, until the sauce has reduced to almost a syrup. Season to taste with salt and pepper. Cut the veal in thick slices, and arrange on warmed plates. Spoon the pan sauce on top, and serve.

Grilled Veal Short Ribs

Amy Kenyon, Skate Creek Farm, New York

Amy Kenyon writes that these ribs can also be made with a more traditional barbecue sauce, instead of Dijon and rosemary. She recommends pairing them with twice-baked potatoes.

SHOWCASE • ON A BUDGET • MINIMUM PREPARATION

SERVES 4 (THIS RECIPE IS EASILY DOUBLED. SIMPLY ALLOW 1 POUND OF SHORT RIBS PER PERSON.)

4 pounds veal short ribs

Salt and freshly ground
    black pepper to taste

1 tablespoon dried rosemary

3 strips thick cut bacon

2 onions, coarsely chopped

4 cloves garlic, minced

1 cup scraped, coarsely chopped carrots

2 bay leaves

2 cups beef or veal stock

4 tablespoons Dijon mustard

2 sprigs fresh rosemary, finely chopped

Preheat oven to 325°F.

Sprinkle the short ribs with salt, pepper, and dried rosemary.

Fry the bacon in a large Dutch oven over medium-high heat. Discard the bacon, and keep the drippings in the pan.

Brown the short ribs on all sides in the bacon fat. Remove the ribs from the pan, and add the onions, garlic, and carrots. Season the vegetables with salt and pepper, and cook until they begin to brown, stirring often. Add the bay leaves, stock, and short ribs. Cover, and bake in the oven for 2 hours.

Meanwhile, combine the mustard with the chopped fresh rosemary to make a paste.

Remove the ribs from the pan, and brush with the mustard-rosemary paste. Put the ribs on a hot grill, and cook until the surface is crispy. Serve with the cooking broth.

Teriyaki Short Ribs

This recipe is adapted from a similar dish called "Korean-Style Oven-Browned Short Ribs," *from Bruce Aidells and Denis Kelly's excellent book* The Complete Meat Cookbook. *It is* *easy to prepare and extremely flavorful.*

ON A BUDGET • MINIMUM PREPARATION • KID-FRIENDLY

SERVES 4 TO 5

¾ cup tamari

1 tablespoon ground ginger

¼ cup honey

3 tablespoons finely chopped chives

3 cups water

2 tablespoons cider or rice vinegar

1 large head garlic, cloves peeled and left whole

3 pounds beef short ribs

4 tablespoons sesame oil

In a large Dutch oven, whisk the tamari, ginger, honey, chives, water, and vinegar; add the whole cloves of garlic.

Add the short ribs. Bring the pot to a boil over high heat, turn the heat to low, and simmer, covered, for 2½ to 3 hours, or until the meat is fork-tender. If you start to run out of liquid, add ⅔ cup water and ⅓ cup tamari. Remove the ribs and keep warm, but continue to allow the broth to simmer, uncovered, on the stove.

Meanwhile, preheat oven to 450°F.

Place the ribs on a roasting pan, meat side up, and brush with sesame oil. Roast for 15 minutes, or until the edges become crispy. Serve in warmed shallow bowls with a few spoonfuls of broth poured on top.

Garlic-Tomato Short Ribs

I made this recipe for a small dinner party one cold January afternoon, using whatever ingredients I had on hand. What a delight these ribs are, especially with the rich sauce spooned over a pile of potatoes mashed with sour cream. This is hearty fare, and a real crowd-pleaser.

SHOWCASE • ON A BUDGET • MINIMUM PREPARATION

SERVES 6 TO 8

2 tablespoons sea salt

1 tablespoon freshly ground black pepper

6 to 7 pounds short ribs

3 tablespoons olive oil

2 medium carrots, scraped, finely chopped plus 3 carrots, scraped and sliced into narrow, 2-inch strips for later use

2 medium onions, finely chopped

16 cloves garlic, peeled and left whole

2 teaspoons dried thyme

2 teaspoons dried basil

2 teaspoons savory

1 teaspoon fennel

1 teaspoon dried lavender heads (optional)

3 tablespoons all-purpose flour

3 cups cabernet sauvignon

3 cups beef broth

1 28-ounce can crushed tomatoes

2 bay leaves

¾ cup oil-cured black olives, pitted

Preheat oven to 300°F.

Combine the salt and pepper in a shallow bowl. Spread mixture lightly on each of the short ribs; set aside on a large platter (depending on your taste, you might want more salt and pepper).

Heat the olive oil in an 8-quart ovenproof pot that can be covered later, add the seasoned ribs in batches, and brown. Set aside.

Add the finely chopped carrots and onions to the drippings, and cook until tender. Toss in the cloves of garlic, the herbs, and flour. Stir well to incorporate the flour. Add the wine and beef broth. Bring to a boil over medium-high heat, scraping up any browned bits from the bottom of the pan. Add the tomatoes and the bay leaves, and return to a boil for 1 minute. Add the ribs and any lingering juices, cover the pot, and bake in the oven for 3 to 4 hours, or until the meat is fork-tender.

Remove the pot from the oven. Remove ribs from sauce and set aside. Add the carrot sticks and black olives to the sauce; simmer on top of the stove, uncovered, for an additional 15 minutes, or until the carrots are tender. Return ribs to sauce and serve. These ribs go well with mashed potatoes and green beans.

Slow-Cooker Version:

As described above, coat the short ribs with salt and pepper, and brown in olive oil. Place the ribs and all the ingredients (except the carrot sticks and olives) in a large slow cooker, and cook on low for 6 to 8 hours, until the meat is fork-tender. Remove the ribs, and keep warm. Add the carrot sticks and olives to the pan juices, and cook on high, uncovered, for 20 minutes, until the carrots are tender and the sauce has thickened slightly.

Boeuf à la Bourguignone (Beef Burgundy)

Lucien Hinkle, Westhaven Farm, Vermont

Lucien Hinkle got this surprisingly simple version of Beef Burgundy from his mother, who adapted it from an old French cookbook. It is easy to prepare and makes a wonderful meal for a chilly day.

ON A BUDGET • MINIMUM PREPARATION

SERVES 4

3 tablespoons olive oil

2 strips bacon, cut into 1-inch pieces

2 pounds stew beef

Salt and freshly ground
    black pepper to taste

12 small white onions, peeled,
    whole (cut in half, if desired)

1 clove garlic, crushed

2 tablespoons all-purpose flour

2 cups dry red wine

2 cups water

2 tablespoons tomato paste

2 teaspoons fresh thyme

1 tablespoon finely chopped parsley

3 bay leaves

7 peppercorns

1 pound mushrooms

Heat the olive oil over a medium flame in a heavy, medium-size stew pot. Add the bacon. Cook for 1 minute.

Sprinkle the beef with salt and pepper, and add to the pot. Cook until browned, turning often, about 7 to 8 minutes. Remove the bacon and the beef; add the onions and garlic, sauté for 2 minutes, and return the meat to the pot. Sprinkle with flour, stir, and cook 2 to 3 minutes longer. Add the remaining ingredients (except the mushrooms), and mix well. Cover, and simmer for 1½ to 2 hours, or until the meat is fork-tender.

Add the mushrooms, and cook, at a slow simmer, 15 minutes longer. Serve over a bed of rice.

Old-Fashioned Beef Stew

Here's a simple, straightforward beef stew recipe—the kind that might have been cooked on top of woodstoves years ago.

ON A BUDGET • MINIMUM PREPARATION • KID-FRIENDLY

SERVES 4 TO 6

1 cup all-purpose flour

2 teaspoons salt

1 teaspoon freshly ground black pepper

1 teaspoon paprika

2 pounds stewing beef, cut into 1-inch cubes

3 tablespoons olive oil

2 large onions, peeled and cut into wedges

1 crumbled bay leaf

1 tablespoon Worcestershire sauce

1 28-ounce can tomatoes, whole or crushed, undrained

2 cups beef broth

2 quarts water

6 to 8 carrots, scraped and cut into chunks

2 small turnips, peeled and cubed

4 boiling potatoes, cut into large chunks

Combine the flour, salt, pepper, and paprika in a shallow bowl.

Dredge the meat in the flour. Heat the olive oil in a large soup pot over medium-high heat. Add the meat, and brown on all sides. Add the remaining ingredients, except the carrots, turnips, and potatoes. Cover. Bring the stew to a boil, reduce the heat, and simmer, covered, for 2 hours.

Add the carrots and turnips, cover, and continue cooking 45 minutes longer. Add the potatoes, cover once more, and cook for another 20 to 25 minutes, or until you can pierce the potatoes with a fork.

Braised Beef with Rich Gravy and Rice

Marcia LeClair, Rocky Meadow Farm, New Hampshire

Here's a homey way to enjoy your stew beef or round steaks. This recipe looks complicated, but it is quite simple. Start by preparing the beef. Once it is simmering in the broth, make the rice with vegetables, then finish off the beef and gravy and serve. From start to finish, this recipe should take only about an hour and a half, with ample downtime for sipping cocktails and nibbling. The ingredients are inexpensive, and the entire meal can be served in one steaming-hot nourishing bowl.

ON A BUDGET

SERVES 4

1 ½ to 2 pounds stew beef or round steak, cut into 1-inch cubes

Salt and freshly ground black pepper to taste

2 tablespoons olive oil

1 medium onion, sliced into thin wedges

2 cups sliced mushrooms (optional)

1 clove garlic, minced

3 cups beef broth plus 1 cup, if needed for gravy

4 tablespoons all-purpose flour

¾ cup ice water

Sprinkle the beef cubes with salt and pepper. Heat the olive oil in a large, heavy skillet. Add the meat, and sauté until well browned; remove to a bowl, and keep warm. In the same skillet, sauté the onions, mushrooms, and garlic until the onions are translucent.

Add 3 cups of the broth, and bring to a simmer, stirring the mixture often and scraping up any browned bits. Return the beef to the skillet, cover tightly, and simmer for 1 hour or more, until the beef is tender. If the liquid starts to boil over, turn the heat down slightly.

Periodically check the stew to make sure there is ample liquid for cooking the meat and for making the gravy afterward. If too much has boiled off, add the fourth cup of broth. If you still need more liquid, add a cup or two of water (you'll want nearly 2 cups of liquid left in the pan after the meat has cooked). During this time, prepare the rice and vegetables (see below).

Once the rice and vegetables are ready, in a separate glass, whisk the flour into the ice water until smooth. Gradually stir this thickener into the simmering beef and broth. Bring the mixture to a slow boil and cook for a few seconds, stirring, until the gravy thickens. Serve over the rice with vegetables.

For the rice and vegetables:

2 cups brown rice (see note)

4 cups warm water

1 teaspoon salt

2 tablespoons unsalted butter

3 stalks celery, coarsely chopped

1 onion, finely chopped

3 carrots, scraped, shredded

2 sweet bell peppers, green or red, diced

2 tablespoons olive oil

½ cup blanched almonds, sliced

Bring rice to a boil, skim off any residue that rises to the top, stir in the salt and butter, cover, lower the heat, and simmer until all liquid is absorbed, about 30 to 45 minutes.

Just before all the water is evaporated, sauté the vegetables in the olive oil until crisp-tender. Stir them into the cooked rice, and add the sliced almonds. Keep warm until you are ready to serve.

Note: I advocate following Sally Fallon's advice (in *Nourishing Traditions)* to soak and ferment grains and legumes in yogurt before cooking them. This does not affect their flavor, but it does allow the enzymes and lactobacilli in the yogurt to neutralize the phytic acid, greatly improving their nutritional properties. If you know when you will be preparing this recipe, simply cover the rice with warm water and 4 tablespoons plain yogurt in an ovenproof casserole and let sit, covered, in a warm place for a minimum of 7 hours. Afterward, cook as instructed above.

Chili Brew Beef Stew with Floating Biscuits

This stew epitomizes comfort food. Adding beer to the broth livens the beefy flavor, and the biscuit topping makes an extra-special treat. My recipe testers believed this would be particularly suitable as Superbowl fare. If your local farmer can provide you with lard (or if you make it yourself following the instructions on page 140), you will have a light, flaky biscuit topping beyond imagination. If lard is not available, butter will work.

ON A BUDGET

SERVES 4

For the dredge:

½ cup all-purpose flour

1 to 2 heaping tablespoons chili powder
(or to taste, depending on the heat you want)

1½ teaspoons salt

1 to 3 teaspoons freshly ground black pepper

Mix all the ingredients in a large, shallow bowl. Use the dredge to coat the beef bones, oxtails, or stew meat.

For the stew:

4 to 7 tablespoons olive oil

1 to 1½ pounds beef soup bones, oxtails, or stew meat, thawed

1 large onion, cut into wedges

3 carrots, scraped, coarsely chopped

1 parsnip or turnip, peeled, coarsely chopped

1 can beer (cheap beer will do; save the good beer for yourself)

2 cups beef stock

2 teaspoons dried thyme

3 bay leaves

In a large Dutch oven or ovenproof pot, heat 4 tablespoons oil over medium heat. Brown the bones or meat on all sides, adding more oil if necessary. Remove and set aside.

If the pan is dry, add a little bit more olive oil. Add the onion wedges, and sauté until translucent, scraping up any brown bits from the bottom of the pan. Add the carrots and parsnips, sauté, and scrape up the brown bits. Sauté for 5 to 7 minutes, until the onion just begins to brown (do not allow any bits to burn).

Return the meat to the pot, add the beer and enough stock to cover everything; add the thyme and bay leaves. Bring to a boil, reduce to a simmer, and cover. Cook the stew for 1 ½ to 2 hours, until the meat is fork-tender. Remove the bones. When they are cool enough, pick off any morsels of meat and return them to the stew. Discard the bones.

For the biscuit topping:

2 cups all-purpose or cake flour

3 teaspoons sugar

4 teaspoons baking powder

1 teaspoon salt

4 tablespoons lard or cold, unsalted butter

1 to 1 ½ cups milk

Preheat the oven to 425°F when the stew is almost ready.

Combine all the dry ingredients for the topping in a mixing bowl. Using a pastry cutter, lightly blend in the lard or butter. Add just enough milk to create a moist, pastelike dough that can be scooped up for the stew. Be careful not to overmix. Gently drop the dough by spoonfuls onto the top of the slowly simmering stew. Try to do this as evenly as possible, but don't worry if you cannot cover the entire top, because the biscuit topping will rise and expand.

Put the stew with its dough topping into the oven, and bake, uncovered, for 10 to 15 minutes until the topping is browned.

Osso Buco

For all the mystique surrounding it, Osso Buco is really nothing more than delicious, easy-to-prepare, fireside comfort food. If you don't have veal shanks, try this recipe with lamb, goat, or beef shanks. The flavor will be different but still satisfyingly good.

SHOWCASE

SERVES 5

½ cup all-purpose flour plus 2 tablespoons

1 tablespoon salt

½ teaspoon freshly ground black pepper

4 tablespoons unsalted butter

4 tablespoons olive oil

4 pounds veal shanks, cut crosswise into 2-inch pieces

1 large onion, coarsely chopped

1 large clove garlic, coarsely chopped

1 cup dry white wine

1 cup lamb, veal, or chicken stock

2 teaspoons dried thyme

2 tablespoons minced fresh parsley

2 tablespoons tomato paste

1½ teaspoons freshly grated lemon zest

4 carrots, scraped, coarsely chopped

2 stalks celery plus leaves, chopped

Combine ½ cup of the flour, salt, and pepper in a shallow bowl. Set aside.

Heat 2 tablespoons of the butter and 2 tablespoons of the olive oil in an extra-deep skillet or flameproof casserole. Dredge the shanks in the flour mixture, and sauté in the butter and olive oil, turning occasionally, until browned, about 10 to 12 minutes. Remove the shanks, reserving any pan juices.

Add the remaining 2 tablespoons olive oil to the skillet. Add the onion, and cook until slightly caramelized; add the garlic, and sauté 1 minute longer. Turn the heat to low, pour in the wine and stock, and simmer 2 minutes, scraping up the browned bits. Return the shanks and accumulated juices to the pan.

Stir in the thyme, parsley, tomato paste, and lemon zest. Cover, and simmer for 2 hours, or until the meat begins to fall off the bone. Stir once or twice during this time. If too much liquid evaporates, add another ½ to 1 cup of stock or water and continue cooking.

Add the carrots and celery, and cook 15 minutes longer, or until the carrots are just tender. Remove the meat to a warm platter, and tent with foil.

Melt the remaining 2 tablespoons butter, and mix in the remaining 2 tablespoons of the flour. Slowly add to the sauce, and simmer, stirring often, until the sauce is smooth and slightly thickened.

For the gremolata:
½ cup crushed walnuts

½ cup minced fresh parsley

2 cloves garlic, minced

1 teaspoon lemon zest

Preheat oven to 350°F.

Place the crushed walnuts in a shallow pan, and roast for 10 minutes, or until they are fragrant. Combine the nuts with the parsley, garlic, and lemon zest in a small bowl. Mix thoroughly. Set aside.

To serve:

Place the meat in warmed, deep dishes or shallow bowls, pour the sauce on top, then sprinkle with the gremolata. Serve with crusty bread or on top of polenta.

Beef Stock

Many of the recipes in this book call for beef stock. It is easy to buy canned broth or bouillon cubes to have on hand, but a good homemade beef stock has richer flavor and is far more nutritious, and you can be assured of the ingredients' safety. Many farmers will sell you reasonably priced soup bones, but also be sure to save the bones from your roasts and steaks, because they will work just as well (in fact, the meatier the bones, the better). Store stock in your freezer until you are ready to use it or until someone in your family comes down with a cold or the flu. A mug full of steaming broth can be amazingly restorative.

Many stock recipes call for removing excess fat, as well as clarifying the stock. I do not find that the extra fat infringes on the quality of my cooking or my waistline, and I find clarifying stock a nuisance. The results of the technique described here will work fine for your recipes.

MAKES 4 TO 5 QUARTS

    4 pounds beef bones

    2 large carrots, cut in very large chunks

    3 ribs celery, cut in very large chunks

    2 onions, peeled and quartered

    7 quarts water

    3 to 4 sprigs thyme

    3 to 4 sprigs oregano

    3 cloves garlic, unpeeled and crushed

    1 tomato, coarsely chopped

    2 teaspoons salt

    2 tablespoons vinegar

Preheat oven to 450°F.

Place the bones and the vegetables in a large roasting pan and roast for 40 minutes, or until the bones have thoroughly browned. Periodically turn them over, and baste the bones and vegetables with any accumulated fat drippings. Pour the bones and vegetables into a very large stockpot.

Set the roasting pan on the stovetop, and pour in 2 cups of the water. Over medium heat, bring the water to a simmer, scraping up the browned bits, and add to the stockpot with any drippings. Tie the thyme and oregano sprigs together, making a bouquet, and add them to the pot along with the garlic, tomato, salt, the remaining $6\frac{1}{2}$ quarts of water, and vinegar. Allow the mixture to rest for 30 minutes.

Bring the mixture to a boil, skimming off any scum that rises to the surface. Reduce the heat to low, and slowly simmer the stock for a minimum of 6 hours. The longer you cook your stock down, the richer it will be. I often simmer stock all day, store it in the refrigerator for the night, and then continue simmering it for several hours the next morning.

Remove all the bones, vegetables, and herbs. Completely cool the stock before pouring it into freezer containers. If you wish, skim off any fat that has risen to the surface before you pack it away.

Note: I also use this technique for making lamb broth, another wonderful ingredient to have on hand. Lamb broth, often substituted for beef broth, is especially delicious in the French Onion Soup on page 80.

French Onion Soup

This is my favorite use for good beef or lamb stock. If you keep stock on hand in your freezer, you can have a memorable lunch or the fabulous first course for a dinner ready in minutes.

SHOWCASE • IN A HURRY • ON A BUDGET • MINIMUM PREPARATION

SERVES 6

4 tablespoons unsalted butter

5 to 6 onions, sliced into thin rings

1 to 2 tablespoons honey

6 cups beef or lamb broth (see page 78)

1 large carrot, scraped, finely diced

1 tablespoon dried thyme

1 tablespoon Worcestershire sauce

½ teaspoon freshly ground black pepper

Salt to taste

6 thick slices of French bread

2 cups shredded Swiss cheese

Preheat oven to 450°F.

Melt the butter in a medium-size soup pot over medium heat. Add the onions, and cook until translucent. Drizzle the honey on top, and sauté 2 minutes longer. Add the broth, carrot, thyme, Worcestershire sauce, and pepper, and simmer for a minimum of 30 minutes. Taste for seasonings, and add salt, if desired.

Toast the bread, and place 1 slice in each of the bottoms of 6 heat-proof bowls. Pour the soup on top, sprinkle each serving with a generous helping of cheese, and bake in the oven for 5 minutes, or until the cheese is completely melted.

Note: This recipe can easily serve fewer people. Just prepare as many slices of toast as you have diners, and store the extra soup in the refrigerator or freezer.

COMMON RETAIL CUTS OF BEEF AND IDEAL COOKING METHODS

CHUCK

Roast	Moist heat, Super slow roast
Steak	Moist heat, Super slow roast
Stew beef	Moist heat
Short ribs	Moist heat
Ground beef	Dry or Moist heat

FLANK

Flank steak	Dry heat
Hanger or Skirt steak	Dry heat

FORE SHANK

Shanks	Moist heat

PLATE

Short ribs	Moist heat
Brisket	Moist heat
Stew beef	Moist heat
Spare ribs	Moist heat, Super slow roast

RIB

Rib steaks	Dry heat
Rib eye steaks (Delmonico)	Dry heat
Rib roast	Dry heat
Short ribs	Moist heat

ROUND

Sirloin tip roasts and steaks	Dry heat, Super slow roast
Top round roast	Dry heat, Super slow roast
Eye round roast	Dry heat, Super slow roast
Bottom round roast	Moist heat, Super slow roast
Sandwich or shaved steaks	Dry heat (pan fry)

SHORT LOIN

Tenderloin roast	Dry heat
Filet mignon	Dry heat
Porterhouse and T-bone steaks	Dry heat
Top loin steaks (NY strip or Kansas City)	Dry heat

SIRLOIN

Sirloin steaks and roasts	Dry heat, Super slow roast
Tri-tip	Dry heat
Kabobs	Dry heat

CHAPTER THREE

$\mathcal{L}$AMB AND GOAT

Sheep and goats were among man's first domesticated animals, dating back at least as far as the Neolithic period ten thousand years ago.[1] This was probably because sheep and goats were extremely useful creatures, surviving on scrublands and pastures and providing meat, milk, textiles, and hides. The meat from these animals has been treasured worldwide for thousands of years; the Bible, for example, refers to the desirability of lamb meat.[2] Still, lamb and goat remain relatively uncommon features on American dinner tables. This is a shame, since grass-fed lamb and goat have delicate flavors, can be raised on lands that are unsuitable for any other sort of agricultural production, and are inexpensive to produce.

The global popularity of these meats means that there is an astounding array of dishes to enjoy. Because sheep and goats are processed at such a young age (generally anywhere between four months old to one year), their meat is very tender, and most of it can be cooked using either dry- or moist-heat methods (although certain cuts do taste better using certain methods; see Table 3 on page 131). The only exceptions would be the shanks and necks, which require moist heat, and the loins and ribs, which are best broiled or roasted.

Goat meat is significantly lower in fat than lamb, and it can toughen easily if it is cooked at temperatures that are too high. Its flavor is quite different, tasting something like venison or beef. Thankfully, because goat meat has not become a popular U.S. agricultural commodity, goats are more commonly raised on grass on small farms and are not subject to the woes of feedlot production.[3] The cooking techniques used for lamb in this chapter apply equally to goat, so the one type of meat can certainly be substituted for the other, although the finished dishes will taste different.

Although a good portion of the imported lamb found in grocery stores has been raised on grass, most of the lamb produced in the United States comes from commercial feedlots located in California, Colorado, Texas, and Wyoming.[4] These commercial feedlots, representing only 2 percent of the nation's lamb producers, are producing more than 50 percent of the lamb and sheep. Still, because sheep are relatively easy to handle and inexpensive to produce, lamb raised on small grass farms is easily found throughout the country.

There is relatively little complete research regarding the flavor differences among the various breeds of sheep. The tastes vary widely, with the darker-faced breeds (such as the very common Suffolks and Hampshires) having a reputation for a somewhat stronger flavor. This is also the lamb meat that is typically found in the supermarket. The lighter-faced breeds, such as Cheviots and Icelandics, are believed to have a milder flavor. Many sheep farmers have experimented with their breeding programs, developing crosses that offer a combination of good muscling and flavor. The desirability of a stronger or a milder lamb flavor is one of personal preference. The best way to find out what tastes best to you is to try lamb from a few different producers.

To evaluate a lamb or goat operation, use the same criteria that you would for beef:

- The pastures should be well managed. Lambs and goats can be turned out to pastures when the grasses are six to ten inches tall and should be moved to fresh fields once the grass is below three inches. Unlike cattle, goats and sheep will graze pastures down to the ground. This can kill off the grasses, so the farmer must be diligent about rotating the animals.

- The animals should experience as little stress as possible before slaughter. The same care taken with cattle should be taken with goats and lambs. Trucking distances should be kept to a minimum, animals should be herded onto the trailer as calmly as possible, and animals should be brought to the plant at a quiet time.

- Although goat and lamb meat does not require the extensive aging that beef needs, lamb meat still benefits from a minimum five-day dry-aging period. Goat meat, due to the animals' minimal fat cover, may dry out too much.

GRASS-FED FOR FLUFFY AND FIDO?

The next time you reach into a bag of pet food to get dinner for your beloved pet, pause for a moment and read a few of the ingredients that appear on the side of the bag. What exactly is "chicken by-product meal"? What is meant by "thickened fat preserved with mixed toco-pherols"? What is "monosodium phosphate"? We know that for people, a good diet requires a variety of healthy, clean, fresh foods, yet why do we assume that a daily regimen of highly processed food from questionable sources is acceptable for our furry family members?

Dr. Richard Pitcairn and Susan Pitcairn, the authors of *Natural Health for Dogs and Cats*, write: "No diet we can formulate from least cost products and process for convenience and long storage will ever rival those mysteriously complex fresh-food diets offered for aeons by Nature herself."[1] They note that in many states, the laws allow pet food makers to use "4-D" sources for pet food, which means animals that are dead, dying, disabled, or diseased upon arrival at the slaughterhouse. As an alternative, the Pitcairns recommend feeding pets a highly varied diet, much like our own, including raw meats, eggs, dairy products, grains and legumes, veg etables, and bones. Their book contains a number of easy-to-prepare recipes to help you create balanced meals using these healthy ingredients.

One of the best sources for many of your pets' nutritional needs is your local farmer. Although you may not want to purchase an expensive rack of lamb or a beef tenderloin for Fido's supper, there are some inexpensive, wholesome options that ensure good nutrition for your pet. Farm-ers periodically have to cull, or remove, old animals from their herds. These animals are often sold at auctions for very low prices. Given a choice, many of these farmers would happily sell you these animals, which can be ground up for clean, nutritious pet food. Processing livestock also generates a surplus of bones that make for nutritious and inexpensive snacks (provided you do not cook them first), as well as organ meats. Consider asking your farmer to sell you a few of these items. I guarantee your pet will reward you with a kiss on the nose or a purr of thanks.

1. Richard H. Pitcairn and Susan Hubble Pitcairn, *Dr. Pitcairn's Complete Guide to Natural Health for Dogs and Cats*, updated ed. (Emmaus, Pa. : Rodale Press, distributed by St. Martin's Press, 1995), 9.

Combining Careers with Passion

Diane Roeder, Sojourner Sheep Farm, Northampton, Massachusetts
Alan Zuschlag, Touchstone Sheep Farm, Amissville, Virginia

Diane Roeder lives on the outskirts of Northampton, Massachusetts, about two and a half hours from downtown Boston. Alan Zuschlag lives sixty-five miles outside of Washington, D.C. Both have professional careers, and both also run small sheep farms, maintaining valuable pastures in the face of urban development pressure. Neither plans to farm full-time. Neither wants to. Diane and Alan are part of a cadre of agriculturists who bear the

title "part-time farmer." Yet they make full-time contributions to the missions of sustainable agriculture by keeping farmland viable, contributing to biodiversity, making healthy local food available, and managing the land in an environmentally responsible fashion.

For many, the transition to full-time farming is a daunting task. Depending on the location, farmland can be exorbitantly expensive, and the return on products can render profits marginal. A person who hasn't spent his or her life working with livestock can take a long time to come up the learning curve. Partners who have off-farm careers may not be able to contribute to the labor force. And finally, current careers may fill too many needs to warrant giving them up.

Both Diane and Alan have found solutions to this dilemma by designing profitable small-scale farming operations. Diane and her husband, William, own only one acre of land, but they rent an additional twenty acres of hillside pasture from a neighbor. There they raise grass-fed lamb and keep thirty-five breeding ewes. Alan owns forty-five acres of pasture in Rappahannock County, Virginia, where he keeps a similar-sized flock. He direct-markets lamb to customers from the Washington D.C. area.

Neither Diane nor Alan opted to begin farming to earn big money. Rather, they were both seeking more fulfillment in their lives and found that they had a passion for raising sheep. Alan, who works as an international development consultant in Washington, D.C., talks about how he came to this realization. "I learned that the more I got involved in a career that took me overseas and did everything I thought I wanted to do, everything I was trained to do, that it really wasn't making me happy. I loved traveling, I loved seeing new people, but I really wanted a place where I could feel completely settled and at home and have roots. And I wanted a creative outlet." When he first purchased Touchstone Sheep Farm, he had no intentions of doing anything more than enjoying quiet weekends in the country, but things soon changed for him. "The image in my mind's eye was always that I wasn't going to be a real farmer. This was going to be a little hobby farm. But the more I got into it and the more I realized what was involved, the more I liked it and the more I wanted to do it. I wanted to prove that you could do this type of agriculture and earn a profit. It quickly became apparent that this is what I was meant to do."

Diane's path of discovery was somewhat different. She calls her evolution into a part-time sheep farmer the result of a "wonderful mid-life crisis." She explains: "I had a fast-track career in medical sales, and it was eating a big hole in me. It was extremely demand-ing, and I didn't always feel that the things I was asked to do were ethical. I was having problems with that, and I felt I was only a spectator in life. I was earning lots of money, and yet I was missing out on life." Today, Diane works part-time in medical sales for a different company and spends the rest of the time with her flock. "This has worked out very well for me, because the job doesn't consume my life. I get to choose the hours and the days that I work, so if I have a problem with the sheep, I can take the morning off and deal with it." Her interest in raising livestock developed after attending a llama show with her father. "I thought, 'Gee, with all this land around here, it would be nice to have livestock.' I drifted away from the idea of llamas, but I really started thinking about sheep."

For both Alan and Diane, whose partners are busy off the farms, sheep were an ideal livestock choice. "I chose sheep because I wanted an animal that wasn't so big I couldn't manage it," says Diane. "I didn't want an animal where I could get hurt. And I wanted one that had food value." Alan echoes her sentiments: "I was out here all by myself, so I figured I needed a small-enough animal that I could manage and handle alone."

Alan and Diane feel that sheep farming is their true passion in life. They love work-ing outdoors, and they love handling the animals. However, each has a different focus. Alan has worked the last six years to develop a flock of purebred Clun Forest sheep, a breed that has now, thanks to shepherds like him, made it to the recovering list of the American Livestock Breeds Conservancy. As Alan says: "Up until the 1970s, the Cluns were one of the backbone breeds of the British sheep industry. Improvements in refrigerated shipping containers from Australia and New Zealand soon had a devastating effect on the British (and American) sheep flocks. Shepherds in those countries could not compete with low-cost imported meat from Down Under." While the Clun has declined in its native Britain, its population is slowly expanding in North America, where smaller flock owners and part-time farmers appreciate its hardiness and its ability to achieve market weights on grass alone. Still, the threat of losing the breed has not yet subsided. "There's a limited gene pool here," Alan explains. "There are two or three thousand animals in North America, but they're all descended from nine rams. That's enough to build a breed on, but we need to diversify those genetics before the breed disappears entirely from Britain." Alan considers the effort to bring back heritage breeds important work. "I'm

fascinated by genetics as a subject. When you look at what people have been able to do over the centuries by breeding animals so they will adapt to certain climates and regions and feeding conditions, that's an incredible genetic legacy that shouldn't be allowed to just disappear."

Diane's flock contains a variety of breeds—some rare, some more common—and some cross-breeds, including Dorsets, Coopworths, Leicesters, Romneys, and Finns. Although she is concerned about issues of genetic diversity, Diane, who once worked as a clinical nurse, is equally concerned about being part of a quality, healthy, local food supply. "When I sell lamb meat," she says, "even though it seems expensive, I'm barely making a profit. But I feel more centered doing what I'm doing." Diane belongs to a local community organization called CISA (Community Involved in Sustaining Agriculture), which encourages people to buy their food locally. "We have so many chronic diseases now," she points out. "What's the matter with us? As a nation we may live to be eighty or ninety, but so many of us can barely walk, and we're so overweight, and we eat all this fake fat. So many people just don't give any thought to where their food comes from, and whether it's nourishing food. And we are not asking, as a culture, if we're making sure the pipeline to nourishing food continues." Diane's work on Sojourner Sheep Farm is her way of helping to keep that pipeline open, by making natural, unadulterated, healthy grass-fed meat available locally. The work is so important to her that she admits it has taken on an almost spiritual meaning. "I think that the closer we are to the natural process, the more divine we are. The more we tinker and improve on nature, the more in trouble we get."

Diane cannot envision expanding her operation. Alan, on the other hand, is growing his very slowly and steadily; each year he retains the daughters of his best-producing ewes. Eventually he hopes to run a flock of around one hundred ewes. Rather than achieving enormous production and sales numbers, both Alan and Diane are keenly aware that to be sustainable, their farms must be workable with only one manager. Both of them are invested in their enterprises for the long haul. "I think I'll always farm part-time," says Diane. "I see myself doing this for as long as I physically can." Alan's sentiments are similar. "I want to keep farming until I die. I've found my dream. I don't need fame or fortune or anything else. I really enjoy what I'm doing, and I can't think of doing anything else."

WHY DO OLDER AMERICANS HAVE AN AVERSION TO LAMB?

When we began sampling our lamb at farmers' markets and food shows, we were surprised to see the number of people who would bristle at our offered samples and quickly respond: "I don't eat lamb." Quite often, these were senior citizens. Finally, one kindly gentleman visiting our farm took the time to give us an explanation. "You see," he said, taking my mother aside as though he were letting her in on a big secret, "many of us had to eat what they called 'lamb' during the war. But it wasn't lamb. It was mutton, and we had few other options for meat. Many people my age swore they'd never eat that stuff again." The good news? That leaves more of this marvelous meat for the rest of us!

PROTECTING LIVESTOCK FROM PREDATORS

Predators are the scourges of pasture-based sheep, goat, and poultry producers throughout the world. The meat that is so delicious to us is also an irresistible treat for coyotes, mountain lions, wolves, bears, domestic dogs, possums, raccoons, foxes, weasels, owls and hawks. Unfortunately, many predator-control devices can raise the ire of animal-rights and wildlife advocates alike, since they include traps, snares, poisons, and guns. Those opposed to these methods are concerned about cruelty to the predators, which are simply following natural instincts; about the other forms of wildlife that are subsequently being killed; and about the elimination of endangered species. What makes these lethal techniques more controversial is their questionable success rates: they are generally believed to result in only six to twelve months of relief.

In recent years, however, many farmers and ranchers have found more reliable and less controversial protection by stepping away from the lethal technologies and adopting an ancient practice: livestock guardians. Livestock guardians are animals that live with the flocks and protect them from intruders. These include guard dogs, llamas, donkeys, geese, and even guinea fowl. These working animals have slightly different guarding styles. Guard dogs mark the territories of their flocks, and then they pursue any uninvited creature until it leaves the area. At this point, the guard dogs return to their flock. If a llama senses danger, it will call an alarm, herd the flock together, place itself between the sheep and the predator, run toward it, and spit, kick, or paw at it. A good guard donkey is particularly fierce toward members of the canine family. The donkey will chase intruders, bray loudly, bite, and rise up on its hind legs to kick and stomp at them. Geese and guinea fowl maintain a vigilant watch, sound ear-piercing alarms, and charge at predators. Each type of animal works best under different conditions, but all have a few common advantages: they bond with their flocks, provide several years of relief, ease the farmers' burden by providing protection day and night, and generally enable the livestock to peacefully coexist with wildlife.

Guardian animals are not a cure-all for predator problems, but they have proven extraordinarily effective in most conditions. In addition to keeping guardians with the flocks, a farmer or rancher can provide further protection by managing his or her pastures responsibly. Excellent pasture management provides habitat for a wide variety of wildlife, both in the fields and in the hedgerows. If this habitat is provided, rodents and other natural predator prey will be in abundance, and predators will have ample culinary options without converting a farmer's pastures into a rib-chop café.

Preserving Family Heritage at Smith Meadows

Forrest, Nancy, and Betsy Pritchard and Ruth Smith-Pritchard, Smith Meadows, Berryville, Virginia

Driving north of Berryville, Virginia, on Route 608, my husband and I saw the sign for Smith Meadows. No house was in sight, only a gravel lane and an old apple orchard. We turned on the lane and proceeded slowly through the orchard, watching the cows browse beneath the laden trees as we passed. When the tree canopy finally opened, we stopped the car and gaped at a massive, federal-style brick home. With our upstate New York sensibilities, we chuckled to ourselves. With an estate like this, we thought, these people could not possibly be *real* farmers. Anyone who owned such a palace surely would never have to work for a living.

We were wrong. As we stood by the car unloading cameras and recording equipment, Betsy Pritchard came out to greet us, balancing her baby, Benson, on her hip. As she began to walk us around the farm, she told us the story of how the estate came to be. The first building was an enormous brick barn, where the farm had begun. Edward Smith—or as Betsy referred to him, "my six greats ago"—fired the bricks to build the barn on the property back in 1822, then used the large brick barn to build the house, named Smithfield, in 1824. Smithfield has remained in the same family for six generations.

Today, the house sits in the middle of 350 acres, flanked by two brick parapet-style "dependencies" (one served as a summer kitchen and the other as a local schoolhouse). Another remaining house had been used as slave quarters. Betsy notes that there were four such houses originally on the property and that between 1850 and 1860, there were more than forty slaves working the estate.

While the Smithfield landholdings seem large compared with other farms, the estate is only one-quarter its original size. When Betsy's grandfather owned it, the landholdings spanned into West Virginia, but on his death, it was divided among his four children. Once the halcyon days of Smithfield had passed, the estate had fallen into considerable disrepair. The house was so rundown that Betsy's grandfather had used it for hay storage. It remained uninhabited for more than forty years. When Betsy's mother, Ruth Smith-Pritchard, inherited the property, many assumed that the boarded-up old house with the caved-in ceilings would have to be demolished. Instead, Ruth spent eleven years restoring the home on the weekends when she wasn't working, and her daughter and her son, Forrest, later joined her on the estate.

Today, Smithfield is once again home for the descendents of the Smith family: Ruth; Betsy and her husband, David, and son, Benson; and Forrest and his wife, Nancy. Betsy and Ruth run the beautiful home as a bed-and-breakfast, and renovations on the various outbuildings continue. But a tour of the land shows that the family is dedicated to restoring more than just the buildings.

Betsy explains that after graduating from William and Mary in 1996 with a degree in English and Geology, Forrest was reluctant to pursue work in an urban area. She says he

read a lot about organic farming and decided to begin pasturing livestock at Smithfield. When he returns from a trip to the butcher, and I ask him to explain his decision not to join his fellow classmates in the nine-to-five workforce, Forrest chuckles briefly and quips, "You didn't see my transcripts."

Regardless of what his grades may have been, Forrest's business and farming acumen deserves an A-plus. The land is much improved under his care. Betsy remarks that they have significantly fewer weeds and that the grass has grown so lush from the grazing that they don't have enough livestock to keep up with it. She adds: "There's very little erosion here, and there's hardly any wear-and-tear on the land, because none of it is tilled." Using grass as the foundation for his herds, Forrest produces beef, goat, pork, veal, poultry, and eggs under the label of Smith Meadow Meats. Although the family had originally hoped to market all the meat directly off the farm, they've found that most of their customers prefer the convenience of having their meat brought to their local farmers' markets. Hence, Forrest and Nancy sell their products at two Washington, D.C.-area farmers' markets every weekend, as well as through a few regional health-food stores. Customers are also welcome to purchase the meat directly from the farm, and guests at the B&B are treated to Forrest's eggs and breakfast meats each morning during their stay. Nancy is hoping to add dinners to the B&B repertoire in the coming year, featuring more of Forrest's meats, as well as other locally grown, organic foods.

Betsy says that one of the challenges they face is balancing their growth with the market demand. Managing a farm, a B&B, and two farmers' markets is difficult for one family. "We can only handle so much product and running up and down the road to the butcher and the markets," she says, "so we have to be careful not to grow too fast or too far. Our hope is to be able to provide meat for between three and four hundred families."

Forrest and Betsy are not new to the agricultural scene. Betsy says that they grew up with their parents in another corner of the former larger estate and that their family raised cattle "the normal way—you know, shooting them full of antibiotics, putting them in feedlots, that whole bad scenario." She justifies Forrest's new direction by adding: "He was just not interested in those big bills, and the chemicals. He wanted to get back to something simpler."

Still, Forrest explains, the portion of Smithfield that his mother inherited could not have been better suited for his type of farming. He is grateful for the legacy his grandfather left him. "When all the other farmers were getting more industrialized, my grandfather chose to hold on to his labor, rather than replacing people with machinery. So all the industrialization never happened here, and we were able to easily leap-frog into a grass-based farm. This 350 acres here was neglected, and that helped us out a lot. A neglected farm is a blessing. It was a liability for the rest of the family, but it was a blessing for us."

Since they are the seventh generation at Smithfield, Betsy says she and Forrest have some advantages over other farmers. "We're really lucky in that we don't have a mortgage. We don't owe money to the bank." Still, she adds, it is not always easy. "There's always a struggle to keep hold of this place. A lot of developers are going all around us, building. So keeping Smithfield in the family is a challenge. People approach us a lot. They say, 'Just name your price,' which is annoying. It's offensive to us, because Smithfield is not for sale. And they say, 'Well, you just let me know when you're ready to sell.' Well, we'll never be ready to sell."

Preserving family heritage while simultaneously building businesses is a big job for two young people like Betsy and Forrest. Betsy, who worked as a geriatric nurse before returning to Smithfield to join her mother at the B&B, feels the effort is worth it. "We wanted to be able to raise Benson on a farm, not in a suburb," she explains. Forrest's decision to not even enter the workforce but to strike out on his own seems equally radical. Yet he disagrees: "When you've got this much tradition and responsibility passed on to you, then the radical choice would be *not* to continue."

SKEWERING DEBATES

Some people vote Republican, some vote Democrat. Some root for the Yankees, some root for the Mets. Some prefer cats, some prefer dogs. And when it comes to preparing skewers for the grill, people are equally divided: some are "sorters," and some are "mixers."

Sorters sort vegetables and meats according to type. All the cherry tomatoes go on one skewer, all the peppers on another, all the onions on a third; the meat has its own skewer. The process can hardly be faulted—meats and vegetables cook at different rates. Using this method, the chef can put the items that need the most time on first and the items that need the least time on last. At the table, all skewers are removed, and a mountain of vegetables and meat can be spooned onto the diners' plates.

Mixers scoff at the trivial fixations of sorters, embracing instead the technical challenge of cutting vegetables to exacting sizes and parboiling others so that they will all cook at the same rate as the meat. Skewers become sites of meat and vegetable integration, where the juices emitted from each blend to create fabulous flavors and a rainbow of color as they are presented on the table. Diners can serve themselves by simply lifting the nutritionally balanced skewers off the platter.

Both methods are perfectly acceptable and can suit the culinary standards of the most exacting chefs. Still, there is yet another school—that of the haphazard grill-master, where people (much like the author of this book) delight in the sumptuous unpredictability of kabob fare. As long as the meat is cooked properly, everything else is an adventure. Vegetables are chopped to a size determined by whoever is drafted into service. Nothing is parboiled because doing so is a pain. Thus, the meat and some of the vegetables are cooked to perfection, and the haphazard grill-master relishes the flavor of the overcharred pineapple in a mélange of undercooked onions and lightly seared peppers.

All of these methods yield suitable dining results. The only rule is to respect the authority of the chef in determining the appropriate procedure.

RECIPES

LAMB AND FETA SANDWICHES 97

LAMB CURRY PIE 98

THIRTEEN MILE LAMB DOGS 100

CHEVON (GOAT) HORS D'OEUVRE 101

LAMB-STUFFED MUSHROOMS 102

SHOULDER CHOPS WITH CARDAMOM, APPLES, AND APRICOTS 103

MEDITERRANEAN GOAT CASSEROLE 104

MOROCCAN LAMB KOFTAS 106

BROILED LAMB CHOPS 107

GRILLED LAMB LOIN 108

SWEET AND SOUR LAMB CHOPS 109

SHISH KABOBS, THE MIDDLE EASTERN WAY 110

TURKISH LAMB SHISH KABOBS 110

ARMENIAN LAMB SHISH KABOBS 111

MOROCCAN LAMB SHISH KABOBS 111

GYROS 112

LAMB RIBLETS IN MUSTARD-ROSEMARY GARLIC PASTE 113

RACK OF LAMB WITH MINT CRUST 114

ROAST LEG OF LAMB 115

LAMB ROAST WITH MOREL GRAVY 116

GRILLED SIRLOIN CHOPS IN A SPICY YOGURT MARINADE 117

HERB-ROASTED BONELESS SIRLOIN 118

STEWED LAMB SHANKS 119

BRAISED LAMB SHANKS 120

TOM CLACK'S DEVILED KIDNEYS 123

LAMB-FENNEL CASSEROLE 124

REBEKAH'S COCONUT CURRY LAMB 125

CURRIED GOAT 126

LAMB STEW 127

HARIRA 128

PEPPER SOUP 130

All recipes without attribution are from Shannon Hayes, Sap Bush Hollow Farm, West Fulton, New York.

Lamb and Feta Sandwiches

Once you've chopped the onions, garlic, and pepper, this meal can be prepared in less than 25 minutes. It works well as a one-dish dinner, and it's perfect for making a little ground lamb go a long way. Leftovers reheat beautifully in a microwave or conventional oven.

IN A HURRY • ON A BUDGET

SERVES 3 TO 4

1 onion, finely chopped

1 clove garlic, finely chopped

1 sweet green or red pepper, diced

3 tablespoons olive oil

1 pound ground lamb

1 ½ teaspoons salt

1 ½ teaspoons freshly ground black pepper

2 tablespoons dried oregano

2 cups fresh spinach, or 10 ounces frozen, thawed and drained

8 ounces feta cheese, crumbled

Pita, sliced whole wheat bread, or English muffins

Sauté the onion, garlic, and diced pepper in olive oil over medium heat in a large saucepan until the onions are translucent. Add the ground lamb, salt, pepper, and oregano. Sauté until lamb browns, 5 to 7 minutes, and add the spinach; cover and simmer for 10 minutes. Stir in the feta cheese, sautéing another 3 to 5 minutes, or just until slightly melted but fully incorporated.

Serve in the pockets of warmed pitas, over toasted bread slices, or on English muffins.

Lamb Curry Pie

Sara Cameron, Cameron Ranch, Wyoming

Here's a wonderful way to use leftover leg of lamb. If you don't have any leftovers on hand, ground lamb also works. If you are going to serve this to kids, it is probably best to use a mild curry powder and leave out the hot pepper.

ON A BUDGET • KID-FRIENDLY

SERVES 5 TO 6

For the crust:

1 cup all-purpose or cake flour

½ teaspoon salt

3 teaspoons curry powder

6 tablespoons unsalted butter, lard, or shortening

3 tablespoons ice water plus 1 or 2 tablespoons more, if needed

Begin by making the crust. Combine the flour, salt, and curry powder in a medium-size mixing bowl. With a fork or pastry blender, cut the butter or shortening into the flour until the mixture resembles coarse crumbs. Sprinkle the mixture with the ice water, and mix lightly with a fork. Continue adding ice water, a little at a time, until the dough is just moist enough to form into a ball. Be sure not to add too much water, because this makes dough tough. Chill in the refrigerator while preparing the filling and sauce.

For the filling:

3 tablespoons olive oil

1 large onion, diced

3 cloves garlic, crushed

¾ cup coarsely chopped celery

¼ cup raisins, soaked in hot water to reconstitute

½ cup coarsely chopped tart apples

½ teaspoon freshly ground cumin

½ teaspoon turmeric

¼ teaspoon freshly ground cinnamon

½ teaspoon dry hot pepper flakes (optional)

¼ teaspoon ground ginger

½ teaspoon curry powder

3 cups diced cooked lamb, or 1 pound ground lamb

Preheat oven to 375°F.

Heat the olive oil in a large, heavy skillet over medium heat. Add the onion, and sauté until translucent. Add the garlic, celery, raisins, apples, and spices and sauté 2 minutes longer. Add the meat, and if you are using leftovers, sauté until heated through; if raw, sauté until cooked to your liking. Turn off the heat, and set aside.

For the sauce:

3 tablespoons unsalted butter

3 tablespoons all-purpose flour

1½ cups milk

½ cup white wine or dry sherry

Salt and freshly ground black pepper to taste

Melt the butter in a 2½-quart saucepan. Use a wooden spoon to blend in the flour, making a paste. Stir over medium heat until the butter and flour begin to foam—about 1½ to 2 minutes. Turn the heat off, and wait for the bubbling to cease. Add milk and whisk to blend thoroughly. Turn the heat to medium-low, and continue to whisk gently (making sure no bits of flour stick to the pot) until the sauce begins to boil. Lower the heat, and simmer for 2 to 3 minutes, stirring constantly and slowly adding the wine. The sauce should be thick enough to coat a spoon. Add salt and pepper to taste.

To bake the pie:

Pour the sauce over the meat mixture, mix gently, and pour all into a 9-inch pie pan. Roll out the pastry dough, and cover the meat mixture. Seal and flute the edges. Cut several slits in the pastry. Place a baking sheet or aluminum foil under the pie pan to catch spills, and bake for 35 to 40 minutes, or until the crust is lightly browned.

Thirteen Mile Lamb Dogs

Becky Weed, Thirteen Mile Farm, Montana

This version of "ground lamb on a stick" is reminiscent of the famous Coney Island corn dogs, though it is infinitely more sophisticated. Look for coarsely ground cornmeal to finish off these lamb dogs.

IN A HURRY • MINIMUM PREPARATION • KID-FRIENDLY

SERVES 4 TO 5

½ cup cooked quinoa (cooked rice or oats can be substituted)

1 egg, beaten

¼ cup tomato sauce, fresh or canned

1½ teaspoons lemon pepper

¼ cup fresh parsley, minced

2 tablespoons fresh mint, finely chopped

1 tablespoon fresh oregano, finely chopped

2 teaspoons fresh rosemary, minced

1 teaspoon salt

½ teaspoon freshly ground black pepper

2 tablespoons stone-ground cornmeal plus extra for coating

1 pound ground lamb

In a medium-size bowl, thoroughly stir together the quinoa, egg, tomato sauce, lemon pepper, fresh herbs, salt, pepper, and cornmeal; add the lamb, and mix well.

Shape into approximately 10 oblong balls. Press the balls onto skewers, and roll them in the extra cornmeal. Grill or broil 3 to 4 minutes on each side or until cooked through.

Chevon (goat) Hors d'oeuvre

Tom and Denise Warren, Stone and Thistle Farm, New York

Here's a flavorful treat to serve at your next cocktail party.

SHOWCASE • IN A HURRY • MINIMUM PREPARATION

MAKES 12 TO 14 MEATBALLS

Zest of ½ lemon or 2 tablespoons chopped lemon balm

2 teaspoons dry sherry

2 teaspoons soy sauce

1½ cloves garlic, minced

1 teaspoon dried thyme or 2 teaspoons fresh, crushed

1 teaspoon salt

1 teaspoon ground black pepper

2 dashes hot pepper sauce

1 pound ground chevon

2 tablespoons olive oil

8 ounces fresh chevre (goat cheese), shaped in logs

Mix together all the ingredients except the olive oil and chevre in a medium-size bowl. Shape into 1½-inch balls. Heat the olive oil in a skillet over medium heat. Add the meatballs—do not crowd—and sauté for 7 to 10 minutes, turning each halfway through. If desired, sprinkle lightly with additional soy sauce.

To serve, cut chevre into thin slices. Serve 1 slice of chevre and 1 meatball on a toothpick.

Lamb-Stuffed Mushrooms

Connie Karstens, Liberty Land and Livestock, Minnesota

These make luscious appetizers or a meal that kids can eat with their fingers.

SHOWCASE • ON A BUDGET • KID-FRIENDLY

MAKES 36 STUFFED MUSHROOMS

36 large mushrooms, washed and dried

½ cup melted unsalted butter plus ¼ cup chilled butter

Juice of 1 lemon

2 tablespoons olive oil

1 pound ground lamb

2 tablespoons minced fresh parsley

2 tablespoons minced onion

½ cup freshly grated Swiss or Parmesan cheese

½ teaspoon salt

Freshly ground black pepper to taste

½ cup dry sherry

¾ cup fine breadcrumbs

Preheat oven to 350°F.

Remove the stems from the mushrooms. Put the caps in a large bowl, sprinkle with the melted butter and lemon juice; toss gently, coating the caps.

Dice the mushroom stems, and sauté in the olive oil with the lamb, parsley, and onion. Drain.

In a bowl, combine the grated cheese, salt, pepper, sherry, and ½ of the breadcrumbs. Add the lamb mixture, and toss lightly.

Shake the butter and lemon juice from the mushroom caps. Fill each cap with the lamb mixture. Sprinkle lightly with the remaining breadcrumbs, and dot each with a bit of the chilled butter. Bake for 15 to 20 minutes, and serve hot.

Shoulder Chops with Cardamom, Apples, and Apricots

Here's a scrumptious way to prepare shoulder chops. The recipe serves two, but you can easily double or triple it.

SHOWCASE • ON A BUDGET

SERVES 2

> Cardamom-Cinnamon Rub (see page 254)
>
> 2 lamb shoulder or leg chops
>
> 2 tablespoons olive oil
>
> 2 onions, cut into ¼-inch wedges
>
> ⅔ cup dried apricots
>
> 1 teaspoon ground ginger
>
> 1 tart apple, peeled and thickly sliced
>
> 1 cup water
>
> 4 teaspoons honey

Rub the Cardamom-Cinnamon mixture into both sides of the lamb chops, and bring the meat to room temperature.

Heat the olive oil in a large pot over medium heat. Sear the chops for 2 to 3 minutes per side, and remove. Add the onions, and sauté until translucent; add the apricots, ginger, apple, and water. Cook over medium heat, stirring constantly for 1 minute; place the chops on top of the onion-fruit sauce. Cover, and simmer over low heat for 2 hours, until the chops are fork-tender.

Turn the heat off, and rest the chops for 5 minutes. Arrange the chops on warmed plates, top with the onion and fruit sauce, and drizzle each chop with 2 teaspoons of honey.

Slow-cooker version:

After searing the chops, stir together the onions, ginger, water (reduce the amount to ½ cup), apple slices, and apricots in a slow-cooker. Place the browned chops on top, and cook on low for 6 hours, or until the meat pulls easily from the bone.

Mediterranean Goat Casserole

This dish, traditionally prepared with ground goat, is equally successful with lamb or beef. It makes super leftovers, even served cold. When working with phyllo dough—usually found in the freezer section of food markets—remove the pastry from the box immediately before you use it, and be sure to keep it covered with a layer of plastic wrap at all times. It dries out very quickly. Once you've taken what you need for this recipe, promptly repackage the leftover pastry, and freeze it for another time.

ON A BUDGET • KID-FRIENDLY

SERVES 4 TO 5

5 medium boiling potatoes, scrubbed and coarsely chopped

1 cup freshly grated Parmesan cheese

6 tablespoons unsalted butter

$\frac{1}{4}$ cup whole milk or half-and-half

5 eggs

$\frac{1}{4}$ cup dried dill

2 tablespoons olive oil

1 large onion, coarsely chopped

1 clove garlic, minced

1 pound ground goat, lamb, or beef

Salt and freshly ground black pepper to taste

2 tablespoons dried parsley

1 tablespoon dried oregano

$\frac{1}{2}$ teaspoon freshly ground nutmeg

$\frac{1}{2}$ pound coarsely chopped spinach

1 14.5-ounce can diced tomatoes or 2 fresh tomatoes, diced

2 sheets phyllo dough

Boil the potatoes until tender. Drain, cool, and mash with $\frac{1}{2}$ cup of the Parmesan cheese, 4 tablespoons of the butter, milk (or half-and-half), 3 of the eggs, and the dill. Set the mixture aside.

Preheat oven to 350°F.

Warm the olive oil in a large skillet over medium heat. Add the chopped onion, and sauté until translucent. Add the garlic, sauté for 1 minute; add the ground meat, sprinkle with salt and pepper, and cook until browned. Add the parsley, oregano, nutmeg, spinach, and tomatoes; simmer for 5 minutes. Allow the mixture to cool for a few minutes; then stir in the remaining 2 eggs.

Melt the remaining 2 tablespoons butter. Brush a 9-x-12-inch casserole dish with half the butter, then lay 1 phyllo sheet along the bottom, folding over any excess phyllo that extends up the sides of the dish. Brush the remaining butter on top, and add the second phyllo sheet. In layers, cover the phyllo sheets with half the potato mixture, all the meat, and the remaining potatoes. Sprinkle the remaining Parmesan cheese on top, and bake for 30 to 40 minutes, or until the potatoes are lightly browned. Allow the casserole to set for at least 15 minutes before serving.

THE TRUTH ABOUT MARINADES

For generations, cooks confronted with tough cuts of meat have turned to marinades in hopes of a tender solution. The idea is that the acids in these mixtures break down the collagen, yielding a tender cut. Many of us suffered in silence when the theory failed to yield positive outcomes, assuming that the resultant tough or squishy meat was due to a lack of culinary prowess. However, the editors of *Cook's Illustrated* have liberated many a self-loathing chef in their book on grilling and barbecuing.[1] After running a number of kitchen trials, they reported that marinades do *not* tenderize meat. At best, an overdose of acidic ingredients can sometimes turn the meat gray and mushy. Instead, the editors advise us to stick to the tried and true principles: use marinades to impart *flavor*, not tenderness. If you want tender meat, match the cut you are using with the appropriate cooking technique.

1. Editors of *Cook's Illustrated* Magazine, *Best Recipe: Grilling and Barbecue* (Brookline, Mass.: Boston Common Press, 2001).

Moroccan Lamb Koftas

Jack Knorek, Oak Moon Farm, Michigan

This is a terrific recipe for afternoon cookouts. If your grill is buried under an avalanche of snow, have no fear: this recipe goes under the broiler as well. For a slightly more "American" variation, check out the recipe for Thirteen Mile Lamb Dogs on page 100.

SHOWCASE • IN A HURRY • MINIMUM PREPARATION • KID-FRIENDLY

SERVES 8

2 tablespoons water	1 ½ teaspoons freshly ground coriander
3 cloves garlic, minced	1 ¼ teaspoons freshly ground cinnamon
2 tablespoons cilantro, finely chopped	¾ teaspoon cayenne pepper
2 tablespoons parsley, finely chopped	1 ¼ teaspoons salt
2 tablespoons paprika	½ teaspoon freshly ground black pepper
1 ½ teaspoons freshly ground cumin	2 pounds ground lamb

Combine all ingredients in a large bowl, and mix well. Shape into approximately 16 oblong "sausages," and press around metal skewers. Grill or broil, 3 to 4 minutes on each side, until cooked through.

Serve each portion on the skewer with grilled pita bread and plain yogurt.

Variation:

2 to 3 teaspoons olive oil, or more if needed

2 large sweet green peppers, cut into wide, lengthwise slices

4 medium onions, quartered

Pour the oil in a medium-size bowl, add the sliced green peppers and onions; gently mix to lightly coat the pieces. Thread on the skewers, alternating with the koftas. Grill or broil, 3 to 4 minutes on each side, until cooked through.

Serve each portion on the skewer with grilled pita bread and plain yogurt.

Broiled Lamb Chops

In my opinion, the simplest way to cook lamb chops is the best way. Here, they are seasoned with just garlic, salt, freshly ground black pepper, and olive oil, allowing the rich flavors of the meat to shine through.

SHOWCASE • IN A HURRY • MINIMUM PREPARATION

SERVES 2

> 4 rib or loin chops, or 2 double lamb chops (English chops),
>   at least 1 ¼ to 1 ½ inches thick
>
> 1 or 2 cloves garlic, cut into fine slivers
>
> Olive oil
>
> Coarse salt and freshly ground black pepper to taste

Pierce the lamb chops on both sides with a sharp paring knife, and insert 4 to 5 garlic slivers into each side of the chops. Brush the chops on both sides with olive oil, then turn them on their sides and brush each side as well (the fat on the chops will crisp up and will taste extraordinary). Sprinkle all sides of each chop, including the fat, with salt and pepper.

Set the broiler on high, and broil for 5 minutes on each side for medium-rare chops.

REHEATING LAMB AND PORK

The next time you have some leftover leg of lamb, fresh ham, or any cuts from lamb or pork shoulders saved for lunch, think twice before you pop them in the microwave. Microwaves have a magical way of turning tender meat rubbery and leaving most of it cold while miraculously melting the dish that was holding your lunch.

Consider instead investing in a tiny, 1½- or 2-quart Dutch oven. Set in the meat, along with any leftover vegetables such as carrots and potatoes, pour in some gravy, pan drippings, or butter to add moisture, put the lid on top, and allow everything to cook in the oven at 350°F for 30 to 45 minutes. The meat will be well-done, piping hot, moist, tender, and delicious—infinitely tastier than microwaved rubber!

Grilled Lamb Loin

A boned-out loin of lamb is not commonly seen, but this elegant piece of meat can be cut to order. It is easy and quick to cook, and there's little waste.

SHOWCASE • IN A HURRY • MINIMUM PREPARATION

SERVES 2

3 tablespoons finely chopped fresh rosemary, or 1 tablespoon dried

1 tablespoon finely chopped fresh oregano, or 1 teaspoon dried

2 cloves garlic, minced

2 teaspoons coarse salt

1 teaspoon freshly ground black pepper

¼ cup olive oil

1 lamb loin roast, about 1 pound

Combine the rosemary, oregano, garlic, salt, pepper, and olive oil to make a thin paste. Rub the mixture into the meat, and let rest for 2 hours at room temperature.

Grill the tenderloin over medium-hot coals (or put it in the broiler set on high) for 8 to 10 minutes per side. When you take it off the grill, the internal temperature should read 120°F for rare meat, 135°F for medium. Tent the meat loosely with foil, and let rest for 5 minutes before serving. The temperature will rise a few more degrees during that time.

Sweet and Sour Lamb Chops

Rae Ellen Freeman, Freeman Homestead, New York

The sweet flavors in this recipe are sure to appeal to your children's palates. If you wish, this entire dish could be served over rice.

ON A BUDGET • MINIMUM PREPARATION • KID-FRIENDLY

SERVES 4

1 teaspoon salt

½ teaspoon freshly ground black pepper

4 lamb shoulder chops, 1- to 1½-inches thick

2 tablespoons olive oil

¼ cup dark brown sugar

¼ cup apple cider vinegar

½ teaspoon ground ginger

½ orange, unpeeled, cut into 4 thin slices

1 lemon, unpeeled, quartered

1 tablespoon cornstarch

1 tablespoon ice water

Combine salt and pepper, and rub into the lamb chops.

Heat a large, heavy skillet over a medium flame. Add the olive oil, and brown the chops, 2 to 4 minutes per side.

Whisk together the brown sugar, vinegar, and ginger; pour over the meat. Top each chop with an orange slice and a lemon wedge. Cover, and simmer over low heat until the chops are fork-tender, 45 minutes to 1 hour. Remove to a platter, and keep warm.

Pour the pan juices into a measuring cup, add enough water to make 1 cup, then return the liquid to the skillet. Turn the heat on low. Mix the cornstarch with ice water until smooth, and add to the juices in the skillet. Cook, stirring constantly, until the mixture boils and thickens. Pour over the chops.

Shish Kabobs, The Middle Eastern Way

Jack Knorek, Oak Moon Farm, Michigan

Jack Knorek, grill aficionado, submitted this series of lamb shish kabob recipes from the Middle East, the home of the shish kabob. The method for cooking all three versions is the same. The only question is deciding which marinade to use. Be sure to plan ahead, because the lamb must marinate for at least 8 hours.

SHOWCASE • ON A BUDGET • MINIMUM PREPARATION • KID-FRIENDLY

SERVES 4 (EASILY DOUBLED)

For the lamb kabobs:

1 ½ pounds boneless lamb (shoulder or sirloin chops,
   or leg of lamb are all acceptable)

Marinade of choice (Armenian, Moroccan or Turkish)

Cut the lamb into 1 ¼ -inch cubes, and then slice each cube partially down the center (about three-quarters of the way), making a butterflied cube. This allows the marinade to better penetrate the meat and to impart more flavor. Prepare a marinade from the recipes below, pour it into a nonreactive bowl, add the lamb, cover, and marinate for 8 hours or overnight.

When you are ready to cook, remove the cubes, and thread them on metal skewers. Grill over very hot coals, uncovered, rotating each kabob one-quarter turn every minute and a half, until the meat is browned (about 6 minutes).

Serve with plain yogurt and grilled pita bread.

TURKISH LAMB SHISH KABOBS

1 cup plain yogurt	3 cloves garlic, chopped
¼ cup olive oil	1 teaspoon coarse salt
1 teaspoon red pepper flakes	1 teaspoon freshly ground black pepper

Whisk all ingredients in a bowl. Transfer the lamb to a nonreactive bowl; pour the marinade over the lamb, and toss until well coated. Cover and marinate in the refrigerator for 8 hours or overnight. Grill as instructed above.

ARMENIAN LAMB SHISH KABOBS

This recipe calls for ground sumac, a popular Middle Eastern spice that has a tart and sour flavor, with overtones of lemon and pepper. It is found in Middle Eastern groceries. If you aren't fortunate enough to have one nearby, try a gourmet food store or a natural-food co-op with a wide spice selection. If you cannot find sumac, either omit it or use a teaspoon of lemon pepper instead.

½ cup dry red wine	1 teaspoon dried marjoram
¼ cup tomato paste	1 teaspoon ground sumac (optional)
¼ cup olive oil	1 teaspoon coarse salt
2 tablespoons red wine vinegar	1 teaspoon freshly ground black pepper
1 large onion, coarsely chopped	½ teaspoon red pepper flakes
3 cloves garlic, chopped	¼ teaspoon freshly ground allspice

Process all ingredients in a blender or food processor. Transfer the lamb pieces to a nonreactive bowl; pour the marinade over the lamb, and toss until well coated. Cover and marinate in the refrigerator for 8 hours or overnight. Grill as instructed on page 110.

MOROCCAN LAMB SHISH KABOBS

¼ cup olive oil	½ teaspoon coarse salt
1 large onion, coarsely chopped	½ teaspoon freshly ground black pepper
3 tablespoons fresh parsley, minced	½ teaspoon paprika
3 tablespoons fresh cilantro, chopped	¼ teaspoon freshly ground cumin
1 clove garlic, chopped	

Mix all ingredients in a bowl; add the lamb cubes, and toss until well coated with the marinade. Cover, and marinate in the refrigerator for 8 hours or overnight. Grill as instructed on page 110.

Gyros

Connie Karstens, Liberty Land and Livestock, Minnesota

Here's a classic lamb favorite that's fun to eat. Kids like making their own gyros when the ingredients are all set out on a plate (but some kids may opt to forgo the raw onion). You may know the ancient Middle Eastern flatbread, pita, as pocket bread or pita pocket.

ON A BUDGET • KID-FRIENDLY

SERVES 4

For the seasoned lamb:

5 tablespoons olive oil

1 tablespoon fresh lemon juice

2 cloves garlic, minced

¼ teaspoon curry powder

½ teaspoon coarse salt

¼ teaspoon freshly ground black pepper

1½ pounds boneless sirloin or leg, cut into 2-inch strips

Whisk together 3 tablespoons of the olive oil, lemon juice, garlic, curry powder, salt, and pepper. Place the lamb in a bowl, add the mixture, and stir until the meat is well coated. Set aside while preparing the cucumber sauce.

For the minted cucumber sauce:

1 cup plain yogurt

1 cup sour cream

½ cucumber, shredded, with excess liquid squeezed and drained

2 green onions, minced

1 tablespoon freshly chopped mint, or 1 teaspoon dried

Mix all the ingredients together, cover, and refrigerate while you prepare the sandwich fillings and cook the meat.

For the sandwiches:

4 pitas

Fresh iceberg lettuce, shredded

1 fresh tomato, thinly sliced

1 cucumber, thinly sliced

1 large sweet onion, thinly sliced

To assemble the gyros:

Preheat a heavy skillet; warm the remaining 2 tablespoons olive oil, add the seasoned lamb mixture, and toss while sautéing to desired stage of doneness.

Warm the pitas, cut off the top corner of the pockets, and place the cooked lamb inside. Add the lettuce, tomato, cucumber, and sliced raw onion. Add a generous portion of minted cucumber sauce, and if desired, garnish with some extra mint.

Lamb Riblets in Mustard-Rosemary Garlic Paste

Lamb riblets, or spareribs, cut from the breast of the lamb, produce very little meat and are not well suited for serving a crowd. Still, they are perfect for two good friends to sit down and devour as a feast. Have plenty of napkins on hand, don't be afraid to eat with your fingers, and remember to enjoy the ribs with a glass or two of red wine. After trying these once, you'll surely find yourself craving them often and perhaps even pleading with your favorite growers to reserve them for you whenever they're processing lamb.

ON A BUDGET • MINIMUM PREPARATION • KID-FRIENDLY

SERVES 2

      1 pound lamb riblets

      Mustard-Rosemary Garlic Paste (see page 256)

Heat oven to 350°F.

Rub both sides of the riblets with the paste. Set them in a shallow roasting pan lined with foil. Roast for 1 to 1 ½ hours, until the meat pulls slightly away from the bone.

Rack of Lamb with Mint Crust

Connie Karstens, Liberty Land and Livestock, Minnesota

In my estimation, a rack of lamb is the perfect Valentine's Day dinner. The original presentation is stately, yet inviting. The couple may begin dining in formal elegance with knife and fork, but as the meal continues, they'll probably pick the ribs up with their fingers and gorge on every morsel of meat that remains. Obviously, the rack of lamb is one of my favorite cuts of meat.

SHOWCASE

SERVES 2 TO 4

3 tablespoons Mint Sauce (see page 115)

3 tablespoons fresh breadcrumbs

1 tablespoon finely chopped fresh parsley, or 1 teaspoon dried

1 clove garlic, crushed

2 teaspoons coarse salt

1 teaspoon freshly ground black pepper

1 egg white

1 rack of lamb, 1 to 2 pounds

Red currant jelly

Preheat oven to 450°F.

Mix together the mint sauce, breadcrumbs, parsley, garlic, salt, pepper, and egg white. Score the surface of the lamb with a sharp knife, and spread the mint mixture over the entire rack. Use a knife to gently press the mixture into the fat and meat.

Put the lamb into a roasting pan, and roast for 10 minutes. Reduce the heat to 350°F, and continue roasting 30 minutes longer, or until a meat thermometer registers 125°F for medium-rare lamb or 135°F for medium. Baste once during this time with the pan juices.

Remove the lamb from the oven, tent with foil, and let rest for 5 minutes. Cut the ribs apart to serve. Warm the currant jelly in the microwave oven or on the stovetop, and serve on the side.

For the Mint Sauce:

The custom of tart, snappy mint sauces originated in Great Britain when early cooks were attempting to mask the strong flavors of mutton. Grass-fed lamb hardly requires such masking, but a good mint sauce makes a nice complement to the flavor.

2 teaspoons sugar	1 cup tightly packed fresh mint leaves
2 teaspoons boiling water	2 teaspoons apple cider vinegar

Dissolve the sugar in the water, and when cool, pour into a blender or food processor. Add the mint and vinegar, and purée. Add additional sugar or vinegar to suit your taste. Allow the sauce to stand, covered, for 15 minutes before serving. Always serve mint sauce at room temperature.

Roast Leg of Lamb

The leg of lamb is a magnificent feast, suitable for only the most appreciative dinner companions. Unfortunately, many people have a tendency to overcook it; it is best served rosy and rare. So if you like juicy lamb, be sure to use your meat thermometer and remove the roast from the oven before it is too well-done.

SHOWCASE • MINIMUM PREPARATION

SERVES 10 TO 12

Rosemary, Thyme, and Mustard Paste (see page 256)

5- to 6-pound leg of lamb

Rub the Rosemary, Thyme, and Mustard Paste all over the leg, and rest the lamb at room temperature for 1 to 2 hours or, covered with plastic wrap, overnight in the refrigerator.

Preheat oven to 500°F.

Place the leg of lamb in a large roasting pan, set it in the oven, and immediately lower the heat to 250°F; continue roasting until a thermometer reads 120°F for a rare roast, 130°F for medium, or 140°F for well-done. Cooking times will vary based on the size of the leg and desired doneness, but allow at least 2½ hours at 250°F for a medium-rare 5½-pound leg.

Remove the lamb from the oven, cover loosely with foil, and rest for a *minimum* of 15 minutes before serving. The lamb will continue to cook during this time, and the temperature will go up another 5° to 10°F.

Lamb Roast with Morel Gravy

Skip and Christy Hensler, The Rock Garden, Washington

Mushroom enthusiasts in your family should delight in the rustic, robust flavors of this recipe. If you're trying to figure out what size roast to purchase, plan on ½ pound of meat per person (you'll have considerable shrinkage in the cooking process). Remember that the larger the roast, the more cooking time it requires. If morels are hard to find in your area, you may substitute porcinis.

SHOWCASE • MINIMUM PREPARATION

SERVES: VARIABLE, DEPENDING ON SIZE OF ROAST; FIGURE ON ½ POUND OF MEAT PER PERSON

1 lamb leg or shoulder roast

Salt to taste

1 cup dry sherry

2 cups water

1 ½ tablespoons garlic powder

1 cup sliced morel (or porcini) mushrooms

2 tablespoons cornstarch

¼ cup ice water

Preheat oven to 325°F.

Bring lamb to room temperature; sprinkle lightly with salt. Place the meat in the center of a roasting pan, pour in the sherry and water, and rub lamb with garlic powder. Add the mushrooms, cover, and roast roughly 30 minutes for each pound of meat.

When the meat is tender, remove from pan, and tent with foil. Bring the remaining juices to a boil over medium heat. Dissolve the cornstarch in ice water, mix until smooth, and pour into the boiling juices, stirring continuously until the gravy thickens.

Grilled Sirloin Chops in a Spicy Yogurt Marinade

If you love leg of lamb but your family is too small to justify buying an entire roast, try grilling the leg chops. They're cut from the sirloin end of the leg, so they have all the great leg meat, with very little waste.

MINIMUM PREPARATION

SERVES 2

> 2 sirloin chops or leg steaks, at least one inch thick
>
> Spicy Yogurt Marinade (page 257)
>
> Salt and freshly ground black pepper to taste

Lay the chops in a shallow bowl, pour the marinade on top, cover, and refrigerate several hours or overnight. Be sure to turn the chops at least once as they marinate.

While the grill is heating, remove the chops from the marinade, pat dry with a paper towel, and sprinkle with salt and pepper.

Grill over a medium flame until they achieve the desired doneness. Remove the chops when they are 5°F below your preferred temperature; tent loosely with foil. They will continue cooking for the next 5 minutes while they rest; the final temperature should be between 120° and 135°F, depending on your preference.

WORKING FROM HOME?

If you've moved your office from a distant institutional building to a spare bedroom in your home, the opportunity to cook wholesome food for your family is greater than ever.

Even if you're putting in long hours, consider the great things you could accomplish. During a midmorning coffee break, you could pop some meat into the oven to slow-roast for dinner; as you work, you could simmer a kettle of broth or soup on the stove; or during a quick afternoon break, you could take something out of the freezer to prepare for tomorrow night's meal. With the added bonus of removing a commute from your busy day, you could prep the vegetables or side dishes and have everything ready to serve up as soon as your family gathers at the table.

Herb-Roasted Boneless Sirloin

Connie Karstens, Liberty Land and Livestock, Minnesota

You won't see boneless sirloin often, but you can get it easily. Just ask your favorite farmers to have their butcher prepare it for you. This tender piece of meat, attached to the leg, averages 2 to 2 ½ pounds. Serve it medium-rare.

IN A HURRY • MINIMUM PREPARATION

SERVES 2 TO 3

> 1 boneless sirloin lamb roast, about 2 to 2½ pounds
>
> 2 teaspoons coarse salt
>
> ½ teaspoon freshly ground black pepper
>
> 1 tablespoon red currant jelly, melted
>
> 1 teaspoon dried rosemary
>
> ½ teaspoon dried oregano

Preheat oven to 350°F.

Bring sirloin to room temperature, sprinkle with salt and pepper, and roast 50 minutes, or until a meat thermometer reads 115°F.

Remove the roast from the oven, brush it with the melted jelly, and sprinkle with the herbs. Return the sirloin to the oven, and continue roasting until the thermometer reads 125°F for medium-rare. Remove, tent with foil, and allow to rest for 5 minutes before serving.

Stewed Lamb Shanks

Diane Roeder, Sojourner Sheep, Massachusetts

Here's a nice, no-fuss way to use an often-overlooked but very flavorful cut of meat.

ON A BUDGET • MINIMUM PREPARATION

SERVES 2 TO 3

  1 pound lamb shanks

  Salt and freshly ground black pepper to taste

  2 tablespoons olive oil

  2 onions, coarsely chopped

  2 cloves garlic, minced

  1 16-ounce can stewed tomatoes with juice

  ¼ cup dry red wine

  1 tablespoon dark brown sugar

  Dash or more of hot pepper sauce to taste

  1 sweet green pepper, chopped into 1-inch chunks

  ½ teaspoon dried rosemary

Sprinkle the lamb shanks with salt and pepper, and set aside.

Heat the olive oil in a heavy, nonreactive pot with a tight-fitting lid. Add the lamb shanks, and sauté until browned on all sides, about 5 to 7 minutes. Add the chopped onions, sauté for 1 minute, add the garlic, and sauté 1 minute more. Stir in the tomatoes, wine, brown sugar, and hot pepper sauce. Cover, and simmer over low heat for 1 hour, or until the lamb is tender. Add the chopped pepper and rosemary, simmer for an additional 30 minutes, and serve.

Braised Lamb Shanks

Alan Zuschlag and Steve Burton, Touchstone Farm, Virginia

Alan and Steve write: "Lamb shanks are often overlooked, yet this humble cut of meat can create a wonderfully rich and hearty meal. This recipe is easy to prepare and slow-cook on a crisp fall day while you're out walking in the woods with the dogs or doing yardwork around the house. It goes very well with red cabbage and Bavarian bread dumplings (recipes follow). Wash it down with a hearty Burgundy or a full-bodied Belgian farmhouse ale."

SHOWCASE • ON A BUDGET

SERVES 6

4 tablespoons olive oil

1 pound medium onions, thinly sliced

5 large shallots, sliced (about 1 cup)

2 tablespoons chopped fresh rosemary, or 1 ½ teaspoons dried

3 to 4 tablespoons all-purpose flour

1 tablespoon coarse salt

½ teaspoon freshly ground black pepper

6 whole lamb shanks

2 ½ cups dry red wine

2 ½ cups beef broth

1 ½ tablespoons tomato paste

2 bay leaves

Pennsylvania Red Cabbage (see page 121)

Bavarian Bread Dumplings (see page 122)

Heat 2 tablespoons of the olive oil in a heavy, large skillet over medium-high heat. Add the sliced onions and shallots, and sauté until caramelized, about 10 to 15 minutes. Mix in the chopped rosemary. Remove from heat.

Combine the flour, salt, and pepper, and use it to coat the shanks. Heat the remaining 2 tablespoons olive oil in the skillet over high heat. Working in batches, add the lamb shanks, and brown on both sides (about 5 minutes per side). Transfer shanks, onions, and shallots to a plate. Add 1 cup of the red wine to the skillet, and simmer for 2 to 3 minutes, scraping up any browned bits. Pour into a Dutch oven (or slow-cooker). Add the remaining $1\frac{1}{2}$ cups wine, beef broth, tomato paste, and bay leaves. Bring to a boil, stirring until tomato paste dissolves. Add the onions and shanks, turning the meat to be sure it is coated with liquid.

Let the mixture come to a boil (or leave on the highest slow-cooker setting for 30 minutes). Reduce heat, cover, and simmer until the lamb is tender, turning occasionally (about 2 hours on the stovetop or 6 hours in the slow-cooker). This can be prepared a day ahead; just cover and refrigerate.

Uncover the Dutch oven, and boil until the liquid reduces to sauce consistency, stirring and turning the shanks occasionally (about 30 minutes). Place the shanks on warmed plates; pour the sauce on top. Serve with Pennsylvania Red Cabbage and Bavarian Bread Dumplings.

For the Pennsylvania Red Cabbage:

SERVES 6

> 2 tablespoons bacon drippings
>
> $\frac{1}{4}$ cup packed dark brown sugar
>
> $\frac{1}{4}$ cup red wine vinegar
>
> $\frac{1}{2}$ teaspoon caraway seeds
>
> $\frac{1}{4}$ cup water
>
> $1\frac{1}{4}$ teaspoons coarse salt
>
> $\frac{1}{8}$ teaspoon freshly ground black pepper
>
> 4 cups shredded red cabbage
>
> 2 cups cubed, unpeeled sweet apples (about 2 medium-size apples)

Heat bacon drippings in a large skillet. Stir in brown sugar, vinegar, caraway seed, water, salt, and pepper. Add cabbage and apples, stirring to coat. Cover, and simmer over low heat, stirring occasionally. For crisp cabbage, cook for 15 minutes. For tender cabbage, simmer for at least 30 minutes (the cabbage can continue to simmer over very low heat until you are ready to serve).

For the Bavarian Bread Dumplings:

SERVES 6 TO 8

> 1 loaf day-old French bread, diced into crouton-size squares
>
> 2 tablespoons unsalted butter
>
> 2 medium yellow or white onions, finely chopped
>
> 1 bundle parsley, finely chopped
>
> 1 cup hot milk (*do not boil*)
>
> ¼ teaspoon freshly ground black pepper
>
> ½ teaspoon freshly ground nutmeg
>
> 1½ teaspoons salt
>
> 2 eggs

Place the diced bread in a large mixing bowl. In a large, heavy frying pan, heat butter, and sauté the onions for 3 to 4 minutes, until translucent. Add the parsley, sauté for 1 minute, and pour mixture over the bread. Add the hot milk, pepper, nutmeg, and 1 teaspoon of the salt. *Do not mix yet!* Allow it to rest for 30 minutes.

Lightly beat the eggs, and pour over the bread mixture. Thoroughly mix, being careful to keep from mashing the diced bread chunks. Divide into 8 portions, and with wet hands, shape into round dumplings.

In a large saucepan, bring 1 quart of water and the remaining ½ teaspoon salt to a boil. Using a slotted spoon, carefully drop the dumplings in the water, and immediately reduce the heat so that the water barely bubbles. Allow the dumplings to simmer uncovered for 15 minutes. Remove dumplings with a slotted spoon. Briefly set on paper towels to soak up water, and serve.

Tom Clack's Deviled Kidneys

Tom Clack, New York

This recipe comes from Tom Clack, one of our favorite customers at Sap Bush Hollow and a true kidney aficionado. You can substitute goat, pork, or beef kidneys for the lamb.

SHOWCASE

SERVES 4 AS AN APPETIZER

8 lamb kidneys (goat, pork, or beef kidneys will also work, just be sure not to exceed ½ pound of meat)

Milk for soaking

2 tablespoons unsalted butter

2 tablespoons Calvados

1 teaspoon all-purpose flour

1 tablespoon Worcestershire sauce

2 tablespoons ketchup

2 tablespoons grainy mustard

¼ teaspoon cayenne pepper

Salt, *very little*, to taste

4 thin slices of Italian or French bread, toasted

Slice kidneys in half lengthwise. Snip out any white fat and tubes with kitchen scissors. Divide each kidney into eighths. Place the kidneys in a shallow bowl, cover with milk, and soak at room temperature anywhere from 10 minutes to 1 hour. Drain the kidneys in a colander, rinse with cold water, and soak in fresh milk once more for 10 minutes. Drain kidneys; pat dry with paper towels.

Melt 1 tablespoon of the butter in a frying pan, add the kidneys, and sauté for 2 minutes. Pour the Calvados over the kidneys, and touch with a lighted match. Stir carefully as the kidneys flambé. Continue to stir until the flame burns itself out.

In a small pan, melt the remaining tablespoon of butter, stir in the flour, and stirring constantly, cook for 1 minute. Add the Worcestershire sauce, ketchup, mustard, and cayenne pepper; stir for about 2 minutes, until well combined and heated through; pour over the kidneys. Salt lightly, and cook the mixture for 2 minutes. Serve on buttered toast.

Lamb-Fennel Casserole

Connie Karstens, Liberty Land and Livestock, Minnesota

Here is an inexpensive way to cook a hearty main dish for your family in little more than an hour. Consider making a double batch, because the leftovers are even more delicious when reheated the second day.

ON A BUDGET • MINIMUM PREPARATION • KID-FRIENDLY

SERVES 4

1 pound lamb, cut into 1½-inch cubes (stew or kabob meat will work)

4 tablespoons all-purpose flour, seasoned with salt and
   freshly ground black pepper to taste

2 tablespoons olive oil

1 medium onion, thinly sliced

1 14.5-ounce can diced tomatoes with the juice

½ cup dry white wine

1 teaspoon dried oregano or 2 teaspoons fresh oregano, minced

Salt and freshly ground black pepper to taste

1 large bulb fennel, cored, cut into 8 wedges

1 4-ounce can button mushrooms, sliced

4 ounces green beans, cut in 2-inch pieces

Coat the lamb in the seasoned flour. Heat the oil in a large, heavy saucepan. Sauté the sliced onion for 2 minutes; add the lamb. Cook until the meat is browned on all sides. Stir in the tomatoes, wine, and oregano; add more salt and pepper to taste, if desired. Add the fennel, cover, and simmer over medium-low heat for 45 minutes, or until the meat is tender. Be sure to stir occasionally during this time. Add the mushrooms and green beans, and cook for 10 more minutes, or until the beans are crisp-tender, and serve.

Rebekah's Coconut Curry Lamb

Rebekah Tanner, New York

My good friend Rebekah Tanner once described this delectable dish to me in detail. Below is my best attempt to transcribe it into a recipe for the rest of the world to enjoy. If you do not live near a store that sells curry paste, simply make your own, page 256 (I find the flavor of the homemade paste much tastier).

ON A BUDGET

SERVES 4 TO 6

> 1 lamb shoulder roast, square-cut or rolled; or
>> ½ leg of lamb roast, or 2 to 3 pounds lamb stew meat
>
> Salt and freshly ground black pepper to taste
>
> 3 tablespoons olive oil
>
> 3 medium onions, sliced into wedges
>
> 2 teaspoons turmeric
>
> 5 medium boiling potatoes, peeled and quartered
>
> Curry Paste (see page 256) or 1 4-ounce can curry paste of your choice
>
> 2 14-ounce cans unsweetened coconut milk
>
> 1 ½ cups water

Preheat oven to 300°F.

Bring the lamb to room temperature. Trim the roast of any excess fat, and sprinkle with salt and pepper. Heat the olive oil in a large, flameproof casserole over medium heat. Brown the roast on all sides, about 3 minutes per side; remove, and set aside.

Toss the onions into the oil, and sauté until translucent; sprinkle onions with turmeric, and sauté 1 minute longer. Turn the heat to low. Add the potatoes, and stir in the curry paste, coconut milk, and water. Mix until well blended.

Set the lamb on top, cover tightly, and roast in the oven for 3 to 4 hours, or until the meat is fork-tender. Serve over a bed of rice topped with the potato-curry sauce.

Curried Goat

This is a simple curry, with seasonings reminiscent of exotic African flavors.

SHOWCASE • ON A BUDGET

SERVES 3 TO 4

¼ cup olive oil

2 pounds goat stewing meat or
    kabobs (lamb will also work)

Salt and freshly ground
    black pepper to taste

1 large onion, chopped

3 to 4 cloves garlic, minced

1 tablespoon grated fresh ginger

2 teaspoons freshly ground cumin

1 teaspoon freshly ground cardamom

2 cinnamon sticks

4 whole cloves

½ teaspoon cayenne pepper

1 teaspoon turmeric

1 can tomato paste

1 cup chicken broth

1 large or 2 small boiling potatoes,
    cut into bite-size chunks (optional)

½ cup chopped fresh cilantro

Heat the oil in a large, deep skillet over medium heat. Sprinkle the goat with salt and pepper, brown on all sides in the oil, remove it to a dish, and keep warm.

Add the chopped onion to the skillet, and sauté until translucent. Stir in the garlic, and cook for 1 minute; add the ginger, cumin, cardamom, cinnamon sticks, cloves, cayenne pepper, and turmeric. Mix thoroughly. Stir in the tomato paste and broth; return the meat to the skillet.

Reduce the heat to low, cover, and simmer until the meat is tender, about 45 minutes to 1 hour. Add the potatoes, cover once more, and cook 30 minutes longer, until easily pierced with a fork. Stir in the cilantro, and simmer, uncovered, for 10 minutes. Remove the cinnamon sticks, and serve over couscous or rice.

Lamb Stew

Kay Castner, Kaehler's Mill Farm, Wisconsin

Here is a simple stew to make on a late wintry afternoon. The meat can be boneless cubed lamb cut from either the shoulder or the shank half of a leg of lamb. If you don't mind bones, use lamb shanks or lamb neck to add extra flavor and body to the stew.

ON A BUDGET • MINIMUM PREPARATION

SERVES 6

2 teaspoons salt

1 teaspoon freshly ground
 black pepper

½ teaspoon sugar

2 teaspoons dried crushed mint

¼ cup all-purpose flour

2 pounds lamb stew meat

2 tablespoons olive oil

2 cloves garlic, chopped

2 cups water

1 cup dry red wine

1 teaspoon Worcestershire sauce

6 to 8 carrots, scraped and
 coarsely chopped

2 medium onions, cut in thick wedges

4 celery stalks, coarsely chopped

2 large boiling potatoes,
 cut into bite-size chunks

Combine the salt, pepper, sugar, crushed mint, and flour in a shallow bowl.

Bring the lamb to room temperature, and mix with the seasoned flour until well coated. Heat the olive oil in a soup pot, add the meat, and sauté until browned. Add the garlic, sauté for 1 minute, and pour in the water, wine, and Worcestershire sauce. Simmer, stirring occasionally, for 45 minutes to 1 hour, until the meat is tender. If too much liquid evaporates, add 1 to 2 cups water. Add the vegetables, and simmer for an additional 30 minutes, until the vegetables are tender.

Harira (Moroccan Lamb Soup)

Alan Zuschlag, Touchstone Farm, Virginia

Alan Zuschlag received this recipe from one of his customers, who explains that this soup is often served during the nights of Ramadan. This is really more of a stew than a soup, and some people claim that it is the best stew in the world.

ON A BUDGET

SERVES 4 TO 6

1 pound dried garbanzo beans

6 tablespoons plus 2 teaspoons fresh lemon juice

¾ cup dried green lentils

1 pound lamb stew meat, cut into 1½-inch cubes

1 tablespoon coarse salt

1½ teaspoons freshly ground black pepper

2 tablespoons olive oil

1 teaspoon ground turmeric

1½ teaspoons ground cinnamon

½ teaspoon cayenne pepper

¼ teaspoon ground ginger

2 tablespoons unsalted butter

4 stalks celery, coarsely chopped

1 yellow onion, coarsely chopped

1 red onion, coarsely chopped

½ cup finely chopped fresh cilantro

1 28-ounce can diced tomatoes, strained and juice reserved

2 quarts water

¼ pound spaghetti, vermicelli or other thin pasta

2 eggs

Ground cinnamon, for garnish

Dried mint, for garnish

1 lemon, cut into wedges

Cover garbanzo beans with warm water. Stir in 4 tablespoons of the lemon juice, cover, and soak for 24 hours. Soak the dried lentils in warm water and 2 tablespoons of the lemon juice for 7 hours. Drain the water from both, and proceed with the recipe.

Bring the lamb to room temperature, and sprinkle with the salt and black pepper. Heat the olive oil in a large, heavy soup pot, add the lamb, and brown it quickly, about 3 minutes per side. Add the turmeric, cinnamon, cayenne pepper, ginger, butter, celery, onions, and cilantro. Cook, stirring frequently, for another 5 minutes. Add the strained tomatoes, and simmer for 10 minutes.

Pour the reserved tomato juice and water into the pot; add the drained lentils and garbanzos. Bring the mixture to a boil, then reduce the heat to simmer. Cover and simmer for 2 hours.

Just before serving, turn the heat up, add the pasta, and cook just a few minutes—the noodles should be al dente. Meanwhile, beat the eggs with the remaining 2 teaspoons lemon juice. When the pasta is ready, lower the heat, and while stirring constantly, slowly add the egg-lemon mixture to the simmering soup. Cook 1 minute longer, being careful to avoid coddling the eggs. Garnish the soup with a dash of cinnamon and dried mint. Serve lemon wedges on the side for those who prefer a more acidic flavor.

Pepper Soup

Recipes for this traditional spicy West African dish vary greatly. Because one of the keys to African cuisine is making the best with whatever is available, go ahead and experiment. Create your own version!

ON A BUDGET

SERVES 6

2 pounds goat or lamb stew meat

¼ cup olive oil

Coarse salt and freshly ground black pepper to taste

2 large onions, finely diced

4 cups water

2 cups chicken broth

2 to 3 hot green chili peppers, seeded, white membranes removed, and finely chopped

3 fresh tomatoes, seeded and chopped

1 can tomato paste

3 boiling potatoes, coarsely chopped

2 teaspoons dried thyme, or 3 teaspoons fresh

2 teaspoons curry powder

Dash cayenne pepper

Bring the meat to room temperature. Heat the oil over medium heat in a large Dutch oven. Sprinkle the stew meat with salt and pepper, and brown on all sides in the olive oil. Add the onions, and sauté until translucent. Add the water and broth, cover, and simmer until the meat is tender, about 1½ hours if you are using goat, 45 minutes to 1 hour if you are using lamb.

Add the remaining ingredients, and simmer 30 minutes longer. Season to taste with additional salt, black pepper, and cayenne pepper. Serve in deep soup bowls as is or over couscous if desired.

COMMON RETAIL CUTS OF LAMB AND GOAT
AND IDEAL COOKING METHODS

BREAST	
Riblets	Super slow roast
Breast	Dry or Moist heat

LEG	
Sirloin chops or roast	Dry heat
Leg steaks	Dry or Moist heat
Leg	Dry or Moist heat
Kabobs	Dry or Moist heat

LOIN	
Double or single loin chops	Dry heat
Loin roast	Dry heat

RIB	
Rib roast or rack	Dry heat
Rib chops	Dry heat

SHANKS	
Whole or cross-cut shanks	Moist heat

SHOULDER	
Chops	Moist heat
Stew meat	Moist heat
Shoulder roast	Moist heat
Ground lamb	Dry or Moist heat

CHAPTER FOUR

$\mathcal{P}$ORK

Few animals have the ability to win over the heart of a casual observer like the pig. Sheep and cows look beautiful grazing in lush green pastures, but a pen full of pigs has an entirely different effect. They're a joy to watch as they run around, chase each other, splash in their wallows, squeal as the farmer prepares their food, chase toys, and plead for scratches. Throw them a ball, and they will be amused for hours. And so will you. If you're visiting a farm and want to see a spectacle that could put the Sea World cast to shame, ask to visit the pigs. However, be careful about approaching them. Though they can look cute and friendly, keep your hands outside the pen unless the farmer says it is OK to touch them. They do nip on occasion.

When you visit the pigs, you'll notice that their living conditions are very different from those of the cows and sheep. The pigs' pastures are not as pristine, and allowances must be made for their unique "piggy" traits. Pigs enjoy rooting around and will quickly make a pasture look like a minefield. Given the opportunity, they'll rapturously attack a farmer's compost pile, rooting for worms and whatever treasures that unappreciative humans may have left behind for them. They're omnivores, so unlike sheep and cows, they cannot live on grass alone. They require supplemental feed and enjoy any number of extra snacks, including nuts, fruits, milk, whey, and table scraps.

The lifestyles of the pastured pig and the pastured pig farmer are measurably different from those of the commodity pigs and the pork producers. Large, vertically integrated corporations produce most of the pork sold in this country. In this system, farmers are no longer independent. Rather, one corporation owns the hogs, the processing facilities, the feed mills, and the distribution system.[1] The corporation contracts with the farmer to raise the hogs, using his or her buildings, facilities, and manure lagoons. In exchange for marginal profits, the farmer shoulders the debt of the operation and all environmental liability, as well as the inevitable health problems that come from working in confinement operations with perilously high levels of carbon dioxide, ammonia, and dust. The pigs' lifestyle isn't any better. They're likely to be despondent, experience respiratory problems, engage in tail biting, have ulcers on their shoulders from rubbing against crates, and suffer from foot and leg problems.

The difference between these two production practices can be tasted in the pork. In an informal taste test performed with *Fine Cooking*'s editor-at-large Maryellen Driscoll, we determined that conventionally produced pork tended to leave a coating in our mouths and with it had an odd, metallic flavor. Braised country ribs did not reflect the flavor of the braising liquids. By contrast, the grass-fed pork had a sweeter, cleaner taste with a nutty finish. The meat was firmer and significantly juicier. When braised, the pork reflected the flavors of the braising liquids. In an article in the *Washington Post,* the food writer Lynn Cowan describes pastured pork as "deep-flavored" and juicy. She writes that pastured pork has a "dense texture, similar to a well-done steak. The flesh is darker, somewhat rosy. It's more moist, so a chop oozes and sputters in a frying pan."[2]

Pastured pigs are active creatures, yet there will be considerable variation in the amount of fat among the breeds, particularly if a farmer is using some of the heritage breeds, which were bred to produce more fat than the more modern, conventional pigs. However, due to the healthy diet of the pigs, the fat is tastier and more nutritious than that of conventionally raised pork meat. In my estimation, to refuse to sample it would be a gastronomical sin. I prefer the fattiest cuts found on the pig; the fresh hams, country ribs, and shoulder chops. Grass-fed pork fat is delicious, and it keeps the meat moist and tender. If you've always shied away from pork fat, now is the time to dig in and give it a try.

Although simply moving pigs into a more natural environment does wonders to improve the meat flavor, a number of heritage breeds are known for being especially tasty, including Gloucestershire Old Spots, Large Blacks, Tamworths (especially known for beautiful bacon), Herefords, and Berkshires. I encourage you to take the opportunity to sample pork from one of those breeds.

Again, pastured pigs live entirely different lives than do cows and lambs. Below are a few items to consider when evaluating a pastured pig operation:

- The pastures will not look like cow or lamb pastures. Pigs like to root around, so they can quickly turn over fields they're allowed to browse in. Because they're so hard on pastures, a farmer may elect to relegate them to the poorest fields. Pigs like short grasses best and require supplemental grain. It's not unusual for a farmer who has planted row crops to release his or her pigs into the fields to harvest the grains directly, rather than incurring the expense of harvesting these crops simply to be later poured into the pigs' feeders. Since the pastures will be a little more beat up, look for evidence that the pigs are being rotated to fresh grass on a regular basis. And even though the soil may be slightly turned, the pigs should not be living in a pure mud pit.

- Speaking of mud pits... Pigs require wallows to stay cool in the summer. These are wet, muddy patches where they can roll around. Thus, if a small portion of the pasture contains a deep muddy area, there's no reason for concern. This is necessary for healthy, happy animals. But again, the distinction should be made between a muddy patch and a pen devoid of grass.

- Pigs generally do not fare well without housing during the winter. Although many of the heritage breeds are significantly heartier than their modern cousins, pigs—unlike other farm animals—do not have thick fur coats. Farmers will often house them on deep straw bedding in a barn or in hoop houses. Either system maximizes warmth for the animals by allowing the manure to compost and generate heat. Even though they're indoors, the pigs will rarely develop the respiratory problems associated with conventional confinement operations because these systems contain plenty of ventilation through open windows and/or entryways. If you're evaluating a farm in the winter months in a cold climate, look to see if this ventilation is present.

- Study the pigs. The best way to tell if they're well-kept is to observe their behavior. Do they run around? Are they playing? Do they respond to you (coming close for inspection, lining up for back scratches, or running away)? Unhappy or unhealthy animals will be less likely to respond to new stimuli.

- Although pigs definitely have their own, unique scent, there should not be an overwhelmingly bad smell when you approach their area, whether indoors or out. A bad odor is an indication that the manure is not being composted properly or that the pastures have not been rotated in a timely fashion.

- Pigs are intelligent and playful, which makes processing day a very sad time for most farmers. Like lamb and cattle, they should be loaded onto the truck as quietly as possible and allowed to calm down before the harvest. Though it is possible for pork to be processed without aging, many farmers feel that a one-week dry-age period helps to guarantee high-quality meat.

HOME-COOKED MEALS AFTER A HARD DAY'S WORK?

The grass-fed meat movement is not only about social justice for farmers, improved livestock conditions, and environmental health. It's also about improving the health of the people who eat the meat, about connecting consumers and local farmers to build stronger community ties, and about bringing families closer together by encouraging them to sit down at the table for a meal.

If fast-food restaurants and the prepackaged food industry were to adopt grass-fed meats, the movement would be only partially successful, since many of the social benefits would be overlooked. The movement will have true success when families are able to sit down together at night to enjoy a nutritious meal grown by the farmers who live and work in their community.

But in today's harried work environment, is such a vision possible? Absolutely. Cooking a meal doesn't need to take significantly more time than ordering take-out pizza or going through the drive-through window. With a few tricks and some advanced planning, anyone can be putting a good meal on the table. Here are some tips:

- Take a few minutes over the weekend to review everybody's schedules for the coming week. What nights will people be home for dinner? What nights will you have time to cook? What nights will be rushed? Make a list of menu items that suit each of these needs. Select a slow-cooker recipe for a night when you won't have much time to cook, choose something a little more complex for nights when you have some time to enjoy being in the kitchen, and plan to make extra for the evenings when people might need to simply reheat their meals and keep running.

- Once you have a menu, go to the freezer on Sunday and take out the meats you will need for the week. Food preparation goes much faster if you don't need to wait for a piece of meat to thaw. Keep the meats in a stainless steel bowl in your refrigerator; they will easily last through the week without spoiling (provided they are grass-fed and fresh-frozen).

- Review the menu plan to determine which ingredients you don't have on hand, and make a point of picking them up on your next shopping trip. Don't let a perpetually empty refrigerator have you always running for convenience foods.

- Don't be afraid to enlist the help of kids in the kitchen. They can learn valuable life skills, enjoy some uninterrupted quality time with you, and help you out immensely.

- Enlist the participation of spouses, partners, and older children by giving them their own night as the family chef. Respect their food choices, and be appreciative of their efforts.

Preparing a meal at the end of the day can be a true creative outlet and a great stress reliever, so long as you plan ahead.

Safeguarding the Land and Biodiversity

Jen Small and Mike Yezzi, Flying Pigs Farm, Shushan New York

While their former Union College classmates are working as doctors, lawyers, and stockbrokers, Jen Small and Mike Yezzi, are busy making faith leap and pigs fly in upstate New York.

Committed environmentalists, Jen and Mike found themselves in a position to practice what they preached very early in their marriage. Jen grew up spending her summers at her father's childhood home in Shushan, a tiny rural hamlet near the Vermont border in Washington County. In 1995, while Mike was still in graduate school, the dilapidated farm neighboring Jen's family home was targeted for development. Jen, a university fundraiser, and Mike, a healthcare attorney, had never imagined that this run-down property might  be their fate. But seeing the threat to their beloved woods, pastures, and Batten Kill River and deploring irresponsible development practices, Jen and Mike pooled what few resources they had and applied for a loan to purchase the farm and save it from being carved into housing lots.

Mike recalls that it was a nerve-wracking experience. "We were in grad school. We didn't have the money to make a mortgage payment and fix up a house." Jen adds "But we *had* to. We didn't have any choice. It was either buy it or lose the land forever." And so, saddled with school loans, a mortgage, and rent payments and armed with only one small income and their bare hands, Jen and Mike set about achieving the impossible. For four years, their newly acquired 1830s farmhouse was not habitable, so they lived near Jen's job and drove to Shushan every weekend and vacation to work at restoring their home. Jen says, "Buying this place was a big blind leap of faith—that somehow, we were going to find jobs out here, that we were going to find a way to pay for this, that we were going to get past not being able to afford the garbage cans we needed to dump the gutting material." Mike adds, "We were making agonizing decisions over how much we could spend on a hammer and how much to spend on a crowbar."

"But you know what?" quips Jen. "It worked out." After four years of painstaking restoration, the couple was finally able to move into a beautiful 1830s farmhouse and turn their attention to the first love that had brought them there: the land. Jen explains that simply holding the land, and not stewarding it, was not an option. "We can talk about protecting land from sprawl all we want, but if nobody wants to farm it, it doesn't matter. Ultimately it must remain in farming, and farming must be economically viable for sprawl to stop." They considered a variety of enterprises, including buffalo, goats, bees, and even llamas and emus. They took their time and endured skepticism and chuckles from the seasoned local farmers. Mike remarks: "People thought we had a nice hobby farm, but the general sentiment we heard was 'You'll never make a go of it. You'll get sick of it in a couple of years, and you'll quit. You'll be real farmers when pigs fly.' "

Coincidentally, that was exactly what happened. In 2000, they decided to try raising three pigs. They enjoyed the experience so much that they're now producing about sixty per year, and their pork is literally flying out of their freezer and into the hands of individuals and restaurants in New York City, almost faster than they can grow it.

But true to their core beliefs, Jen and Mike didn't settle for simply marketing the typical pink, hairless pig bred to endure factory-farming conditions. Rather, they found a unique market niche that enabled them to continue with their environmental mission by increasing biodiversity. They began raising heritage-breed pork. Today, a visit to their farm is like walking into a small pig zoo, with the variety of species including Gloucestershire Old Spots, Tamworths, and Large Blacks. By building a market and increasing the demand for heritage-breed pork, Jen and Mike are working to save valuable pig breeds from extinction while helping to ensure that the factory pig does not take over the porcine gene pool.

Even today, Jen is surprised that she and her husband raise meat for slaughter. "I never, ever imagined myself raising an animal to kill it. I still can't believe it!" she exclaims. However, raising their animals in a natural environment, on grass, has helped her gain perspective about the life and death of farm livestock. "I know that our animals have a fabulous life. And I also know that they have a very quick death. So if I'm going to eat meat, this is the kind I want."

Mike relishes treating the livestock with the respect and care they deserve. "It's simple. If you give animals space and good things to eat and a good place to sleep, then you don't have any of the problems experienced on conventional [factory] farms. Look at the way pigs are raised and the way they're treated and penned up in conventional farm settings. It is amazing to observe the *lengths* people will go to treat the problem behaviors that happen. They dock all the pigs' tails because otherwise, they bite each other. People think that the pigs are having a problem, so they cut off their tails. They disregard the fact that the animals are overcrowded in a tiny pen, and that's why they are biting each other."

Equally exciting for this couple is how the animals have improved their land. By moving pigs carefully through their pastures and with additional help from some sheep and chickens, Jen and Mike delight in the changes in their fields. The excess brush is cleaned up, the pastures become lusher each year, the wild-life habitat is improving, and the carrying capacity of the land steadily grows. "Every year, it gets even better," says Jen, "and that's a great success for us."

It's a lot for two people to have accomplished. Together, Jen and Mike saved a section of their community from development, they restored the land, they're part of a movement to bring back rare-breed pigs, and they've built a viable business. But they're quick to admit that it has taken a lot of hard work. "It's not easy," says Jen. "We believe that you don't have to inherit a farm or be wealthy to get into farming. But it's hard. We have to work full-time off-farm jobs. It's not uncommon for us to come home from our jobs and then work on the farm until ten or eleven at night, plus the weekends." Still, she says, they feel their efforts are worthwhile, especially with their weekly trips to the Grand Army Plaza and Borough Hall Green Markets in Brooklyn. "We go to the farmers' market, and our customers are waiting for us. And they tell us how great our product is and how much they appreciate what we're doing. And that's very rewarding."

DON'T LET THAT PORK FAT GO TO WASTE!

When butchers process hogs, a considerable amount of fat must be trimmed from the meat and thrown out. However, in the days before margarine, lard was a prized product, and pigs were selected based on their ability to produce this wonderful fat. When farm families harvested hogs in the fall, they promptly set about rendering the fat into lard to be used for baking and for making soap.

In our family, we've found that good lard makes the best fried food, pie crusts, and biscuits. We also use it to make a gentle and long-lasting soap. If you order a whole or half pig from your farmer, consider asking for some of the fat and rendering it into lard. The process is a bit time-consuming, but the results are well worth it. However, be sure that your kitchen is well ventilated so that your house is not inundated with the smell of melting pork fat.

What you'll need:[1]

    10 to 20 pounds of pork fat (This makes enough for about a one-year supply of lard.)

    ½ teaspoon baking soda (Even if you make a half batch of lard, use the same amount.)

    large cauldron with a lid

    colander

    large piece of cloth for straining

    large metal bowl

    freezer containers

Slice the pork fat into strips no wider than two inches across, and toss them into the cauldron. Do not fill the cauldron more than halfway, since the fat will splatter as it starts to melt. Sprinkle the baking soda on top, then cover the pot with the lid, leaving it slightly ajar to allow the water to escape.

Turn the heat on the lowest setting possible, and periodically stir the fat, making sure to not put your face directly over the cauldron (the fat can splatter very suddenly and burn). Allow the fat to cook until the bits of meat and cracklings are browned and floating on the surface—about 12 to 24 hours. If you're concerned about leaving a pot on the stove during the night, simply turn the heat off and resume the rendering process in the morning. Use a slotted spoon to remove the cracklings to brown paper to drain (sprinkled with a touch of salt, they make a wonderful snack).

Line your colander with the piece of cloth, and set it over the large metal bowl. Pour the melted fat into the colander, and allow it to strain through the cloth and into the bowl. Allow the fat to cool slightly before pouring it into containers. Chill the lard quickly, and then freeze it until you are ready to use it.

1. Carl Emery, *The Encyclopedia of Country Living* (Seattle: Sasquatch Books, 2003)

$\mathcal{R}$ECIPES

PORK SAUSAGES WITH POTATOES AND ROSEMARY 142

MAPLE-BRAISED PORK SAUSAGES 143

LUCHON PORK PÂTÉ 144

HONEY-ROASTED PORK CHOPS WITH APPLES AND ONIONS 146

SPICY MARINATED PORK CHOPS 147

MAPLE- AND CIDER-BRINED PORK WITH CREAMED LEEKS AND APPLES 148

BROILED COUNTRY HAM STEAK 150

PORK TENDERLOIN MEDALLIONS SAUTÉED WITH MUSHROOMS AND POTATOES 151

CLASSIC PULLED PORK 152

HOMEMADE BARBECUE SAUCE 153

HONEY-GINGER BRINED PORK 154

FRESH HAM 156

BARBECUE-STYLE PORK RIBS 157

MOROCCAN SPICED PORK LOIN WITH PEAR-RAISIN CHUTNEY 158

ORANGE PORK SHOULDER ROAST 159

HONEY-GLAZED PORK RIB ROAST WITH APPLE-WALNUT STUFFING 160

GLAZED HAM IN A MAPLE-RAISIN SAUCE 162

ARTICHOKES AND BACON 163

BRANDIED PORK SHOULDER CHOPS WITH APRICOTS AND PRUNES 164

PORK LIVER AND APPLES 165

BOSTON BAKED BEANS WITH HAM HOCKS 166

BRAISED PORK HEART 168

All recipes without attribution are from Shannon Hayes, Sap Bush Hollow Farm, West Fulton, New York.

Pork Sausages with Potatoes and Rosemary

Nancy Pritchard, Smith Meadows, Virginia

Nancy Pritchard developed this recipe for veal sausages, but it works deliciously well with sweet Italian pork sausages.

ON A BUDGET

SERVES 6

> 4 tablespoons olive oil
>
> 8 large-link pork sausages (or veal)
>
> ¼ cup coarsely chopped onion
>
> 8 medium-size baking potatoes, cut into large wedges
>
> 1 teaspoon salt
>
> ¼ teaspoon freshly ground black pepper
>
> ½ teaspoon cayenne pepper
>
> 1 cup dry white wine
>
> 4 large sprigs of fresh rosemary

Preheat oven to 350°F.

Heat 2 tablespoons of the olive oil over medium heat in a large ovenproof pot or Dutch oven (as long as it is not cast iron). Brown the sausages for 3 to 5 minutes per side. Remove, cut into large chunks about the same size as the potatoes, and set aside. Pour off the fat, add the remaining 2 tablespoons olive oil and the onion, and sauté until transparent. Add the potatoes, and cook for about 5 minutes on high heat, stirring frequently to be sure the potatoes don't stick.

Return the sausages and their juices to the pot, and add the salt, pepper, and cayenne pepper. Stir in the wine and rosemary, cover, and bake for approximately 1 hour, until the potatoes can be pierced easily with a fork.

Maple-Braised Pork Sausages

This is one of the easiest, most delicious recipes for sweet Italian sausage you'll ever see. It requires only a few minutes in the kitchen, and everyone you serve it to will remember it always. I like it with winter squash mashed with butter and herbes de Provence and steamed broccoli tossed with toasted walnuts.

SHOWCASE • ON A BUDGET • IN A HURRY • MINIMUM PREPARATION • KID-FRIENDLY

SERVES 5

2 tablespoons olive oil

2 pounds link sweet Italian pork sausage or
   2 pounds bulk sweet Italian pork sausage, formed into 8 large patties

6 tart apples, cored and quartered, but not peeled

¼ cup maple syrup

Preheat oven to 350°F.

Heat the olive oil in a flameproof casserole over medium heat. Brown the sausages, about 3 minutes per side. Remove from the heat, and add the apples. Drizzle the maple syrup on top, cover, and roast for 30 to 45 minutes, or until the apples can be pierced easily with a fork. Serve in a shallow bowl with the apples and the pan sauce spooned on top.

Luchon Pork Pâté

Marc Fournier, Sap Bush Hollow Farm

Americans have come to expect pâté to be smooth and creamy—more like a mousse than a true pâté. This rustic, traditional pâté is surprisingly easy to make. If you can make meatloaf, you can make this. The only difference is that pâtés must be made a day in advance, allowed to mellow in the refrigerator, and served cold. We've passed many splendid summer evenings at Sap Bush Hollow sipping wine and spreading this luscious pâté on crackers or French bread. It makes a fabulous appetizer or, paired with a salad, a light dinner. Bake this pâté in standard 9-inch loaf pans. Even though this recipe makes three loaves, one will serve 4 to 6 people. Thus, when you're preparing to serve it, pop the other loaves out of their pans, wrap them in plastic, and keep them in your freezer for your next dinner party or pâté craving.

SHOWCASE

ONE PAN SERVES 4 TO 6 PEOPLE; RECIPE MAKES 3 PANS

1 ¼ pounds pork liver (or chicken or beef liver)

3 pounds ground pork breakfast sausage

1 egg

½ teaspoon freshly ground nutmeg

1 ½ tablespoons coarse salt

1 teaspoon freshly ground black pepper

1 tablespoon cornmeal

1 onion, minced

3 cloves garlic, minced

3 tablespoons Armagnac or Cognac

½ pound lard or melted unsalted butter for topping patés (optional)

Preheat oven to 320°F.

Purée the liver in a food processor or grind it in a meat grinder; place the liver in the bowl of a large electric mixer. (If you don't have an electric mixer, you can mix by hand.) Add the sausage, egg, nutmeg, salt, pepper, cornmeal, onion, garlic, and Armagnac. Beat until well blended (use a splatter screen if you have one).

Coat each of the loaf pans generously with some softened butter. Divide the pâté evenly among the pans. Cover each loaf with a sheet of buttered wax paper, and cover with foil. Bake 1½ hours, or until a meat thermometer reads 162°F. Remove the pâté from the oven, spread with half the lard (or melted butter), and cool for 1 hour. Spread with the remaining lard, and refrigerate. Allow to sit for 1 full day in the refrigerator before serving.

To serve, set the loaf pan in a bowl of hot water for a minute to loosen the pâté. Unmold onto a platter, and garnish with fresh herbs. Serve with bread or crackers.

SIFTING SALTS

A walk through any gourmet store these days offers the home cook a world tour of the types of salts available. Simple table salt and kosher salt, once kitchen standards, are now being trumped by infinitely more expensive salts from a variety of exotic locations: black sea salt, red sea salt, French sea salt, Celtic sea salt, and fleur de sel are just a few of the current offerings.

According to an article in *Cook's Illustrated*,[1] each of these salts is distinguished by the amount of minerals and clay attached to the sodium chloride crystals. Personal flavor preferences vary, but coarser salts work better when flavoring meat because they coat the cuts more evenly. However, in her book *Nourishing Traditions*,[2] Sally Fallon points out that one of the important issues to pay attention to is how salt is processed. Most industrial salt processing removes important magnesium salts as well as naturally occurring minerals. She adds that in order to keep salt dry, refiners often use additives, such as aluminum compounds. In the case of ordinary table salt, the natural iodine salts that are removed are replaced with potassium iodide and dextrose and then a bleaching agent is used to restore the whiteness. Fallon points out that most sea salts are produced by industrial methods; therefore, the best salts are those that are extracted using natural processes (which make use of clay-lined vats placed in the sun). By these standards, the best salts are red sea salt, Celtic sea salt, or sea salt from Brittany.

1. Anna Kasabian and Meg Suzuki, *"The Emperor's New Salt,"* Cook's Illustrated, September-October 2002, pp. 26-30.

2. Sally Fallon, with Mary G. Enig. *Nourishing Traditions: The Cookbook That Challenges Politically Correct Nutrition and the Diet Dictocrats* (Washington, D.C.: New Trends Publishing, 1999).

Honey-Roasted Pork Chops
with Apples and Onions

A homey dinner for two, this is a nice way to enjoy a fall harvest of apples and onions. It takes only 10 minutes to prepare, then fills your kitchen with sweet scents while you relax as the chops cook.

SHOWCASE • ON A BUDGET • MINIMUM PREPARATION

SERVES 2

1 tablespoon salt

1 teaspoon freshly ground black pepper

3 teaspoons rubbed sage

1 tablespoon olive oil

2 pork chops (rib, shoulder, loin, and country ribs are all okay to use)

$\frac{1}{3}$ cup apple cider or juice

1 tart, firm apple, cored and cut into thick slices, but not peeled

1 small onion, thinly sliced into rings

$\frac{1}{4}$ cup raisins

2 tablespoons honey

Preheat oven to 350°F.

Combine the salt, pepper, and sage; rub into the meat.

Pour the olive oil into a heated ovenproof skillet, and sear the chops over medium heat, 1 minute per side or until browned. Remove from the heat, add the cider, sliced apple, onion, and raisins. Drizzle with honey, cover, and roast for 1 $\frac{1}{2}$ hours or until fork-tender.

Spicy Marinated Pork Chops

Pam Millar, Zu Zu's Petals, New York

Pam Millar warns that these pork chops are not for the meek, but that the smoky richness of the marinade pairs exquisitely with the pork. I think they're an absolute delight.

ON A BUDGET • MINIMUM PREPARATION

SERVES 4

> 4 pork chops, 1 ½-inches thick
>
> Ancho-Chipotle Marinade (page 257)
>
> Salt and freshly ground black pepper to taste

Place the chops in a stainless steel bowl, pour in the marinade, cover, and refrigerate overnight.

Remove the meat from the marinade, blot dry, sprinkle with salt and pepper, and grill or broil over medium-high heat for 5 to 6 minutes per side (for 1 ½-inch-thick chops), or until the internal temperature reaches 145°F. Remove the chops from the grill, tent with foil, and let rest for 5 minutes before serving.

Maple- and Cider-Brined Pork with Creamed Leeks and Apples

Judy Pangman, Sweet Tree Farm, New York

Here's an elegant recipe that celebrates many of New York State's finest products. One of my recipe testers recommended pairing this dish with a cider wine.

SHOWCASE

SERVES 4

For the brined pork:

1 cup maple syrup

4¼ cups apple cider

3 tablespoons coarse salt

6 allspice berries

1 bay leaf

4 bone-in, center-cut pork chops, or 5 to 6 country ribs

Bring maple syrup, 4 cups of the cider, salt, allspice, and bay leaf to a boil in a large saucepan, stirring to dissolve the salt. Boil for 1 minute. Cool completely. Place the pork in a 13-x-9-x-2-inch glass baking dish, pour in the brine, cover, and refrigerate, soaking the chops or ribs overnight.

For the creamed leeks:

4 tablespoons (½ stick) unsalted butter

6 large leeks (white and pale green parts only), thinly sliced crosswise

1 cup whipping cream

Salt and freshly ground black pepper to taste

Olive oil

Melt 2 tablespoons of the butter in a heavy, large skillet over medium-low heat. Add the leeks, and sauté until tender, about 7 minutes. Add the cream, and simmer until slightly thickened, about 3 minutes. Season to taste with salt and pepper. Creamed leeks can be made 1 day ahead. Cover and chill.

For the apple and Calvados sauce:

1½ pounds Granny Smith apples, peeled, cored, halved, each cut into 4 wedges

2 tablespoons granulated maple sugar or white sugar

½ cup chicken stock

⅓ cup Calvados

Melt the remaining 2 tablespoons butter in a large, nonstick skillet over medium heat. Add the apples, and sauté for 10 minutes. Add the sugar, and sauté until the apples are golden, about 6 minutes longer. Add the stock, then the Calvados and the remaining ¼ cup cider. Simmer until the liquid thickens slightly and the apples are tender, stirring occasionally, about 5 minutes. Set aside.

For the barbecue:

Prepare the barbecue grill (medium heat) or preheat the broiler. Drain the pork, rinse under cold water, and pat dry. Brush the meat with olive oil (use only a scant amount if meat will be broiled). Grill or broil to desired doneness, about 5 minutes per side for medium.

Meanwhile, rewarm the leeks, thinning the sauce with 1 to 3 tablespoons water, if necessary. Bring apples to a simmer. Spoon leeks onto warmed plates. Top with pork, then apples.

Broiled Country Ham Steak

Anton Burkett, Early Morning Organic Farm, New York

Whether you're in a hurry to cook dinner for the family or you're having guests over and want to serve a special dinner, this is a great treat. If you need to feed more people, simply add another steak and double the recipe.

SHOWCASE • ON A BUDGET • IN A HURRY • MINIMUM PREPARATION • KID-FRIENDLY

SERVES 2 TO 3

1 teaspoon Dijon mustard

1 tablespoon apple cider vinegar

¼ cup pear, apple, or peach jam

1 smoked ham steak, about 1-inch thick

Whisk the mustard, vinegar, and jam until completely blended.

Preheat the broiler.

Bring the ham to room temperature. Make several 1-inch cuts around the perimeter of the ham steak. Brush the steak on both sides with the glaze, and place on a pan about 3 inches below the heat element. Broil ham for 5 minutes on the first side. Remove, turn it over, brush the second side with additional glaze, and broil for 3 more minutes, or until heated through. Remove the steak from the oven, top with the remaining glaze, and serve.

Pork Tenderloin Medallions
Sautéed with Mushrooms and Potatoes

Pork tenderloin medallions lend themselves to a wide variety of flavors and recipes. This sauté makes a fast but satisfying meal based on simple, comforting flavors.

SHOWCASE • IN A HURRY

SERVES 2

6 tablespoons unsalted butter

2 small onions, cut into wedges

8 mushrooms, quartered

½ teaspoon dried or 2 sprigs fresh tarragon

1 cup chicken stock

3 medium boiling potatoes, cut into small chunks

Salt and freshly ground black pepper to taste

1 pound pork tenderloin medallions

½ cup dry white wine

½ cup heavy cream

To make the sauce, heat 2 tablespoons of the butter in a heavy, deep-sided skillet. Add the onions, and sauté for 3 minutes. Add the mushrooms, and cook 2 minutes longer. Add the tarragon and chicken stock, and simmer over low heat for 15 minutes.

Meanwhile, heat 2 tablespoons of the butter in a second skillet, add the potatoes, and sauté until browned. Season with salt and pepper, and continue sautéing for 15 minutes until tender. Remove from the heat, but keep warm.

Pour the contents of the first skillet into a small bowl. With the skillet back on the burner, turn the heat to medium-high, and add the remaining 2 tablespoons of butter. Sprinkle the medallions with salt and pepper, and toss into the butter. Sauté the meat for about 3 to 4 minutes per side; add it to the potatoes. Pour the sauce into the empty skillet; add the wine, and simmer, scraping up any browned bits, until the mixture is reduced by almost half. Add the heavy cream, and mix well over low heat. Stir in the potatoes and meat, and serve immediately.

Classic Pulled Pork

This was adapted from Cook's Illustrated *magazine's* Best Recipe: Grilling and Barbecue book.[3] *I like this recipe because it captures a true smoky flavor but doesn't mask the great taste of the meat. Prepare this recipe for a summer dinner party, when you will have a full day to tend to the meat and a full crowd to laud your efforts. This is not difficult to prepare, but it will require some attention every few hours.*

SHOWCASE • ON A BUDGET

SERVES 8

½ cup Barbecue Spice Rub (see page 253)

1 bone-in pork shoulder roast, 6 to 8 pounds

4 cups mesquite or hickory chips

1 cup barbecue sauce (for a homemade sauce recipe, see page 153)

Rub the spices into the meat, cover with plastic wrap, and rest at room temperature for 2 to 3 hours.

If using a charcoal grill, place the coals (about 2½ pounds) on one side of the grill and light. Place the mesquite chips on a large square of aluminum foil, and fold up the edges to make a sealed packet. Cut six holes, about 1 inch in diameter, in the top. Place the foil packet directly on the coals when they are covered with a thin layer of ash. Make sure the bottom vent of the grill is open.

If using a gas grill, soak the wood chips for 20 minutes in a pan of water; pour off the water, and put the chips in a tray made from aluminum foil. Turn all burners on high, place the foil tray over the primary burner, close the grill lid, and wait until the chips begin smoking heavily, about 20 minutes. Turn the primary burner to medium, and turn off all the other burners.

Place the pork roast in a disposable pan, and set on the coolest part of the grill. Close the lid. If the lid has vents, position them so that they are a little more than halfway open, on the side *opposite* the wood chips (this will draw the smoke through the meat). Cook for 3 hours. The temperature of the grill should be about 275°F. If you are using a charcoal grill, maintaining this temperature requires that you add about 8 coals every hour.

At the end of 3 hours, preheat your oven to 325°F.

Bring the pork inside, cover it tightly with aluminum foil, and bake until fork-tender, about 2½ hours.

Slide the foil-wrapped pan into a brown paper bag. Roll the bag shut, seal it with a couple of clothespins or plastic clips, and rest the meat for 1 hour. Open the bag, and cut or "pull" the meat to shreds.

To serve, mix the pan juices with ½ cup of the barbecue sauce, and pour over the meat. Pour the remaining ½ cup barbecue sauce into a small bowl, and serve separately.

Homemade Barbecue Sauce

LeeAnn VanDerPol, Pastures A'Plenty, Minnesota

Barbecue sauce is surprisingly easy to make. Try this recipe, and then develop your own signature version by adding whatever you like—minced raw onion, extra Tabasco, chili powder, honey—your possibilities are endless.

MAKES 1 TO 2 CUPS

　　　1 cup ketchup

　　　½ to 1 cup red wine or tarragon vinegar (depending on your taste preference
　　　　　and the strength of your vinegar)

　　　½ cup molasses or dark corn syrup

　　　2 teaspoons sugar

　　　½ teaspoon coarse salt

　　　¼ teaspoon garlic powder, or 2 large cloves, minced

　　　¼ teaspoon onion powder (or 2 teaspoons finely chopped onion)

　　　¼ teaspoon Tabasco sauce

Combine all ingredients in a saucepan over high heat; whisk, and blend until smooth. Bring to a boil, reduce heat, then simmer, uncovered, for 30 to 45 minutes. To obtain thicker sauce, cook longer; if too thick, thin by adding extra vinegar.

Honey-Ginger Brined Pork

Carol Clement, Heather Ridge Farm, New York

Carol Clement is a huge fan of brining meats. She began using this method with pork more than twenty years ago. She writes, "It immediately appealed to me, not only because of the possibilities of enhanced flavoring and juicier roasts but also because it works well for my lifestyle. Having no microwave oven for quick defrosting, but lots of frozen pork, I defrosted everything slowly in the refrigerator. By putting a frozen roast in refrigerated brine for days, I accomplished the dual purpose of defrosting and creating a succulent, flavorful roast. And I had a flexible range of days in which to cook it." This recipe works as well with all kinds of pork roasts—shoulders, hams, or loins. Thus, no matter what your budget, you are sure to have a delicious meal. Also, kids are likely to enjoy this recipe, especially if you let them help you mix up the brine.

SHOWCASE • ON A BUDGET • KID-FRIENDLY

SERVES 6

8 cups water, approximately

½ cup coarse salt

½ cup honey

3 slices of fresh ginger, each about the size of a quarter

2 large cloves garlic

Zest of 1 to 2 oranges, cut into wide strips (use 1 orange for a smaller roast, 2 for a larger one)

1 tablespoon coriander seed

1 tablespoon freshly ground black pepper

1 tablespoon mustard seed

1 bay leaf

2 stalks lemon grass (optional)

1 pork roast (loin, shoulder, or ham), 4 to 6 pounds

In a covered pot large enough to submerge the roast later, heat the water to a boil. Remove from heat, and stir in the salt and honey until both are dissolved. Add the remaining ingredients, except for the pork. Cool the mixture to room temperature. Add the roast (fresh, defrosted, or frozen), and weigh it down so that it is totally submerged in the brine. A plate with a weight (such as a plastic container full of water) works well. Cover and refrigerate. For a mild flavor, leave the roast to brine for 24 hours. For a more intense flavor, allow it to brine for 2 to 7 days, turning it several times. (If the roast was frozen when you put it in the brine, give it an extra day.)

Preheat oven to 400°F.

Remove the meat from the brine, and wipe it dry. Roast for 15 minutes, then lower the temperature to 300°F. Roast until the internal temperature of the meat is 145° to 155°F. Remove the roast from the oven, and tent it loosely with foil. Allow the meat to rest for 10 minutes before serving. The internal temperature should rise another 5° to 10°F.

The meat will be so tender, juicy, and flavorful that you won't need gravy. However, if you'd like to make gravy from the pan scrapings, you will have a terrific sauce. If you have a bone-in roast, use the bone for soup. It too will have absorbed the brine flavor and will make great stock.

Fresh Ham

Fresh ham, particularly fresh ham with cracklings, is one of the most impressive roasts you will ever cook. It is the perfect Christmas Day feast because it is large enough to serve an army of guests yet extremely easy to prepare. Fresh hams are cut in all sizes. The recipe below is for a half leg, about a 7- or 8-pound roast, but farmers often have them quartered, creating smaller roasts that are better suited to small family dinners. If you like roast pork but don't like the expense of loin roasts, this is a good way to go. If you need to feed more people, order a whole leg, and double the herb rub recipe. Just be sure to use an internal meat thermometer so that you take the roast out at the right time.

Ask your farmer to have the butcher leave the skin on for you. Once roasted, the skin becomes cracklings, which I think is the finest part of the feast (in our house, this part is usually consumed by the cooks in the kitchen, and very few cracklings make it to the table).

SHOWCASE • ON A BUDGET • MINIMUM PREPARATION

SERVES 8

½ leg of pork (about a 7- or 8-pound fresh ham), preferably with the skin on
Sage and Thyme Pork Rub (see page 256)

Preheat oven to 325°F.

Bring the ham to room temperature. Set the ham on a large cutting board, widest side down, skin side up. If the skin is still on the roast, use a very sharp knife to cut a series of 1-inch gashes all over the skin. Try to cut down to the meat without piercing it, and make about 30 to 40 gashes. Stuff the Sage and Thyme Pork Rub into these gashes, then rub the remainder on the bottom of the roast and any other exposed meat. Do not rub any of the mixture directly on the skin. If the roast does not have the skin, simply rub the herb mixture all over the meat.

Set the meat in a large roasting pan, insert a meat thermometer, and roast until the internal temperature registers 145° to 148°F, about 3 hours, or 20 to 22 minutes per pound. Remove the roast from the oven, tent loosely with foil, and allow it to rest for 20 to 30 minutes before serving. The internal temperature should rise 5° to 10°F.

Note: Many days when we're out working, we cook a quarter of a fresh ham for our lunch. We coat it with the herb rub around 7 in the morning, roast it for 30 minutes at 250°F, then use the super-slow method and cook it at 170°F for several hours until lunchtime. It is very hard to overcook pork roast using this method. If the temperature is not quite high enough when we're ready to eat, we simply turn up the heat for the last few minutes while we prepare a salad and set the table.

Barbecue-Style Pork Ribs

My husband is a somewhat picky eater, but whenever these pork ribs hit the table, they're gone before I even get my napkin on my lap. This is a delicious way to prepare a barbecue-style dinner—even if you don't own a grill. The ribs are best when you let them sit in the dry rub overnight in your refrigerator.

SHOWCASE • ON A BUDGET • MINIMUM PREPARATION

SERVES 4

> Barbecue Spice Rub (see page 253)
>
> 4 country-style pork ribs or shoulder chops, or
>   3 to 4 pounds spare ribs or baby back ribs
>
> ¾ cup Homemade Barbecue Sauce (see page 153)

Thoroughly coat the ribs with the Barbecue Spice Rub, cover with plastic wrap, and let sit overnight in the refrigerator.

Preheat oven to 200°F.

Bring the ribs to room temperature; place the ribs in a shallow baking pan in the middle of your oven. Roast the ribs for about 3½ to 4 hours, until tender. Coat them generously with the Homemade Barbecue Sauce, and cook 30 minutes longer before removing from the oven. Brush once more with Barbecue Sauce before serving.

Moroccan Spiced Pork Loin
with Pear-Raisin Chutney

Here's another elegant roast with exotic seasonings, sure to impress the fussiest guests and their children as well.

SHOWCASE • KID-FRIENDLY

SERVES 5 TO 6

> 5 tablespoons Moroccan Spice Rub (see page 255)
>
> 1 pork tenderloin, about 3 to 4 pounds
>
> Pear-Raisin Chutney (see below)

Rub the Moroccan Spice Rub into the meat. Cover, and refrigerate overnight.

Preheat oven to 325°F.

Put the pork in a shallow roasting pan, and cook for about 1 to 1 ½ hours, or until the internal temperature reaches 145° to 155°F. Meanwhile, prepare the chutney.

Remove the roast from the oven, tent with foil, rest for 10 minutes, and serve with the Pear-Raisin Chutney.

For the Pear–Raisin Chutney:

2 tablespoons butter	1 cup golden raisins
1 onion, diced	2 cloves garlic, minced
4 pears, peeled, cored, and diced	1 teaspoon grated fresh ginger root
½ cup honey	1 tablespoon Moroccan Spice Rub
½ cup cider vinegar	(see page 255)

Melt the butter in a medium-size saucepan. Add the diced onion, and sauté until translucent. Add the pears, and sauté for 3 minutes. Stir in the honey, cider vinegar, raisins, garlic, ginger, and Moroccan Spice Rub. Bring the mixture to a boil, reduce the heat, cover, and simmer for 20 minutes. Taste, and add more honey, if desired. Continue to simmer, uncovered, a few minutes longer to allow the chutney to thicken.

Orange Pork Shoulder Roast

Wendy Gornick, Sweet Grass Farm, New York

This delightful sweet and savory dish is easy to prepare.

ON A BUDGET • MINIMUM PREPARATION • KID-FRIENDLY

SERVES 4 TO 8

2 to 4 pound pork shoulder roast (Boston butt, pork shoulder butt, rolled tied boneless butt, or any boneless shoulder roast will work)

2 tablespoons olive oil

½ cup fresh orange juice

2 tablespoons dark brown sugar

1 teaspoon Worcestershire sauce

½ teaspoon powdered mustard

½ teaspoon rosemary, crushed

¼ teaspoon coarse salt

⅛ teaspoon freshly ground black pepper

3 sweet potatoes, peeled

Preheat oven to 325°F.

Bring the pork roast to room temperature. Heat the olive oil over high heat in a Dutch oven. Brown the meat on all sides, about 2 to 3 minutes per side; finish browning with the fat-side up. Whisk together the orange juice, brown sugar, Worcestershire sauce, mustard, rosemary, salt, pepper, and pour over the roast. Cover tightly, and bake for 1 hour, basting occasionally.

Meanwhile, cut each of the potatoes into 8 wedges. After 1 hour, scatter the potatoes in the sauce around the roast. Cover, and continue roasting until the potatoes are tender and the internal temperature of the meat registers 150° to 155°F on an instant-read thermometer. Allow the meat to rest for about 10 minutes before serving (the temperature should rise to about 160° to 165°F).

To serve, move to a warm platter, slice the meat, arrange the potatoes alongside, and spoon the sauce on top, allowing some to dribble over the potato wedges.

Honey-Glazed Pork Rib Roast
with Apple-Walnut Stuffing

Pork rib roasts really encourage flashy cooking, so here's a recipe to dazzle your dinner guests.

SHOWCASE

SERVES 4

1 tablespoon coarse salt

2 teaspoons freshly ground black pepper

4 teaspoons rubbed sage

1 four-bone pork rib roast

4 tablespoons unsalted butter

1 small onion, minced

1 small tart apple, peeled and finely diced

½ cup raisins

¼ cup dry white wine

¼ cup coarsely chopped walnuts

½ cup honey

¼ cup fresh lemon juice

¼ cup olive oil

1½ cups chicken broth

Combine the salt, pepper, and 3 teaspoons of the sage, and rub it into the pork roast. Cover, and refrigerate overnight.

Melt 2 tablespoons of the butter in a skillet over medium heat. Add the onion, and sauté for 1 minute. Add the apple and raisins, and cook a few minutes longer, until the onions are translucent. Add the wine, and simmer until the raisins are soft and most of the liquid is absorbed. Stir in the remaining teaspoon of the sage and walnuts, and set aside to cool.

Preheat oven to 450°F.

Using a long, sharp knife (a fillet knife will work well for this), carve a ¾-inch-wide hole through the meatiest part of the roast. Dice the meat that you carved out to make the hole and set it aside in the refrigerator. Firmly pack the apple-walnut stuffing into the hole, making sure it comes through to the other side of the roast. Set the meat in a roasting pan. Reserve any extra stuffing that did not fit into the roast.

Whisk together the honey, lemon juice, and olive oil; brush the mixture on the pork to coat. Put the roast in the oven, and immediately lower the heat to 300°F. Bake the meat, basting 2 or 3 times with the pan juices, for about 2 hours and 45 minutes, or until an instant-read thermometer inserted into the thickest part of the meat—but not the stuffing— registers 150°F. Thirty minutes before the meat is done, transfer the extra stuffing to a small, ovenproof dish, cover with foil, and place in the oven. Once the internal temperature of the meat reaches 150°F, transfer the roast to a cutting board, and tent loosely with foil.

Set the roasting pan over two burners on the stove over medium heat. Add the remaining 2 tablespoons of butter and the reserved diced pork. Sauté for 2 minutes, or until the meat is cooked through. Add the chicken broth, thoroughly blend it with the pan drippings, and then simmer until the liquid is reduced to 1 cup, scraping up any browned bits.

To serve, carve the pork by cutting between the ribs to form chops, spoon the pan sauce on top, and sprinkle with the extra stuffing.

Glazed Ham in Maple-Raisin Sauce

A smoked ham once implied that the chef of the house was cooking a meal for twenty and was probably going to have leftovers. However, today's smoked hams are cut in a variety of sizes, enabling cooks to prepare dinner for groups of all sizes. Here's a basic maple-glazed ham recipe that you can use whether you're preparing dinner for five or twenty-five.

SHOWCASE • KID-FRIENDLY

NUMBER OF SERVINGS VARIES BASED ON THE SIZE OF THE HAM

1 smoked ham or smoked picnic ham, preferably bone-in, any size

1 ½ cups maple syrup or honey (you will need only 1 cup if your ham is 4 pounds or less)

Preheat the oven to 325°F.

Bring ham to room temperature, place in a roasting pan, and bake until heated through (the internal temperature need not be more than 130°F). As a guide, a whole ham (about 14 pounds) will take about 2½ hours, and a half ham (about 7 pounds) will take about 1½ hours. Remove the ham from the oven, and increase the heat to 425°F.

Using a knife, score the outside of the ham by making a series of crisscross cuts. Brush on ½ cup of the maple syrup (if you are using a ham that is 4 pounds or less, use ¼ cup syrup), return the ham to the oven for 20 minutes, and baste 2 or 3 times with the pan juices.

Remove the ham from the oven, set it on a cutting board, and brush with another ½ cup of syrup (again, if your ham is 4 pounds or less, use ¼ cup). Tent loosely with foil, and let rest while you make the raisin sauce.

For the maple-raisin sauce:

If your ham is less than 4 pounds, halve all the ingredients.

1 cup water

½ cup raisins

1 teaspoon freshly ground cinnamon

¼ teaspoon freshly ground nutmeg

2 tablespoons unsalted butter

2 tablespoons fresh lemon juice

1 tablespoon cornstarch or arrowroot

$\frac{1}{4}$ cup ice water

To make the sauce, place the roasting pan on two burners over low heat. Pour in the cup of water and the remaining $\frac{1}{2}$ cup maple syrup and simmer, scraping up any browned bits. Add the raisins, cinnamon, nutmeg, butter, and lemon juice; bring to a boil, stirring constantly. Reduce the mixture by about a third, and lower to a simmer. Whisk the cornstarch or arrowroot and ice water until smooth, and slowly pour into the sauce. Continue to cook, and stir 1 to 2 minutes longer, until the sauce has thickened. Carve the ham, and serve the sauce separately.

Artichokes and Bacon

This is an ideal meal for anyone suffering from a cold. The garlicky broth and thick-cut, flavorful bacon penetrate the stuffiest heads and noses and nourish the spirit.

IN A HURRY

SERVES 3

3 tablespoons olive oil

1 medium-size onion, sliced in thin wedges

5 cloves garlic, minced

$\frac{1}{3}$ to $\frac{1}{2}$ pound bacon or jowl bacon

2 13$\frac{3}{4}$-ounce cans artichoke hearts in brine, quartered

Heat the oil in a large pan. Add the onion, and sauté over medium-high heat. Add the garlic, and sauté for 1 minute; add the bacon, and sauté for 2 minutes; add the quartered artichokes with the brine. Cover, and simmer over medium-low heat for 25 minutes. Serve in soup bowls.

Brandied Pork Shoulder Chops
with Apricots and Prunes

Here's a simple slow-cooker recipe to make a tasty dinner while you're out for the day. Kids should enjoy the fruit and fork-tender meat; grown-ups will appreciate the moistness and the balance of sweet and savory flavors.

MINIMUM PREPARATION • KID-FRIENDLY

SERVES 4

4 pork shoulder chops or country-style ribs

Mustard Sage Rub (see page 255)

1 onion, cut into wedges

1 leek, finely sliced, white part only (optional)

3 to 4 carrots, scraped and finely chopped

½ cup pitted prunes (dried plums)

½ cup dried apricots

¼ cup dry sherry

1 cup beef or chicken stock

¼ cup brandy

2 bay leaves

Coat the pork chops with the Mustard Sage Rub. Cover with plastic wrap, and refrigerate overnight, or allow them to sit for 2 hours at room temperature.

Place the onion, leek, and carrots in the bottom of a large slow-cooker. Set the shoulder chops on top, then cover with the prunes and apricots. Pour in the sherry, stock, and brandy; add the bay leaves. Cook on low for 6 to 8 hours, until the meat falls from the bones.

Pork Liver and Apples

Extremely nutritious liver was weekly fare in many households until concerns about cholesterol and toxins threw it off the American menu. However, the availability of liver from grass-fed animals answers this issue and permits liver to return to our tables.

ON A BUDGET • MINIMUM PREPARATION

SERVES 2 TO 4

> 1 pound pork liver (beef, veal, venison, goat, or lamb will work)
>
> 1 cup fresh lemon juice
>
> 3 tart, firm apples, cored and finely diced, but not peeled
>
> 1 large onion, finely chopped
>
> $\frac{3}{4}$ teaspoon coarse salt
>
> $\frac{1}{4}$ teaspoon freshly ground black pepper
>
> 2 tablespoons unsalted butter
>
> 4 slices bacon
>
> $\frac{1}{4}$ cup hot water
>
> $1\frac{1}{2}$ teaspoons paprika

Slice the pork liver into strips, about $\frac{1}{2}$-inch wide. Place the strips in a small bowl, soak in the lemon juice, adding more if necessary. Cover the bowl, and marinate the meat several hours or overnight in the refrigerator.

Preheat oven to 350°F.

Mix the apples, onion, salt, and pepper. Heat the butter in a frying pan, and sauté the mixture until the onion is translucent and the apples are crisp-tender, about 5 to 6 minutes; set aside.

Remove the liver from the lemon juice, pat dry, and place in the bottom of a buttered baking dish. Pour the apple and onion mixture over the liver. Arrange the bacon slices on top, and pour in hot water. Sprinkle with the paprika. Cook for 20 to 30 minutes, or until the liquid is bubbling and the apples are soft. Serve immediately.

Boston Baked Beans with Ham Hocks

There's no way around it. Baked beans, done well, are an all-day and overnight project. They can be cooked faster in a pressure cooker, but I am loath to trust anything that promises to cook food at speeds faster than food naturally cooks. Still, baked beans are an all-day treat for the senses. They fill your home with warmth from the time you start them on the top of the stove until the time you pull them from the oven and serve them to your family. In my estimation, the secret to superlative baked beans lies in using plenty of ham hocks. They impart incredible flavor and make for heartier fare. Always be sure to soak your beans in water, with a little yogurt added overnight before you begin cooking them. This helps neutralize the phytic acid, making them easier to digest.

ON A BUDGET

SERVES 6

1 pound navy beans,
    soaked overnight

2 tablespoons plain yogurt
    or whey (optional)

3 quarts water

1 medium onion,
    cut into thick wedges

½ cup molasses

2 tablespoons dark brown sugar

½ teaspoon powdered mustard

¼ teaspoon ground ginger

¼ teaspoon freshly ground allspice

2 to 3 pounds smoked ham hock
    or salt pork

Honey mustard

Rinse beans, pour them into a bowl or pot, and cover with warm water. Add yogurt or whey, and mix lightly. Cover, and soak overnight. The next day, pour off the water, rinse the beans thoroughly, and place them in a large, ovenproof pot or Dutch oven (if cast iron, make sure it is coated). Pour in 2 quarts of the water, bring to a boil, and simmer over low heat for 1 hour. Drain the beans once more. Return them to the large pot, and add the remaining 1 quart water with the rest of the ingredients except for the honey mustard. Bring to a boil; simmer, uncovered, over low heat for 2 hours.

Preheat oven to 300°F.

Cover the beans, and roast in the oven. When the beans are tender, usually after 3 hours, remove the lid, and continue baking until the liquid is mostly evaporated and the beans are soft, generally an additional 2 hours.

If you are using salt pork, discard it before serving the beans. If you are using ham hocks, remove them, cool slightly, and then pull off the skin to reveal the smoked meat. Pull off this meat and stir it into the beans before serving. Serve with a dollop of honey mustard.

WHAT DOES IT MEAN IF MY HAMS AND BACONS ARE LABELED "NO NITRITE"?

Few people can think of pork without envisioning pink cured hams and bacons. Although today this meat is popular for its smoky flavor, the curing process came about as a way to preserve pork without refrigeration.

Curing is the process of adding either nitrates (NO_3) and/or nitrites (NO_2) to meat in order to prevent the growth of botulism. This is also what gives the processed hams and bacons their pink color. However, the use of these chemicals is a double-edged sword. Used properly, these nitrates and nitrites keep smoked meats safe to eat. Used in excess, these chemicals are potentially carcinogenic.

According to Dennis Shaw, a meat scientist at Cornell University, nitrates, in the form of sodium or potassium salts, were traditionally used to cure meats. Through a bacterial reduction process, nitrates (NO_3) would be reduced to nitrites (NO_2) as the meat was cured. However, this was a lengthy process, and many processors eventually stopped using the nitrates and switched to directly incorporating the nitrites into the meat. For nitrites to work properly, ascorbates or erythorbates must be added to the meat as well.[1] (Shaw)

Some people are concerned about the use of nitrites, ascorbates, and erythorbates in their cured meats. However, by definition, all cured meats must contain nitrites, although some contain them as a result of a natural chemical breakdown and some contain them as an added chemical. When hams or bacon are labeled "no nitrite," this means that the butcher has used a more traditional curing process, one in which the meats are treated with a natural source of nitrates (NO_3), such as sea salt, which is allowed to slowly break down into nitrites (NO_2). Although this traditional process is more costly and time-consuming, many people prefer purchasing cured products that have not had the nitrites and other chemicals directly added to the meat.

1. Taken from the printed proceedings of a sausage-making workshop. See Dennis Shaw, Han Sebald, Cameron L. Faustman, Ridge Shinn, and Robert Weybright, *Sausage Making and Good Manufacturing Practices*: (Storrs, Conn.: University of Connecticut, 2002)

Braised Pork Heart

Heart is chewy muscle meat, much like some of the tougher cuts of meat in the shoulders of pork, lamb, and beef. Thus, if your family won't sample a recipe containing heart alone, try removing the hard parts, chopping it up, and adding it to your stews. Your spouse and kids will never know the difference. In any event, the recipe below is mildly sweet and savory and, well,… hearty!

ON A BUDGET

SERVES 4 TO 6

2 pork hearts; or 1 beef, veal, or
    venison heart; or 4 lamb or
    goat hearts

8 tablespoons all-purpose flour

3 teaspoons salt

1 teaspoon freshly ground
    black pepper

4 strips bacon

1 onion, finely chopped

1 clove garlic, minced

1 green bell pepper, coarsely diced

1 ½ cups tomato juice

2 tablespoons red wine vinegar

2 tablespoons molasses

1 bay leaf

1 teaspoon dried basil

1 teaspoon dried savory

1 ½ cups beef stock

4 to 6 cups cooked rice

Remove any hard parts from the heart, and slice across the fibers into ½-inch strips.

Combine 4 tablespoons of the flour, ½ teaspoon of the salt, and ½ teaspoon of the pepper in a shallow bowl. Dredge the strips of meat in the flour, and set aside.

Heat a Dutch oven (not cast iron) or midsize soup pot over medium heat. Add the bacon, and cook until crisp. Remove the bacon to a paper towel to drain, and add the heart strips to the sizzling bacon drippings. Sauté until browned. Add the onion, garlic, and green pepper, and continue sautéing until the onion is translucent. Stir in the tomato juice, vinegar, molasses, the remaining 2 ½ teaspoons salt, and the remaining ½ teaspoon pepper.

Cover the pot tightly, and allow it to simmer for 1 ½ hours, or until the meat is nearly tender. Add the bay leaf, basil, and savory to the sauce, and simmer for 1 minute. Whisk the remaining 4 tablespoons flour into the beef stock until smooth, and pour into the sauce. Crumble the bacon, and stir it into the sauce. Continue simmering, uncovered, for another 5 to 10 minutes, or until the sauce thickens. Serve over rice.

T A B L E 4

COMMON RETAIL CUTS OF PORK AND IDEAL COOKING METHODS

LEG	
Fresh ham	Dry heat
Smoked ham	Dry or Moist heat
Smoked ham slice or steak	Dry heat

LOIN	
Blade, Rib, Loin or Sirloin chops	Dry or Moist heat
Country style ribs	Moist heat
Sirloin roast	Dry heat
Loin roast	Dry heat
Rib roast	Dry heat
Tenderloin	Dry heat
Canadian bacon	Dry heat
Smoked pork chops	Dry heat

SHOULDER	
Boston butt	Dry or Moist heat
Picnic roast	Dry or Moist heat
Shoulder steaks or chops	Moist heat
Sausage	Dry or Moist heat
Hocks	Moist heat

SPARERIBS AND BELLY	
Spareribs	Dry or Moist heat
Bacon	Dry or Moist heat

CHAPTER FIVE

POULTRY AND RABBITS

Saturday night in our home is not appropriately observed without listening to *A Prairie Home Companion* and roasting a chicken. My husband and I have shared many wonderful times together, but nothing comes close to our Saturday rituals, when the cabin fills with the smell of roasting chicken as we sip martinis and foxtrot in the living room—or out on the porch in midsummer. In our home, as in many others, a roasting chicken is synonymous with enjoying family time, with slowing down, with tuning out the world and tuning in to each other.

Of all the different meats, poultry seems especially linked to family time: the Thanksgiving turkey, the Christmas goose. Not surprisingly, poultry is the meat most often consumed in the United States. According to the USDA, the average American ate 77.5 pounds of chicken in 1999, more than the consumption of beef, pork, or lamb. Per-capita consumption of all poultry is 95 pounds per year. Thankfully, pastured poultry is the least expensive of all the pastured meats, so there's no better way to start treating your family better than by buying them real chickens, turkeys, geese, and ducks.

Although pastured poultry and rabbits are lower in fat than conventionally grown birds and rabbits, there's very little variation in cooking requirements. Use the same cooking temperatures you've always used in your family recipes; just be sure to use a meat thermometer, because with the reduced fat, the meat will cook faster. Aside from quick cooking times, the only other difference between pastured and conventional poultry is the flavor, which is nothing short of amazing. I guarantee that after trying one pastured chicken, your family will never allow you to buy a grocery-store roaster again. Compared with the fat-laden and flavorless grocery store meat, pastured poultry has a clean, fresh, more assertive flavor. The meat is firmer and remains moist and juicy after it has been roasted.

If you're lucky enough to have a farmer near you producing rabbit, be sure to take an opportunity to sample this delicious, delicate meat. Rabbits are usually marketed as fryers (under twelve weeks old), roasters (under six months old), or stewers (over six months old). Roasters and stewers will be tougher because they have reached sexual maturity, and they will thus require long periods of moist-heat cooking. Most rabbits you find will be fryers, which will be the most tender. Rabbit meat can dry out easily, so it tastes best if allowed to simmer in liquids or sauces. You can generally substitute rabbit for many chicken dishes, and several of the recipes in this book work especially well, including Chicken with 40 Cloves of Garlic, Suvilla's Melt-on-Your-Tongue Chicken, Chicken Fricassee, or Poulet aux Oignons. If you want to roast a rabbit, use a fryer, and consider wrapping it first in pork fat or brushing the meat with oil and then wrapping it in foil before putting it in the oven.

The trick to buying the best poultry and rabbits is to understand the various labels under which it is marketed. Gourmet food stores may carry high-end poultry, but the quality will not be the same as pastured poultry unless the meat is labeled *pastured*. Other labels, such as *free-range* and *organic,* can be misleading. *Free-range* means only that the animal has had access to fresh air (but may have been raised on a concrete slab). According to the National Organic Standards, the *organic* label requires that animals be raised outdoors, but the standards do not guarantee that the animal has constant access to fresh pasture. However, standards set by many independent certification agencies are more stringent, so it is best to check with them if you have questions about pasture requirements. The key to flavorful, sustainable, juicy poultry and rabbits is the pasture. Chickens, turkeys, geese, ducks, and rabbits need to be allowed to browse on grasses, bugs, and legumes in order to acquire their wonderful, characteristic flavor.

Since most poultry and rabbits are processed and sold on the farm, it's easy to inspect an enterprise in order to find out if the meat will be first-rate:

- Don't be surprised if the birds or rabbits are in pens on the grass. Birds and rabbits easily fall victim to predators, so farmers must provide adequate movable housing that protects against wind and rain and against wild animals yet simultaneously allows them access to fresh air, grass, and sunshine. Although pens are generally movable, rabbits are occasionally raised in immovable, floored cages, with the grasses brought to them.

- Depending on the size of the grazing area and the foraging characteristics of the birds, the farmer should be moving them to fresh pasture every one to three days. The grass may appear trampled toward the end of a rotation, but there shouldn't be excessive bare patches with exposed soil, indicating overgrazing. One important fact to remember, however, is that chickens like to scratch up some soil to enjoy a dust bath. These areas generally appear closer to the chickens' shelter. An occasional dust bath, like a hog wallow, is just part of the life of a happy chicken. However, the bare patches should not be predominant in the fields, nor should the grassy areas be feces-laden.

- Poultry (and all livestock, for that matter) require a continuous supply of water. Check to see that the waterers have not been allowed to run dry. Birds deprived of water do not gain weight properly. Like pigs, poultry cannot live on grass alone, so do not be surprised to see that the birds' diets are supplemented with grain.

- Do not be alarmed if you see a farmer administering probiotics to the birds. Probiotics, which are doses of positive or healthy bacteria that naturally occur in a bird's intestine, are different from antibiotics, which are intended to kill existing bacteria. Farmers may administer probiotics, such as Lactobacillus acidophilus, to help reduce stress on the birds and increase disease resistance, especially during times of extreme weather fluctuations.

- In many states, farmers are able to process limited quantities of poultry on the farm as long as they market the poultry directly to the consumer. Many farmers feel that on-farm processing is more humane for the animals. Furthermore, they believe they can maintain more sanitary and higher-quality standards by processing the birds themselves rather than sending the poultry off to a federally inspected plant. Thus, do not be shy about asking how the birds are processed. Ideally, the birds are not electrocuted but are instead "cone-killed": they are put upside-down in cones, an incision is made to the jugular, and the animal is allowed to bleed out thoroughly, a more humane and significantly cleaner technique. You can tell if a bird has not been properly bled out if you find a lot of black-clotted blood around the bones.[1] The skin of the processed birds should not be slimy, and the internal cavity should be pristine. Good farmers are willing to share the details of poultry processing with you and will even occasionally welcome visitors on processing day to provide added assurance that their procedures are clean and humane.

Farming as a Community Affair

Melvin and Suvilla Fisher, The Organic Grass Farm, Rockville, Indiana

Melvin and Suvilla Fisher enjoy a brief respite from the late August sun beneath a shade tree in front of their home. Sonoma, their two-year-old daughter, cuddles in her mother's lap and watches as I take notes on my pad. Rueben, eleven, their oldest son, sits nearby and closely follows our conversation while his three younger brothers—Leon, eight, Christian, six, and Melvin Junior, four—play in a nearby barn filled with benches from yesterday's Sunday church gathering. They holler in an old German dialect and periodically creep close to investigate my recording equipment.

Melvin and Suvilla are talking about the hardships they've faced this summer. "We're still not selling enough chicken to make a living at it," Suvilla confesses. Melvin explains: "We didn't have enough market, and we ran out of money—again. But we still want to make it. There's no sense in going on with the business if it doesn't pay for itself... I sometimes think that we're about ready to fly out in blue skies, but you never know."

All around them, the farm is a testament to their creativity and their reverence for the land. The pastures are lush in spite of the recent drought, an organic garden is bursting with vegetables and flowers, the animals graze peacefully, and the children exude a robust health: their eyes are bright, their skin glows, and they seem to possess an almost unnatural amount of energy for such a stifling day. The happiness and health of this farm and all its inhabitants—animals, plants, and people alike—cannot be overlooked.

Four years ago, Melvin and Suvilla made a monumental decision. After working seven years with their family's iron-craft business in Lancaster County, Pennsylvania, they had saved enough money to make a down-payment on a farm and to move to a new Amish community in Rockville, Indiana. In spite of the farming practices they had learned growing up, they elected to forgo conventional, chemical-intensive agricultural techniques and opted instead to run an organic, grass-based farm.

Melvin and Suvilla do not feel that being organic farmers is the cause of their financial trials. Living in one of the poorest counties in the state, Suvilla is quick to observe: "Other people have a hard time too." They both note that commodity farming prices are so low that getting started in farming full-time is difficult no matter which practices a person adopts. And any doubt they may have about their success is fleeting. Melvin and Suvilla are not ashamed to discuss their difficulties, mainly because their concerns are mitigated by a layer of confidence and optimism that stems from the support they receive from their customers and the surrounding community. "Actually, for a time we were wondering, can we get on? And that's when the support we got really encouraged us," Suvilla explains. "We had people say they just would be so sorry to see us go out. They don't know where they'd get this good food if we couldn't get on doing this."

Melvin adds, "Our parents wholeheartedly support us, and a lot of the people in our community do the same." Even though the Fishers' farm is the only one of its kind in Rockville, Melvin says that their Amish neighbors support their ideas. "We have a lot of great people who cheer us on," he says. The level of support they describe in their Amish community is heartwarming. Melvin's father assists if they fall too far behind with bills. A fellow Amish member arranges to buy their extra chicken legs and thighs to use for a community bridge festival in the fall. Local youth come to the farm to assist with chores and poultry processing. Chefs they market to in Indianapolis conscientiously support their efforts.

The result is a small family farm that is poised for success. In the four years they've operated this farm, Melvin and Suvilla have built a substantial market. They produce eggs, chickens, turkey, and beef, and they sell their goods to five health food stores and seven restaurants in the Indianapolis area, as well as to a number of customers who buy direct from the farm. They've built a federally inspected processing plant, and they process five hundred chickens every week to supply their market.

Beyond that, their farm is bursting with the type of innovations that will enable them to help other farmers realize similar dreams. Melvin has adapted portable chicken-house designs so that his workhorses can pull the houses. He has installed extra-long eaves that provide shade on hot days and that can be dropped down to protect the birds from inclement weather. He and his helpers have built rollaway nesting boxes for the laying hens; the boxes contain privacy curtains as well as angled nests so that the eggs gently roll away from the hens, easing the chore of gathering them. He has padded the nests for the chickens' comfort, added Astroturf to help keep the eggs clean, and constructed the houses so that they can be shut at night, preventing the hens from roosting inside and soiling the area. He has trained five dogs to live harmoniously with the various flocks, guarding them from predators. Furthermore, he has worked out an ingenious arrangement with his local turkey vultures. Standing in his pastures, my husband and I noticed several "buzzards" perched in dead trees, spaced evenly around the fields. Melvin explained that when a chicken dies prematurely, he leaves the carrion just outside the pens, where the buzzards can find it. In exchange, he deduces they patrol the territory and keep hawks from coming in and preying on the live birds.

Melvin and Suvilla are both eager for their farm to take flight so that they can have an opportunity to return all the help they've received. Both of them hope that organic, grass-based farming becomes more common in the Amish community. Suvilla wants to see as many people as possible have access to good-quality food. "I feel so bad when I see people go to the store and come home with loads of cheap junk, and they feed this junk to their families. I just hope we can help."

Growing good food—and helping others learn to do the same—is their deepest ambition. Melvin explains why they started their farm: "We decided we wanted to produce the best food possible." They don't aspire to become rich in their business. Rather, Melvin says, "I would like to see a network of farmers producing this type of food." For himself and his family, he'd like to reach a comfort level where he could maintain a family farm. Toward this aim, they work with apprentices, and they hope to be able to assist each of their children in starting on-farm enterprises. Their eldest son, Reuben, has already begun raising rabbits. The younger children have yet to select their entrepreneurial ventures.

Until that time, Melvin and Suvilla carry on, their willingness to work hard and their love of good food apparent in their fields, as well as on their table.

THE GRUESOME TRUTH ABOUT CHICKENS

Farmers often get many strange questions from their customers, but one classic question is asked regularly. A new customer walks up and patiently waits until the farmer is standing alone. He or she looks furtively about, then leans forward and asks in a whisper, "Do the chickens really run around when you chop off their heads?"

The answer is yes—and no. If chickens are processed the old-fashioned way, in which they are carried out to the chopping block to meet their fate by way of an ax, the adrenaline that is released in the muscle tissue will cause the bird's body to have convulsions. If the farmer releases his or her grip on the bird, it will indeed flap about as though it were still alive.

But this is not the preferred way to process chickens. First, to guarantee the quality of the meat and to reduce the flow of adrenaline, farmers will do everything in their power to keep the animals calm and stress-free. Processed humanely, chickens are placed upside-down into snug-fitting cones, which help keep the animal contained and relatively calm. An incision is made in the jugular, and the chicken is allowed to bleed out. A chicken that has been allowed to run about after losing its head is not bled out properly, and the quality of the meat will suffer. Some chickens will still flap about during a cone-kill process, but for the most part this procedure is much more tranquil, and the quality of the meat is significantly better because the birds remain "unruffled."

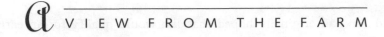

Farming with Kids

Pam, Jim, Kate, Luke, Emerson, and Alta Millar
Zu Zu's Petals, Spencer, New York

If you ever want the honest truth about what it's like to raise livestock, never ask a grown-up. Kate, Luke, Emerson, and Alta Millar, who range in age from twelve to five, pile indoors and sit with me on a frigid October afternoon. They don't hesitate to dole out the straight facts about what it's like to spend all day on a farm:

"The cows get out."

"Sometimes the dogs chase the pigs into the pond, and we have to get them out."

"It's hard counting out change with customers standing over you watching, or finding a cut of meat for them in the freezer while they stand around waiting."

"You always have to be nice to customers, even if they're mean and you don't like 'em."

"Even when it's raining and freezing, you still have to go out and move the animals."

Obviously, these four kids are no strangers to the realities of agricultural life. They run Zu Zu's Petals farm day in and day out with their mom, Pam Millar, in Spencer, New York. Pam and her husband, Jim, made the decision to home-school their children long before their eldest child was of school age. They felt it would enable their children to pursue their curiosity. "If our kids want to really sink their teeth into something and really learn, to explore, they can," explains Pam.

Formerly a suburban girl from Wilmington, Delaware, Pam hadn't expected that the greatest exploration would be running a farm in partnership with her children. She confesses that she and Jim "never really considered farming." She explains: "We had lots of different ideas about what to do with our land, but not farming. We were vegetarians!" However, when a neighbor gave them a few baby chicks, their lives changed forever. Today, Zu Zu's Petals spans ninety-three acres, and Pam and her four children raise 13 steers, 30 lambs, 1,000 broilers, 50 turkeys, and 15 pigs each year.

Pam and Jim had originally hoped that Jim would qualify for an early retirement from his company and could come home to join the family full-time on the farm. When it became clear that this was not yet possible, Pam decided that she would make some adjustments. Today, in spite of the market potential, she works hard at controlling the growth of her business. "It seems silly to grow it beyond my ability to do it alone with the kids," she explains. But the work she can accomplish with the enthusiastic involvement of her children is amazing.

When home-school is not in session, Pam's children manage all the farm sales on their own, they assist their parents on chicken-processing days by weighing and bagging the birds, they throw the hay, they feed and water the chickens, they move fences, and they even help herd the animals to fresh pasture. When asked how they feel about their lifestyle, the kids readily agree that they do a great deal of hard work, but that they enjoy it. Kate talks about how she likes taking care of the animals, how they are content when she brings them feed and hay, and how she enjoys caring for them when they're sick. Luke excitedly explains that if the cows break out while the children are having lessons, they get to stop and chase the cattle. And all of them will happily discuss the things they've learned while helping their mom. They talk about running the sales at their farm stand, where they build their math skills and where they learn the importance of being polite, communicating, finding products, and being in control. Kate says that with all the things they do on the farm, they've had "to learn to be patient with everybody and everything: animals, people, situations." She adds: "It's really easy to get mad. A fence gets tangled, or you don't want to go outside, but you have to; or you don't want to work, you want to play." Luke and his sisters talk about learning how to move fences and put them together and how to herd the livestock without frightening them (a skill that many seasoned farmers have yet to master). And they talk about the compassion they have for the animals in their care. At the end of this discussion, Emerson chimes in with one more important lesson: "I learned you always have to turn the fence back on!"

A daily regimen of herding cows, tending lambs, feeding chickens, and selling meat may seem normal for the four Millar children, but they are keenly aware of how different their lives are from those of their peers. They laugh as they talk about playing Saturday-morning soccer while their mom and dad process chickens in the summer. Because Jim and Pam are busy, the children must get rides to the games from the parents of their teammates. Explaining to the other moms and dads why they need rides has become a source of amusement of the family. Luke prefers to give the other parents a slightly exaggerated, more graphic explanation. "They're killing chickens," he says. "There's blood flying, and there's feathers everywhere!" Kate, in an effort to minimize alarm, opts for a more simple answer. When asked why her mom can't drive her to games, Kate simply says, "She's working." Pam admits that farm life can occasionally be embarrassing for the kids, especially when their mom shows up to bring them home from games and has bits of chicken viscera clinging to her arms or is sporting Carhartt overalls. "I don't look like the other soccer moms," she laughs.

It's hard to say how many years Zu Zu's Petals will continue in operation. Pam says that when her kids grow up, she would like to spend some time seeing the world with Jim. Although she'll always want to produce meat for her family, she's unsure if she'll be able to justify continuing the farm on a commercial scale. "I guess it's going to depend on what happens with us in terms of getting farm help," she says. "We've thought about getting interns, but we don't know. I guess it will depend somewhat on what my kids are doing. I'd like to be able to travel and farm. You know, the ideal world would be to farm and have somebody else here doing it some of the time so we could go somewhere." Here she calls attention to one of the biggest challenges facing many of today's farmers. "Farming is hard. It's like getting married. There's no more dating. When you decide to farm, it means you might not be able to go on vacations, or sometimes, not even a day trip. It's mutually exclusive to almost every kind of fun you might have in another life. It's a real choice you have to make."

Still, given the option, the Millar children wouldn't give up their farm for anything. If Zu Zu's Petals shut down, all of them said they would be sad. Emerson adds that she "would miss doing the chores." Pam agrees. "There are days when it just really sucks. And some days, it's exquisitely fun. And I think mostly, it's been a fun ride for us." As she says this, Pam gets up to go add more wood to the stove. When she returns, she turns to her youngest child, Alta, who has sat quietly drawing while her brother and sisters chat. Pam asks, "Do you like being a farmer, Alta?" There is a long pause as Alta looks away from her mom and watches the snow blow past their window. She sighs, looks her mother directly in the eyes, and says, "I think it's pretty cold out there." Everyone laughs. In spite of yet another brutally honest assessment of farm life, there is plenty of fun to be had.

RECIPES

SHANNON'S FAVORITE HERB-ROASTED CHICKEN 182

SUVILLA'S MELT-ON-YOUR-TONGUE CHICKEN 183

SWEET-AND-SOUR CHICKEN 184

HONEY-GLAZED CHICKEN 185

CHICKEN WITH 40 CLOVES OF GARLIC 186

CHICKEN FRICASSEE WITH WILD RICE (OR WITHOUT) 188

KENTUCKY BAKED CHICKEN 190

POULET AUX OIGNONS 191

BUTTERFLIED HIGH-ROAST CHICKEN WITH CRISPY POTATOES 192

BASIC CHICKEN NUGGETS 194

PARMESAN CHICKEN NUGGETS 195

PASTA WITH CHICKEN AND SQUASH 196

BASIC CHICKEN BROTH 198

TERIYAKI CHICKEN HEARTS 199

CHICKEN POT PIE WITH HERBED CRUST 200

TERRINE DE FOIES DE VOLAILLE 202

LEMON CHICKEN WINGS 204

HERB-ROASTED TURKEY WITH GIBLET GRAVY 205

ROAST GOOSE WITH SHERRY AND ORANGES 208

ASIAN-STYLE DUCK WITH PEANUT NOODLES 210

BRAISED RABBIT WITH MUSTARD AND ROSEMARY SAUCE 212

SMOKED HAM AND POTATO FRITTATA 213

ONION PIE 214

DONEY'S EGGNOG 216

All recipes without attribution are from Shannon Hayes, Sap Bush Hollow Farm, West Fulton, New York.

Shannon's Favorite Herb-Roasted Chicken

My simple recipe will fill your house with great smells and have your friends begging to stay for dinner. The pan juices are wonderful served plain or made into a gravy. We pour the leftovers, along with the chicken bones and meat, into a soup pot to make the Chicken Broth listed on page 198. Soup made from the carcass will be enough for 6 to 8 servings.

SHOWCASE • ON A BUDGET • KID-FRIENDLY

SERVES 4

> 2 tablespoons Chicken Herb Rub (see page 254)
>
> 1 clove garlic
>
> ¼ cup olive oil
>
> 1 whole chicken, approximately 4 pounds

Preheat oven to 350°F.

Place Chicken Herb Rub in a food processor with the garlic and olive oil, and purée into a smooth paste.

Rinse the chicken, and pat it dry with paper towels. Rub the herb paste all over the chicken, being sure to get underneath as well as on top of the skin. Allow to sit for 2 hours in the refrigerator, or roast immediately, roughly 1 ½ hours, until the legs are loose, or until the internal temperature of the breast reads 160°F and the internal temperature of the thigh reads 165° to 170°F. Let rest for 10 to 15 minutes before carving.

HOW MUCH CHICKEN SHOULD YOU BUY?

When preparing a whole chicken, figure 1 pound of bird per person. A 4-pound chicken usually serves 4 people, 2-pound birds are ideal for 2, and so on. Most of the recipes here are for birds in the 3-to-5-pound range. These recipes will work just as well with 6-pound birds—assuming you are lucky enough to find a farmer willing to sell you one, since we like to keep the biggest birds for ourselves. Simply allow a little more cooking time, using your meat thermometer to gauge when it is done.

Suvilla's Melt-on-Your-Tongue Chicken

Suvilla Fisher, The Organic Grass Farm, Indiana

Suvilla Fisher uses this slow-cook method to prepare chicken for her Amish family when everyone is busy and no one has time to spend in the kitchen. I don't generally advocate cooking chicken in a covered pot because the skin does not get nice and crisp. However, while visiting her farm, she served me a piece of cold chicken cooked with this technique. It was unbelievably moist and delicious! While this dish is meant to be served warm from the oven, in my opinion, if you like to have cold chicken on hand to serve for lunches, this is the best method.

ON A BUDGET • MINIMUM PREPARATION

SERVES 4 TO 5

> 3 teaspoons coarse salt
>
> 1 ½ teaspoons freshly ground black pepper
>
> 1 tablespoon paprika
>
> 2 teaspoons celery powder
>
> 1 broiler, 3 to 5 pounds
>
> 5 large baking potatoes, cut in quarters

Preheat oven to 200°F.

Combine the salt, pepper, paprika, and celery powder in a small dish. Rinse the chicken, pat it dry with paper towels, and then rub the spice mix on the chicken and underneath the skin. Place the chicken in a roasting pan, arranging the potato quarters around it. Cover tightly, and bake for about 8 hours.

Suvilla notes: "This recipe is for young broilers. If you want to cook that ornery old rooster, just give it more cooking time, like 12 hours or so."

Sweet-and-Sour Chicken

Penny Gioja, Joy of Illinois Farm, Illinois

After raising nine children on their family farm, Penny and Les Gioja have figured out how to make a little food go a long, long way. Their appetizing recipe makes an old stewing hen or duck a favorite family treat.

ON A BUDGET • KID-FRIENDLY

SERVES 8 TO 10

1 4-pound stewing hen or duck

1 20-ounce can chunk unsweetened
    pineapple, drained and juice reserved

½ cup red wine vinegar

2 tablespoons soy sauce

1 teaspoon coarse salt

¼ cup cornstarch

½ cup dark brown sugar

2 carrots, scraped and thinly sliced

2 green bell peppers, cut in strips

2 medium onions, thinly sliced

Other vegetables of choice,
    such as peas or green beans

8 to 10 cups hot cooked rice

Early in the morning, rinse the chicken, and put it in a large kettle. Cover with water, bring to a boil, and simmer all day, until about 1 hour before you are ready to serve. Alternatively, put the bird in a slow-cooker with 1 quart water, and cook on low for about 8 hours.

In the late afternoon, remove the chicken. Pull off the skin and bones, discard, and cut the meat into bite-size pieces. Set aside. Pour 2 cups of the cooking broth into a soup pot (reserve the rest of the broth for another use). Add the pineapple juice, vinegar, soy sauce, and salt.

In a small bowl, thoroughly combine the cornstarch and brown sugar (if it isn't mixed properly, you will have lumps of cornstarch in your dinner), and add to the seasoned broth in the pot. Simmer over medium heat, stirring often, until the mixture thickens and is noticeably darker. Add the carrots, meat, and pineapple chunks, and cook for 4 to 5 minutes. Add the green pepper, onions, and any other vegetables you've fancied, and cook until all are just crisp-tender. Serve over rice.

Honey-Glazed Chicken

Rae Ellen Freeman, Freeman Homestead, New York

The honey and lemon on this chicken make it memorable.

ON A BUDGET • KID-FRIENDLY

SERVES 4

> ¾ cup all-purpose flour
>
> 1½ teaspoons coarse salt
>
> ¾ teaspoon freshly ground black pepper
>
> 1 3- to 5-pound chicken, cut up
>
> 4 tablespoons unsalted butter, melted
>
> ¼ cup dark brown sugar
>
> ¼ cup honey
>
> ¼ cup fresh lemon juice
>
> 1 tablespoon soy sauce
>
> 1½ teaspoons curry powder

Preheat oven to 350°F.

Combine flour, salt, and pepper in a medium bowl. Rinse the chicken, pat it dry with paper towels, and then dip the pieces into the flour mixture, turning until they are thoroughly coated. Place on a rack, and set aside.

Pour the melted butter into a 9-x-13-inch baking pan. Add the chicken pieces, turning until they are coated with the butter. Bake, uncovered, for 30 minutes.

Mix together the brown sugar, honey, lemon juice, soy sauce, and curry powder. Pour over the chicken, and bake 45 minutes longer, basting occasionally with the pan drippings.

Chicken with 40 Cloves of Garlic

Stacey Muncie, of Grazey Acres in Indiana, suggested that I add the sage, rosemary, and whole peppercorns to this recipe. Adding these spices really brings out the subtle flavors in the meat. This is a scrumptious way to prepare chicken. If you're fortunate enough to have leftovers, they'll reheat beautifully in a covered casserole in your oven. Be sure that you do not prepare this recipe in a cast-iron pan; wine will interact with the metal and give foods an off-flavor.

SHOWCASE • ON A BUDGET

SERVES 4

1 chicken or rabbit, 3 to 4 pounds, cut up

3½ teaspoons coarse salt

2½ teaspoons freshly ground black pepper

2 tablespoons unsalted butter

2 tablespoons olive oil

40 cloves of garlic, peeled

3 sprigs fresh thyme

1 sprig fresh rosemary

2 sprigs fresh sage

10 whole black peppercorns

½ cup dry white wine

Rinse the chicken, and pat it dry with paper towels. Combine the salt and ground pepper in a small dish, then rub into the chicken parts. Heat the butter and olive oil in a large Dutch oven or sauté pan over medium-high heat. Add the chicken, and brown, about 5 to 7 minutes per side. This can be done in batches to avoid crowding.

Remove the browned pieces to a warm shallow bowl. Lower the heat, and add the garlic. Stir constantly to pick up any browned bits of chicken and to prevent the garlic from burning. Continue cooking for about 10 minutes, until the garlic is soft. Using a slotted spoon, remove the garlic to a small bowl (smaller cloves will need to come out sooner, larger ones can stay in longer). Return the chicken and any juices that might have drained off back to the pan. Add the herbs, peppercorns, and wine, and pour the garlic cloves on top. Bring to a boil, then lower the heat until the liquid is just lightly simmering. Cover and cook, for 25 to 30 minutes, basting occasionally (a baster works better than a brush).

Serve the chicken with mashed potatoes, being sure to top both with a few spoonfuls of the juices and soft garlic.

PRESERVING HERITAGE-BREED TURKEYS

The industrialization of agriculture throughout the world has had a devastating effect on the genetic diversity of livestock breeds. According to the United Nations Food and Agriculture Organization, 300 out of 6,000 livestock breeds worldwide have become extinct in the last fifteen years; currently, 1,350 breeds are facing extinction. One look at the North American turkey industry illustrates this concern. A single breed of turkey dominates the industry: the Large White, a bird with an inordinately enormous breast, custom-designed to dominate the Thanksgiving table in the United States.

Relying solely on one particular breed of bird is an unwise practice. It erodes the gene pool, creating animals that are particularly susceptible to the same types of illnesses and calamities. Conversely, wide genetic diversity results in a variety of birds suited to a variety of conditions and able to withstand a broad array of mishaps, resulting in greater food security. In addition, genetic diversity means that breeders are more easily able to develop strains of turkeys that are uniquely suited to small, pasture-based farms.

As part of the battle against the industrialization of the food system, the Slow Food USA organization (http://www.slowfoodusa.org) has undertaken the enormous task of working to recover a number of North American heritage turkey breeds that were near extinction, including the Narragansett, American Standard Bronze, Jersey Buff, and Bourbon Red. By coordinating with consumers and chefs, small farmers, breeders, processors, and distributors throughout the country, Slow Food has built up a nationwide network for producing and distributing these unique and delicious birds throughout the country.

Such an initiative does more than simply build up the turkey gene pool. These breeds have cultural importance; they are part of our agricultural heritage. Just as we preserve historic landmarks and artifacts to better understand our past, so too should we safeguard the artifacts of our agricultural history.

Chicken Fricassee with Wild Rice (or without)

Karen Bumann, Sweetland Farm, Wisconsin

When my husband and I tested this recipe, we found we preferred this dish without rice because then there was more yummy sauce left on our plates for dipping the meat. Still, if you prefer the traditional route, cook up some wild rice while the chicken is simmering, pair this with a salad, and your meal is complete. This recipe should appeal to the entire family. However, if your children are very young, watch out for loose bones when you dish up their portions. Rabbit also works in this recipe, as does stewing chicken.

SHOWCASE • ON A BUDGET • KID-FRIENDLY

SERVES 4 TO 5

1 chicken or rabbit, 3 to 5 pounds, cut into 8 pieces

1 ½ teaspoons coarse salt

1 onion, cut into 1-inch slices

1 tablespoon fresh thyme or 1 teaspoon dried

2 sprigs fresh rosemary or ¾ teaspoon dried

1 bay leaf

2 teaspoons fresh sage or ¾ teaspoon dried

2 cups chicken broth

1 cup Chardonnay

1 ½ quarts water

5 cups cooked wild rice

Rinse the chicken. Place the chicken, salt, onion, herbs, broth, and Chardonnay in a large pot. Pour in just enough water to cover the bird. Bring to a boil, skimming off any foam that rises to the surface. Lower the heat to a simmer, and cook the bird for 1 ½ to 2 hours, until the meat is fork-tender. Meanwhile, prepare the wild rice. Transfer the meat to a hot platter to keep warm, reserve the cooking stock.

Strain the stock through a colander into a pot. Bring to a boil, and cook until reduced to about 2 cups.

For the sauce:

3 tablespoons unsalted butter

3 tablespoons all-purpose flour

2 cups reduced chicken broth (from above)

3 egg yolks

¼ teaspoon freshly ground nutmeg

1 teaspoon freshly ground black pepper

1 cup heavy cream

Melt the butter in a 2½-quart saucepan. Add the flour, and using a wooden spoon, mix to make a smooth paste. Stir over medium heat until the butter and flour begin to foam, about 1½ to 2 minutes. Turn the heat off, and wait for the bubbling to cease. Add 1½ cups of the reduced broth, and whisk to blend thoroughly.

Combine the egg yolks, nutmeg, pepper, and cream in a bowl, and whisk until well blended. Temper the yolk and cream mixture by slowly stirring in the remaining ½ cup of hot broth. Pour the yolk mixture into the sauce. Cook, stirring constantly, over medium-low heat until the sauce has thickened; if necessary, after 3 to 5 minutes, gradually increase the heat to speed thickening. Pour over the chicken pieces, and serve alone or with wild rice.

WORKING WITH DRIED HERBS

The simplest and most flavorful way to cook many grass-fed meats is to rub salt, pepper, some chopped garlic, and a few dried herbs into the meat before cooking it. For this technique to be successful, you must be sure to buy high-quality, preferably domestic, organically grown or wild-crafted herbs. I've found that the best sources of good-quality herbs are local food co-ops and health food stores, where they are often sold in bulk. Although some people warn that bulk herbs may not be sterile (which could lead to "off" flavors or spoiled food), I've not found this to be the case. The bulk herbs I buy seem fresher, and I pay only for the herbs themselves— not the excessive packaging used for commercial, grocery-store herbs.

When buying bulk herbs, make sure they're good quality. The dried plants should still have much of their original color, and they should have a strong scent. Be sure the herbs don't smell musty or dusty, which could mean that they have gotten damp or moldy. Don't purchase any herbs that are faded or yellowed, since these are too old and will have lost their flavor. Dried herbs will keep for several months if stored properly. Keep them in airtight metal or glass containers in a cool, dry, dark place. Don't hesitate to toss any herbs that have begun to lose their color—they're simply taking up valuable kitchen space and offer no seasoning value.

If you find yourself working with a recipe that calls for fresh herbs you don't have on hand, substitute dry herbs at a rate of 1 teaspoon dried for 1 tablespoon fresh.

Kentucky Baked Chicken

Dave and Pat Griffith, Bar 7 Ranch, British Columbia, Canada

Once you've cut up your chicken, your kids might enjoy helping you put this recipe together.

ON A BUDGET • KID-FRIENDLY

SERVES 4 TO 6

> 2 cups plain yogurt
>
> 2 cups dry bread crumbs
>
> ¾ cup freshly grated Parmesan cheese
>
> ¼ cup minced fresh parsley or 1 ½ tablespoons dried
>
> 1 tablespoon coarse salt
>
> 1 chicken, 4 ½ to 5 pounds, cut up

Preheat oven to 325°F.

Line a 9-x-12-inch baking pan with foil, and set a flat wire rack inside.

Pour the yogurt into a shallow bowl. Combine the breadcrumbs, cheese, parsley, and salt in a separate shallow bowl.

Rinse the chicken, and pat it dry with paper towels; dip the chicken pieces into the yogurt, then into the crumb mixture. Set chicken pieces on the wire rack. Bake for 1 to 1 ½ hours, or until the juices of the meat run clear. The legs and wings will cook faster than the thighs and breasts, so removing them early is advisable. Place on a warm platter, and tent them with foil. Remove the thighs and breasts when an internal thermometer reads 165°F.

Poulet aux Oignons
(Chicken Caramelized in Onions)

Marc Fournier, a shepherd from the Pyrenees Mountains and a dear friend, taught me how to make this. The chicken gets a hearty sweetness from the onions, making this one of my favorite dishes.

SHOWCASE • ON A BUDGET

SERVES 4

> 1 chicken or rabbit, 3 to 4 pounds, cut into 8 pieces
>
> Coarse salt and freshly ground black pepper to taste
>
> 4 tablespoons olive oil
>
> 5 to 6 medium onions, sliced into thin rings

Rinse the chicken, and pat it dry with paper towels; sprinkle liberally with salt and pepper.

Heat a large Dutch oven or wok over medium heat. Add the olive oil, and brown the chicken on both sides, about 5 to 7 minutes per side. If necessary, this can be done in batches to avoid crowding. Remove the chicken, set aside, and keep warm.

Add the onions, and sauté until translucent, scraping up any brown bits from the chicken. Return the chicken to the pot, turning to mix it with the onions. Simmer, uncovered, over very low heat for about 1 hour, until the onions caramelize and the chicken is done (the juices will run clear). When serving, be sure to spoon the caramelized onions and the rich juices over the chicken.

Butterflied High-Roast Chicken
with Crispy Potatoes

Maryellen Driscoll, Free Bird Farm, New York

Maryellen writes: "This chicken is roasted at a high temperature, which normally creates a lot of smoke. But here, thin-sliced potatoes are layered underneath the bird so that they absorb the chicken renderings—tempering the smoke and, even better, sopping up the flavor. This dish is easy and quick enough to serve on weeknights but fantastically delicious enough to serve to guests."

Note: One of my recipe testers remarked that this recipe also worked really well with a brined chicken.

SHOWCASE • ON A BUDGET

SERVES 4

1 whole chicken, about 4 pounds, giblets removed

Coarse salt

Freshly ground black pepper

2 branches of fresh rosemary or fresh thyme, 3 inches long

1 fresh lemon, cut into 4 thin slices

2 cloves garlic, thinly sliced

2 pounds Yukon Gold potatoes, sliced into ⅛-inch-thick rounds

1 tablespoon olive oil

Preheat oven to 475° F.

Using heavy-duty kitchen shears or poultry shears, cut along both sides of the chicken's backbone and remove it. Save the backbone for homemade stock. Breast side up, spread the chicken open, and press down with the palms of your hands to splay out flat. Rinse the butterflied chicken, and pat it dry with paper towels. At the top of the breast, loosen the skin so that you can insert your fingers between it and the meat. Spread about ½ teaspoon salt and a few good grinds of pepper under the skin of each breast half. Then insert a branch of rosemary, 2 lemon slices, and half the garlic slices under the skin of one breast and toward the thigh as far as you can reach, being careful not to tear the skin. Repeat with the other breast. Sprinkle the rest of the chicken with salt and pepper.

Gently toss the thin-sliced potatoes with the olive oil until thoroughly coated, and season with salt and pepper. In the bottom half of a broiler pan, overlap the potato slices, like fallen dominoes, in rows the length of the pan, and covering the entire bottom.

Place the slotted half of the broiler pan over the base, and set the chicken, skin side up, on top. Press to flatten. Roast until the skin is golden-crisp and the juices of the bird run clear, about 50 minutes to 1 hour; an instant-read thermometer should read 160°F in the thickest part of the breast and about 165° to 170°F in the thickest part of the thigh. Set the chicken aside on a cutting board, and let rest for 10 minutes before carving.

Meanwhile, if the potatoes have not turned a crispy golden brown around the edges, return them to the oven while the chicken rests. Carve the chicken and serve with the potato slices.

JUST HOW FRESH DO YOU WANT YOUR FRESH CHICKEN?

When we first started raising and processing chickens at Sap Bush Hollow Farm, we looked forward to a fresh chicken on processing day. In the morning, my father would take a newly processed bird from the cold-water bath and would present it to me to take inside and cook. However, by noon, the mood would turn black. The chicken I had roasted would be too tough to enjoy. My father and mother would glare at me. How could I mess this up? Here I was, an aspiring epicurean, and I couldn't even cook a chicken. Then one day, I neglected to roast the fresh bird until the day *after* processing day. And on that day, the angels sang, the flowers bloomed, and we licked our plates clean. The chicken was as tender as we expected it should be.

What was the difference? Whereas some chickens are tender almost immediately, others require more time for proteolytic enzymes to break down the connective tissue in the meat. For this to happen, freshly processed chickens need to be refrigerated for twenty-four hours before cooking or freezing. So the next time you venture out for a fresh chicken, make sure it's not *too* fresh, or you may be unpleasantly surprised.

Chicken Nuggets

Chicken nuggets are easy to eat and appeal to children—they're a good idea for a birthday party. There are two variations of this recipe below; one features breadcrumbs and Parmesan cheese. Leftovers are terrific in a salad.

BASIC CHICKEN NUGGETS

Rae Ellen Freeman, Freeman Homestead, New York

IN A HURRY • KID-FRIENDLY

SERVES 8 TO 10

> 8 boneless, skinless chicken breast halves, cut into $1\frac{1}{2}$-inch pieces
>
> 1 cup all-purpose flour
>
> 4 teaspoons seasoned salt
>
> 1 teaspoon paprika
>
> 1 teaspoon poultry seasoning
>
> 1 teaspoon ground mustard
>
> $\frac{1}{2}$ teaspoon freshly ground black pepper
>
> $\frac{1}{4}$ cup vegetable oil

Rinse the chicken, and pat it dry with paper towels. Combine the dry ingredients in a zipper-seal plastic bag; place the chicken pieces inside, a few at a time, and shake to coat.

Meanwhile, heat a large cast-iron skillet over medium heat, and add the vegetable oil. When the oil is hot but not smoking, begin frying the chicken pieces in batches, 6 to 8 minutes per batch. Stir and turn frequently until the chicken is browned and the juices run clear.

PARMESAN CHICKEN NUGGETS

David and Sheila Roth, Roth's Greener Pastures, Missouri

IN A HURRY • KID-FRIENDLY

SERVES 3 TO 4

> 3 boneless, skinless 6- to 8-ounce chicken breast halves,
>   cut into bite-size chunks
>
> ½ cup Italian breadcrumbs
>
> ¼ cup freshly grated Parmesan cheese
>
> 1 teaspoon paprika
>
> ½ cup unsalted butter, melted

Preheat oven to 400°F.

Rinse the chicken, and pat it dry with paper towels. Combine the breadcrumbs, Parmesan cheese, and paprika in a shallow bowl. Dip the chicken chunks into the melted butter, then into the crumb mixture. Bake for 15 minutes, turning once.

Eat alone, or dip into a variety of sauces, such as blue-cheese or ranch dressing, barbecue sauce, or Dijon mustard.

Pasta with Chicken and Squash

Rae Ellen Freeman, Freeman Homestead, New York

Although this recipe calls for chicken breasts, it also works well with leftover chicken. Simply shred the leftovers, and cook with the seasonings just until heated. For a lighter dinner, skip the rich cheese sauce, and toss the pasta, veggies, and chicken with ¼ cup good olive oil and some coarse salt.

ON A BUDGET • KID-FRIENDLY

SERVES 6

1 pound spiral pasta

2 cups whipping cream

1 tablespoon unsalted butter

2 cups shredded cheddar cheese

1 small onion, chopped

1 garlic clove, minced

5 tablespoons olive oil

2 medium zucchini, julienned

2 medium yellow squash, julienned

1¼ teaspoon salt

⅛ teaspoon freshly ground black pepper

1 pound skinless, boneless chicken breasts, or 2 cups cooked leftover chicken

1 teaspoon coarsely chopped fresh basil, or ¼ teaspoon dried

¼ teaspoon finely chopped fresh marjoram, or just a pinch dried

1 teaspoon finely chopped fresh rosemary, or ¼ teaspoon dried

½ teaspoon finely chopped fresh sage, or ⅛ teaspoon dried

Bring a large pot of salted water to a boil, add the pasta, and boil until al dente. Meanwhile, heat the cream and butter in a heavy large saucepan over medium heat until the butter melts. Add the cheese, stirring until melted.

Thoroughly drain the pasta, and mix with the cheese sauce. Cover, and keep warm. In a large skillet, sauté the onion and garlic in 3 tablespoons of the olive oil until the onions are translucent. Add the zucchini and yellow squash, and quickly sauté until crisp tender; be very careful not to overcook. Sprinkle with 1 teaspoon of the salt and the ⅛ teaspoon pepper, remove from the heat, drain off any excess liquid, and keep warm.

Add the remaining 2 tablespoons oil to the skillet. If you are using raw meat, rinse the chicken breasts. Toss the chicken, herbs, and remaining salt into the skillet. If you are using leftover chicken, sauté until the chicken is thoroughly warmed; if you are using raw chicken, sauté until the juices run clear. Place the pasta on a warm serving platter, and top with the chicken and squash.

A HUMBLE OPINION (AND CONFESSION) ON STOCKS AND BOUILLON

In her book *Nourishing Traditions,*[1] Sally Fallon extols the virtues of properly prepared meat stocks. As Fallon writes, meat stocks "are extremely nutritious, containing the minerals of bone, cartilage, marrow and vegetables as electrolytes, a form that is easy to assimilate. Acidic wine or vinegar added during cooking helps to draw minerals, particularly calcium, magnesium and potassium, into the broth."

I couldn't agree more, and I discourage all home cooks from discarding cooked bones without first boiling them for stock. After cooking our Saturday chicken, my husband and I boil the carcass with vegetables and a splash of vinegar to make a rich broth that we package and store in the freezer, to be used in cooking or to be heated up for soup if one of us is feeling under the weather.

Still, I will confess that in the darkest corner of my cupboard, hidden from view, sits a container of beef and chicken bouillon cubes. Those evil little cubes host a wallop of unsavory ingredients, including monosodium glutamate, mysterious oils, and exotic forms of sodium. I also know that a few of my health-conscious friends keep store-bought canned broth hidden on their pantry shelves. Ideally, when using a recipe that calls for stock, I'm able to go to the freezer and pull out a quart of nourishing, homemade broth. But the truth is that I don't always have my act together, and I may not have broth on hand. At those times, I wait until no one is looking, and then I reach for my secret cubes. I figure that in the long run, it's far better to prepare a home-cooked meal for my family with a little "cheater" ingredient than it is to give up on a recipe and take the family out for fast food. So although homemade stock is by far the best way to go, don't feel ashamed to keep some back-up broth on hand to use in a pinch.

1. Sally Fallon, with Mary G. Enig, *Nourishing Traditions: The Cookbook That Challenges Politically Correct Nutrition and the Diet Dictocrats* (Washington, D.C.: New Trends Publishing, 1999), 116.

Basic Chicken Broth

Stacey Muncie, Grazey Acres, Indiana

Here's a super way to use your leftover chicken. If you don't plan to use the broth right away, store it in your freezer, and take it out when you want to make soup. I firmly believe that good broth is the best cold and flu remedy in the world. Try drinking a mug of hot chicken broth the next time you're under the weather. The vinegar added to this recipe draws more nutrients from the bones.

ON A BUDGET

MAKES ABOUT 3 QUARTS OF STOCK

> 1 medium onion, coarsely chopped
>
> 3 celery stalks, coarsely chopped
>
> 2 carrots, scraped and cut into large pieces
>
> 1 bay leaf
>
> 2 tablespoons white vinegar
>
> 4 quarts water
>
> 1 leftover chicken carcass and pan drippings

Place all ingredients in a large stockpot. Allow everything to sit, with the heat off, for 30 minutes. Turn the heat on high, bring to a boil, then lower the heat and simmer the broth for a minimum of 6 hours—the longer the broth simmers, the richer it will be.

Strain the liquid, discarding the vegetables but reserving the carcass. Place broth in a container, cover tightly, and refrigerate. When it is chilled, skim the fat from the surface.

Pick off the remaining meat from the carcass, and either return the meat to the broth for chicken soup or use it to make something else (such as chicken and rice).

Teriyaki Chicken Hearts

Here's an easy way to cook up a few chicken hearts for a super-nutritious meal.

ON A BUDGET

SERVES 4

½ cup tamari

½ cup sherry

2 teaspoons ground ginger

2 tablespoons honey

2 cloves garlic, crushed

½ pound chicken hearts, quartered lengthwise

2 to 4 tablespoons olive or peanut oil

2 carrots, scraped and cut into thin diagonal slices

2 stalks celery, coarsely diced

1 green bell pepper, coarsely chopped

1 onion, cut into ¼-inch slices

⅓ cup whole raw cashews

Combine the tamari, sherry, ginger, honey, and garlic in a small saucepan. Simmer, stirring constantly, until the liquid is reduced to about ⅔ cup; cool for a few minutes, then pour over the chicken hearts. Refrigerate for 2 to 3 hours.

Remove the chicken hearts from the marinade. Pour the marinating liquid into a small saucepan, and simmer until it is thick and syrupy, about 6 minutes.

Heat 2 tablespoons oil in a large sauté pan or wok. Add the chicken hearts, and sauté over high heat, about 3 minutes. Pour the marinade over the hearts, and continue to cook over high heat 3 minutes longer. Remove the chicken and the liquid to a bowl, and keep warm.

If necessary, add more oil to the pan. Add the carrots, and sauté over medium heat for 2 minutes. Add the remaining vegetables and cashews, and sauté 2 minutes more, or until all the vegetables are crisp-tender. Return hearts and sauce to the pan, stirring to mix with the vegetables. Serve immediately, alone or over rice.

Chicken Pot Pie with Herbed Crust

No chapter on cooking poultry would be complete without a recipe for one of the world's greatest comfort foods—and another way to use leftover chicken or turkey to warm your belly on a chilly day.

ON A BUDGET

SERVES 6

For the herbed pie crust:

1 ½ cups all-purpose flour, plus some extra for rolling out the dough

¾ teaspoon salt

¼ teaspoon freshly ground black pepper

1 teaspoon dried thyme

½ teaspoon dried oregano

8 tablespoons butter or lard

6 to 8 tablespoons ice water

Combine the flour, salt, pepper, and dried herbs in a medium bowl. Use a pastry blender or fork to cut the butter or lard into the flour mixture until it is crumbly. Add the ice water gradually, mixing quickly with a fork until the dough is just moist enough to hold together. Be careful not to add too much water. You may not need the full 6 tablespoons. Shape the dough into a ball, then place on a floured surface and roll out to a rectangle at least 9 x 13 inches.

For the filling:

6 tablespoons unsalted butter

3 small stalks celery, coarsely chopped

3 carrots, scraped and finely chopped

1 large onion, sliced into thin wedges

½ teaspoon coarse salt

¼ teaspoon freshly ground black pepper

¾ cup fresh or thawed whole corn kernels

½ cup fresh or frozen peas

3 cups cooked chicken or turkey, shredded

½ cup all-purpose flour

2 cups chicken broth

1 cup whole milk

½ cup half-and-half

1 teaspoon dried thyme, or 1 tablespoon fresh

2 tablespoons dry sherry

Preheat oven to 400°F.

Melt 2 tablespoons of the butter in a large, nonreactive saucepan, then sauté the celery, carrots, and onions over medium-high heat until they are crisp-tender, approximately 4 to 5 minutes. Remove to a large bowl, and keep warm. Add the salt, pepper, corn, peas, and shredded chicken or turkey to the vegetables, and stir gently until well combined.

Melt the remaining 4 tablespoons butter in the saucepan. Turn off the heat, add the flour, and stir in quickly. The mixture will be pasty. Over medium heat, stir in the broth, milk, half-and-half, and thyme. Bring the liquid to a boil, stirring occasionally; lower the heat and simmer, stirring often, until the sauce is thick and rich. Stir in the sherry.

Pour the sauce over the meat and vegetables, and mix gently. Season to taste with additional salt and pepper. Pour the entire contents of the bowl into a 13-x-9-inch baking pan, and top with the herbed pie crust. Fold down and crimp overlapping edges so that the crust fits inside the pan. Pierce the top several times with a sharp knife, and bake for 35 to 45 minutes, or until the top is golden brown and the filling is bubbling.

Terrine de Foies de Volaille (Chicken Liver Mousse)

Sean Hayes, Sap Bush Hollow Farm, New York

My brother picked this recipe up somewhere during his world travels, and it sits folded up in the family recipe box, the paper heavily creased and grease-spotted from use. It is a recipe to-die-for. The only problem is that it is very hard not to be a glutton and consume the entire thing, by yourself, in one sitting. Even though preparation involves a few different phases, the end result is worth the effort. If you are going to serve this as an appetizer for dinner, you must start early in the morning or one day before the event.

SERVES 6 AS A MEAL, 12 AS AN APPETIZER

PART I

      1 medium onion, sliced thin

      1 cup chicken stock

      ½ teaspoon coarse salt

      1 pound fresh chicken livers

Place all the above ingredients in a saucepan (make sure it is not aluminum, or the liquid will be off-color). Bring to a boil, then lower the heat and simmer for 10 minutes. Remove from the heat, let rest for 10 minutes, and strain through a colander, taking care to reserve the liquid. This liquid, called "stock," will be used in forming the aspic you will make in Part III.

PART II

      ¾ pound (3 sticks) unsalted butter, very soft

      2 teaspoons coarse salt

      ¾ teaspoon freshly ground white pepper,

      3 tablespoons cognac, Armagnac or any other good brandy

      ½ cup heavy cream

Place ⅓ of the strained liver-and-onion mixture in a blender. Add one stick of the butter, ½ teaspoon of the salt, ¼ teaspoon of the pepper, and 1 tablespoon of the cognac. Blend until very smooth. Transfer to a bowl. Repeat until all the butter, liver, salt, pepper, and cognac have been used. Place the mixture in the refrigerator for 15 minutes. Remove, mix thoroughly with a wooden spoon, then return to the refrigerator for 10 more minutes.

Meanwhile, whip the cream until stiff peaks form, and gently fold it into the liver mixture. Pour the mixture into a decorative terrine or a bowl lined with plastic wrap. Cover with plastic wrap, and refrigerate.

PART III

> 1 envelope unflavored gelatin
>
> 1 cup (approximately) of the reserved stock that you made in Part I
>
> 1 egg white

Mix the gelatin and the stock in a small, nonreactive saucepan. Beat the egg white with a wire whisk for 1 minute, then add to the liquid. Cook mixture over medium heat until it comes to a boil, stirring occasionally to prevent scorching. As soon as the liquid boils, strain it through a double layer of cheesecloth (a crust will have formed on the top of the liquid). Allow the liquid to cool until it has the consistency of heavy syrup. Pour over the top of the mousse. Chill in the refrigerator for a minimum of 4 to 5 hours, or overnight. If the mousse has been made in a decorative terrine, serve it as it is. Otherwise, unmold onto a plate, remove the plastic wrap, and garnish with fresh vegetables.

Lemon Chicken Wings

Karma and Michael Glos, Kingbird Farm, New York

If you buy your chickens cut up and have plenty of recipes for the thighs, drumsticks, and breasts but only a few for wings, here's one that makes a delightful meal for four or a tasty appetizer for a larger gathering.

SHOWCASE • MINIMUM PREPARATION

SERVES 4

4 pounds chicken wings

½ cup lemon juice

½ cup olive oil

6 cloves garlic, minced

2 tablespoons minced fresh rosemary, or ½ teaspoon ground dried

1 teaspoon coarse salt

½ teaspoon freshly ground black pepper

Rinse the wings, pat dry with a paper towel, and then tuck back the tips (if you prefer, feel free to snip the tips for a neater presentation). Mix all the above ingredients (except the wings) in a stainless steel or other nonreactive bowl. Add the chicken, and marinate overnight.

Preheat oven to 350°F.

Roast the wings, uncovered, for 1 hour. Serve promptly alone as an appetizer or, for a meal, over cooked barley or Yukon Gold mashed potatoes.

Herb-Roasted Turkey with Giblet Gravy

Grass-fed turkeys come in all shapes and sizes, so it's not possible to give precise cooking times. The only sure way to have a properly cooked turkey is to use an internal meat thermometer. The chart on page 217 gives approximate cooking times to help you determine when the bird should go in the oven, but due to the variation in fat and size, there is no substitute for a good meat thermometer. The estimated times given are for unstuffed birds. If you plan to stuff your turkey, add at least 30 minutes to the cooking time. Make sure that your stuffing reaches 165°F before you remove it from the bird.

If you are ordering a turkey for Thanksgiving, you've probably learned that attaining your exact desired weight is not always possible when buying from a small farm. You should be willing to accept 5 pounds more or less than what you ordered.

SHOWCASE

FIGURE ON ABOUT 1 POUND PER PERSON FOR A NORMAL THANKSGIVING FEAST AND 1½ POUNDS PER PERSON IF YOU WANT LEFTOVERS.

For the giblet broth:

2 tablespoons olive oil

Turkey giblets, including the neck, gizzard, heart, and liver

1 medium carrot, scraped and coarsely chopped

1 medium onion, coarsely chopped

1½ quarts chicken broth (or turkey broth, if you have it on hand)

1 tablespoon dried thyme, or 3 tablespoons fresh

2 teaspoons dried parsley, or 2 tablespoons fresh, finely minced

Start your turkey by making the giblet broth one day ahead, if possible. If not, remove the giblets, and make the broth while roasting the turkey as directed below.

Heat olive oil in a small soup pot. Rinse the giblets, and sauté in the oil until they are lightly browned, about 4 to 5 minutes (this can be done in batches, if necessary). Add the carrot, and sauté 1 minute longer. Add the onion, and sauté until translucent. Reduce the heat to very low. Cover, and simmer for 10 minutes. Add the chicken broth, thyme, and parsley, and bring to a boil. Reduce the heat, and simmer for 30 minutes longer.

Strain the broth, making sure to reserve the giblets. When they are cool enough to handle, remove any gristle, then dice the gizzard, heart, and liver; pull off the neck meat. Refrigerate all these bits of meat separately from the broth until you are ready to use them.

For the herb butter:

This makes enough to accommodate up to 18 pounds of turkey. If your bird is larger, scale up the proportions to suit your taste. If it is 24 pounds or more, consider doubling the recipe.

1 tablespoon coarse salt

1 tablespoon freshly ground black pepper

4 cloves garlic

1 tablespoon fresh thyme

2 tablespoons finely minced fresh oregano

1 tablespoon minced fresh rosemary

1 teaspoon dried lavender

¼ pound unsalted butter, softened, or 1 cup olive oil

Combine all in a food processor, and purée until smooth.

For the turkey:

1 turkey

3 medium onions, coarsely chopped

2 carrots, scraped and coarsely chopped

2 stalks celery, coarsely chopped

4 to 6 springs fresh thyme

2 sprigs fresh sage

2 sprigs fresh marjoram or oregano

4 tablespoons unsalted butter, melted

Preheat oven to 325°F.

Rinse the turkey, inside and out, and pat dry with paper towels.

Place the oven rack in the lowest position, and rub one-quarter of the herb butter under the skin on the breast. Rub the remainder all over the bird—on the back, on the breast, on the legs, and on the thighs.

Set the turkey, breast side down, on a well-oiled rack in a large roasting pan. Toss half the chopped onions, carrots, and celery into the cavity of the bird. Add half the fresh herbs and 1 tablespoon of the melted butter. Scatter the remaining vegetables and herbs in the bottom of the roasting pan. Pour 1 cup of water over the vegetables (*not* on the turkey). Roast the turkey for the estimated amount of time listed on the chart on page 217, basting every hour. Early in the roasting, before you have pan juices, use the remaining 3 tablespoons melted butter to baste the bird. If the vegetables in the pan look dehydrated, periodically add another ½ cup water until the turkey starts releasing pan juices. Halfway through the estimated cooking time, pour the reserved giblet broth into the bottom of the pan; carefully turn the bird breast side up. Continue roasting, basting regularly with the pan juices, until the thigh registers 170° to 175°F.

Remove the bird from the oven, transfer it to a warm platter, tent loosely with foil, and let rest for about 30 minutes while you make the gravy.

For the gravy:

4 tablespoons unsalted butter

¼ cup all-purpose flour

1 cup dry white wine

Coarse salt and freshly ground black pepper to taste

Pour the pan juices into a large measuring cup or bowl. Strain and discard the vegetables and herbs.

Heat the butter in a large saucepan over medium heat. Whisk in the flour, stirring constantly, until it turns a deep caramel color. Pour in all but 1 cup of the pan juices. Keep stirring the mixture until it comes to a boil. Reduce the heat, and simmer the gravy for about 5 minutes, until it is slightly thickened. Be sure to stir the mixture frequently.

Set the roasting pan over two stove burners. Add the wine to the pan, and bring to a simmer, scraping up any browned bits. Add the gravy, and continue cooking until the sauce is reduced by almost one-third (approximately 5 minutes). Add the remaining broth and chopped giblets, and return the mixture to a boil, stirring constantly. Adjust the seasonings for salt and pepper. Serve gravy alongside the carved turkey.

Roast Goose with Sherry and Oranges

Here it is… a sweet and savory recipe for the crown prince of poultry, the holiday goose. Your dinner preparations should begin one day in advance by quickly boiling the bird to render as much of the subcutaneous fat as possible and to ensure crisp, delicious skin.

SHOWCASE

SERVES 4 TO 6

1 goose, roughly 8 to 10 pounds

2 tablespoons unsalted butter

1 goose neck

3 shallots, sliced

1 ½ cups dry sherry

4 oranges, quartered

1 quart chicken broth

1 cup fresh orange juice

1 tablespoon cornstarch

1 tablespoon honey

1 tablespoon fresh lemon juice

Coarse salt and freshly ground black pepper to taste

Using a metal skewer, prick the goose skin all over, but avoid piercing the meat. Submerge as much of the goose as possible in a large pot of boiling water. Hold it there for 1 minute. Remove the bird, return the water to a boil, then submerge the other part. Hold it for 1 minute longer. Drain the bird, and thoroughly dry it inside and out with paper towels. Lay it on a rack in a roasting pan, and refrigerate for 24 hours. Do *not* cover. The intent is to dry it out as much as possible.

Preheat oven to 325°F.

Melt the butter in a large saucepan over medium heat. Brown the goose neck, about 2 ½ minutes per side. Add the sliced shallots, and sauté until translucent. Pour in ¾ cup of the sherry, and add 1 of the quartered oranges. Simmer until the liquid is reduced by one-fourth, scraping up any browned bits. Pour in the chicken broth and the orange juice, and simmer until the sauce is reduced to 2 cups. Strain out the shallots and orange quarters. Remove the neck, and when cool, pull off the meat, shred it, and return it to the sauce.

While the sauce is simmering, place the goose, breast side down, in an oven rack in a large roasting pan. Roast for 1 hour. Remove the bird from the oven, and spoon off the fat from the bottom of the pan, being careful to leave behind any browned bits. Turn the bird over, breast side up, and roast 1 hour longer, or until the skin is puffy and the meat inside the drumstick is fork-tender (the meat is adequately cooked when it reaches 170°F in the thigh, but for it to be tender, it needs to cook longer). A slice at the base of the thigh should reveal no pink juices whatsoever.

Remove the goose to a large baking pan, increase oven temperature to 400°F, and continue roasting until the skin is deep brown and crisp, about 15 minutes longer. Meanwhile, add ½ cup of the sherry to the original roasting pan. Heat it on the stovetop over low heat, scraping up any browned bits. Pour in the sauce made from chicken broth and orange juice. Simmer for 2 minutes. Dissolve the cornstarch in the remaining ¼ cup of sherry, stirring until smooth. Whisk this mixture into the sauce, and boil until thickened, about 5 minutes. Stir in the honey and lemon juice, and season to taste with salt and pepper.

Remove the goose from the oven and let rest for 30 minutes, uncovered, before serving. Carve the goose, garnish with the remaining orange quarters, and pass the sauce separately.

Asian-Style Duck with Peanut Noodles

East meets West in this method of preparing duck. Traditional Chinese cooking requires that a duck first be cured and then steamed before roasting. Although the results are legendary, the process is labor-intensive and takes many hours. This recipe calls for familiar Asian seasonings but, to make things easier, uses the simpler Western technique of roasting a duck. Peanut noodles are a popular accompaniment.

SHOWCASE

SERVES 2 TO 3

$\frac{1}{2}$ cup tamari

$\frac{1}{2}$ cup honey

$\frac{1}{4}$ cup dry white wine

1 duck, about $4\frac{1}{2}$ pounds

3 whole cloves garlic, peeled

1-inch piece fresh ginger, peeled

Preheat oven to 350°F.

Line a roasting pan with foil. Whisk together the tamari, honey, and wine. Set aside.

Rinse the duck, and pat it dry with paper towels. Using a sharp knife, prick the skin of the duck repeatedly to pierce through the layer of fat that lies underneath the skin, taking care not to puncture the meat. Set the duck, breast side up, on a rack in a roasting pan; place the garlic cloves and ginger in the cavity. Brush the duck with the tamari sauce, and roast for $1\frac{1}{4}$ hours. Remove the pan from the oven, brush the duck with more tamari sauce, and roast 20 minutes longer. Brush the duck with tamari sauce once more and increase oven temperature to 500°F. Continue roasting the duck until the skin becomes crisp, about another 15 minutes.

Remove the duck from the oven, loosely tent with foil, and let rest for 15 minutes before carving. Pour the tamari sauce into a saucepan, and whisk in $\frac{1}{2}$ cup of the pan juices. Bring the mixture to a boil over high heat, then lower the heat and simmer the sauce until reduced by half. Pour the sauce over the carved duck, and serve with Peanut Noodles.

For the Peanut Noodles:

½ pound vermicelli or soba noodles

1 tablespoon sesame oil

1 cup creamy peanut butter

½ cup strong black tea

½-inch piece fresh ginger, peeled and finely minced

2 cloves garlic, minced

2 teaspoons honey

Dash of pepper sauce

4 scallions, thinly sliced

Cook the spaghetti until al dente. Rinse under cold water to stop cooking, drain thoroughly, toss with the sesame oil, and set aside.

Put the peanut butter in a small saucepan, and slowly whisk in the tea. Heat the mixture until just melted, promptly remove from the heat, and stir in the ginger, garlic, honey, and pepper sauce.

Just before serving, toss the noodles with the peanut sauce and scallions, using your hands to ensure even coating.

Braised Rabbit with Mustard and Rosemary Sauce

Many recipes that work for chicken also work for rabbit. This elegant dish, wonderful with chicken, is especially so with meaty rabbit flavors.

SHOWCASE • ON A BUDGET • IN A HURRY

SERVES 4

1 cup all-purpose flour

2 teaspoons coarse salt

1 teaspoon freshly ground black pepper

1 rabbit, about 3½ pounds, cut into 8 pieces, or 1 chicken, cut up

4 to 6 tablespoons unsalted butter

1 onion, coarsely diced

1 cup dry white wine

2 cups chicken broth

½ cup Dijon mustard

2 tablespoons finely chopped fresh rosemary

Combine the flour, salt, and pepper in a shallow bowl. Dredge the meat in this flour mixture, and set aside. Heat 2 tablespoons of the butter in a heavy, deep skillet. Brown the rabbit on all sides, about 4 minutes per side, remove to a dish, and keep warm. If necessary, add more butter to the skillet while browning the meat.

Add the remaining 2 tablespoons butter to the skillet. Sauté the onions over medium heat until translucent. Add the wine and broth, and simmer until the sauce is reduced by one-third, scraping up any browned bits. Return the rabbit to the skillet, cover, and simmer over medium-low heat for 45 minutes, or until tender.

Remove the rabbit to a warm platter, and tent loosely with foil. Continue simmering the sauce until reduced by half, stirring often and scraping up any browned bits. Whisk in the mustard and rosemary. Simmer until thickened. Spoon the sauce over the rabbit, and serve.

Smoked Ham and Potato Frittata

Nancy Pritchard, Smith Meadows, Virginia

This frittata is another quick and easy way to create a nourishing one-dish dinner for your family.

ON A BUDGET • IN A HURRY

SERVES 6

      1 cup diced baking potatoes

      1 green bell pepper, diced

      1 red bell pepper, diced

      2 cups shredded Monterey jack, mozzarella, or cheddar cheese, or a combination of the three

      2 cups shredded smoked ham

      ¼ cup finely sliced green onion

      8 eggs, beaten

      2 12-ounce cans evaporated milk or evaporated skim milk

      ¼ teaspoon finely ground black pepper

      ⅛ teaspoon salt

      ⅓ cup finely chopped fresh rosemary, thyme, and chives, mixed together (optional)

Preheat oven to 350°F.

Coat a 3-quart baking dish with butter. Arrange the potatoes and peppers evenly on the bottom, then sprinkle with the cheese, ham, and green onion. In a medium-size mixing bowl, combine eggs, evaporated milk, pepper, salt, and herbs. Pour the egg mixture over the potatoes and cheese. (This recipe can be made ahead and refrigerated at this point for several hours or overnight. When cooking, however, it will need to bake for about 1 hour.)

Bake, uncovered, for 40 to 45 minutes, or until the center appears set and the edges are golden brown. Let stand for 5 minutes before serving.

Onion Pie

Stacey Muncie, Grazey Acres, Indiana

For those who are counting carbs, Stacey writes that this recipe makes an appealing side dish without the biscuit crust. Adding other veggies, such as roasted red peppers or chopped spinach, makes this dish even more exciting.

ON A BUDGET

SERVES 6

For the biscuit dough:

1 cup all-purpose flour

1 ½ teaspoons baking powder

½ teaspoon coarse salt

2 tablespoons shortening

½ cup milk

Preheat oven to 350°F.

Sift the dry ingredients together. Cut in the shortening with a fork. Add milk, and mix quickly just until incorporated, being careful not to overwork the dough.

Using a floured surface, roll the mixture into a rectangle large enough to fit the bottom and sides of a 9-x-13-inch pan. Place the dough in the pan, fold the excess under, and flute the edges. To prevent the crust from bubbling or shrinking during baking, cover the crust with a layer of dried beans or rice. Bake 5 minutes, remove the pan, pour the beans or rice out (save them for your next crust-baking event); increase the oven temperature to 400°F.

For the filling:

8 slices of bacon

3 tablespoons unsalted butter

4 cups thinly sliced onions

8 eggs

1½ teaspoons coarse salt

Freshly ground black pepper

2 cups sour cream

Sauté the bacon in a skillet over medium heat until crisp; drain the bacon on paper towels. Drain the fat from the skillet, add the butter, and melt it over low heat. Add the onions, and sauté, stirring constantly, until soft.

Put the onions in a large mixing bowl. In a separate, smaller bowl, beat the eggs lightly, and add to the onions. Add the salt, pepper, and sour cream, and mix gently, but avoid overbeating—the mixture should remain light and airy.

Pour into the partially baked crust. Cut the bacon into ½-inch pieces, and place evenly over the top of the pie. Bake at 400°F for 20 to 30 minutes, until the crust is light brown or until the onion-egg mixture is set to your liking.

EGGS FROM PASTURED HENS

One of the easiest—and least expensive—ways of incorporating the healthful benefits of grass-fed products into your diet is to enjoy eggs from pastured hens. Eggs from grass-fed hens are relatively easy to find at farmers' markets and natural food stores; many farmers keep a flock of laying hens. If you have never compared grass-fed and conventional eggs, you will discover that the flavor, texture, and color differences are staggering. Grass-fed egg yolks are deep-yellow or orange, they stand up higher when cracked into a frying pan, and they have an astonishingly rich flavor.

Doney's Eggnog

The best way to enjoy wonderful grass-fed eggs and milk is in eggnog—not the corn syrup junk that you find in supermarkets but real eggnog made with real eggs. Although this may traditionally be a holiday treat, my husband requests it all year long. One taste of this stuff, and you'll understand why!

SHOWCASE • ON A BUDGET

MAKES 2 QUARTS

7 eggs

½ gallon milk

½ cup pure maple syrup

¼ teaspoon coarse salt

2 tablespoons vanilla

2 cups whipped cream

1 cup dark rum (optional)

Dash freshly grated nutmeg (optional)

Whisk together the eggs, milk, syrup, and salt in a large saucepan. Cook over low heat, stirring constantly, until the mixture thickens and will coat a spoon, about 1 hour. Pour the mixture into a bowl, and refrigerate for several hours.

When you are ready to serve, whip the cream and fold it into the eggnog. If you wish, stir in 1 cup rum and garnish with a few shakes of freshly ground nutmeg.

Note: My Aunt Katie has a shortcut for this recipe. She heats the milk until it is just lukewarm, or "baby-bottle warm," then whisks in the eggs, syrup, salt, and vanilla. This cuts the cooking time down to about 20 to 30 minutes. However, be careful that you don't heat the milk too much, because the eggs will cook when you add them rather than blending with the other ingredients.

ESTIMATED COOKING TIMES FOR TURKEY

SIZE OF TURKEY	ESTIMATED COOKING TIME
12 to 14 pounds	2¼ to 3 hours
15 to 17 pounds	3 to 3½ hours
18 to 20 pounds	3½ to 4 hours
21 to 22 pounds	4 to 4½ hours
23 to 24 pounds	4½ to 4¾ hours

CHAPTER SIX

Dairy and Desserts

The sweetest milk, the finest cheeses, and why you need a Gustav...

If, on some blustery midwinter afternoon, you long for warmer days, ask a dairy farmer to tell you about summer's milk. You may see the lush, green pastures of summer reflected in his eyes as he describes the butter-yellow color and the remarkable sweetness of milk from grass-fed cows.

The nutritional value and complex flavors that distinguish grass-fed meats extend to dairy products as well, with a few added extras. Like meat from grass-fed animals, milk from grass-fed animals offers exceptional health benefits, due in large part to the proper ratio of omega-3 and omega-6 fatty acids and the high levels of conjugated linoleic acid (CLA). As a result of their pasture-based diet, the milk of grass-fed cows is naturally high in vitamins A and E and rich in beta-carotene, which contributes to its characteristic buttery color. (The exception is milk from goats and Ayrshire cows, which do not process beta-carotene.)

Through her research, Jo Robinson, author of *Why Grassfed Is Best* and *Pasture Perfect*, has uncovered significant findings pointing to the cancer-fighting properties of grass-fed dairy products. A recent Finnish study she cites, for example, concludes: "A diet composed of CLA-rich foods, particularly cheese, may protect against breast cancer in postmenopausal women."[1]

The virtues of grass-fed dairy products are best understood when compared with the products from conventional dairy systems. Cows used in industrial dairies—the source for most store-bought dairy products—are selectively bred, fed special rations, and are treated with hormones (such as recombinant bovine growth hormone, or rBGH) to boost their milk production far beyond their natural capacity. Although confinement-feeding practices may boost the profit margin for large corporate farms, this comes at the expense of the nutritional value of the milk. A study in the *Journal of Dairy Research* reports that the more milk a cow produces, the lower the concentration of nutrients that milk contains.[2]

In addition to producing milk of less nutritional value, the cows from industrial dairy farms have a significantly shorter lifespan than do grass-fed cows. Whereas the pastured cow on a small dairy farm typically enjoys a life (which I believe is much happier) of roughly eight to ten years, the "industrial" cow lives only about half as long before she is exhausted and is shipped to the auction.

Unless you can purchase milk directly from the farmer (which in many cases is illegal in this country), it's difficult to know if milk is coming from pastured cows. Dairy farmers typically market their milk through cooperatives, where truckloads of milk from many farms are pooled together before being processed. Although National Organic Standards require that organic dairy cows be kept "on pasture," they do *not* require that the animals' *diet* be from those pastures. According to the standards, dairy cows could be let out on overgrazed fields (which provide little-to-no sustenance), but their primary diet could still come from grain. (The standards of other private organic certification agencies are often more stringent and may contain specific grazing requirements; check with the agency named on the certification label.)

Fortunately, a growing number of dairy companies are moving to fill the widening niche for grass-fed milk and dairy products. Natural By Nature, a brand of milk produced by Natural Dairy Products Corporation of West Grove, Pennsylvania, states that the cows that produce its milk are both certified organic *and* grass-fed. Butter and cheese from Ireland and New Zealand (Kerry Gold is a common brand in many grocery stores) generally comes from pasture-raised animals. Further, a growing number of small farmers in the United States and Canada also produce grass-fed dairy products; many of them are registered on Jo Robinson's Web site at www.eatwild.com.

The impact of pasture on dairy production isn't limited to cows. Goat and sheep milk producers will tell you the same thing: the more pasture in the diet, the sweeter the milk. In fact, pastures affect milk flavor so profoundly that the characteristics of the finest cheeses may be determined by exactly *which* pastures the animals graze on. In his quintessential cheese text, *The Cheese Primer,* the master cheesemonger Steve Jenkins discusses the Vacherin Mont d'Or—a soft, unpasteurized French cheese that must be made from milk of cows that have grazed exclusively on winter fodder. Indeed, a true fanatic can taste a slice of cheese and tell you whether the animals grazed on clover, buttercups, or even fenugreek leaves.

Like fine wine, dairy products directly reflect the region where they were produced, hence the multitude of fine and artisanal cheeses that can be found in most gourmet food markets and farm stands in this country and around the world. Navigating the world of grass-fed cheeses can be a true gastronomic adventure. However, it can also be costly if you find yourself shelling out money for cheeses that you soon discover you don't like or for cheeses that are delicious alone but that fall flat when you present them in a cheese course.

This brings me to a very important point (and confession): before working on this book, I was, well, a cheddar chick. Although I'd long ago surrendered my childhood Velveeta obsession, my gourmet cheese experiences were limited to bricks of decent extra-sharp cheddar, perhaps served with a crisp fall apple or on a salad with toasted walnuts, dried blueberries, and a balsamic vinaigrette. Occasional bouts of bravery led me to artisanal cheeses that I purchased directly from the farmers who produced them, but whenever I needed a wide selection, I would head to a gourmet cheese market. Unfortunately, those establishments often left me flustered and embarrassed by my own pretenses of appreciation for the many foul-smelling cheeses offered by the in-house cheesemongers. Many a wretched $20/pound cheese has turned green and gray in my refrigerator.

My life in cheese was altered when I met Gustav Ericson, of the Honest Weight Food Co-op in Albany, New York. My time with Gustav taught me that a good cheese guide contributes as much to the quality of my life as a good chiropractor or hairdresser. That person doesn't need to be a master cheesemonger or *maitre-fromager,* but he or she definitely needs to love cheese. Gustav epitomizes the perfect cheese guru. He's humble, open-minded, and generously tolerant of cheddar chicks like me. And like all other good cheesemongers, he understands that an uneducated palate is not a *stupid* palate. Before venturing too far into the world of cheese, I suggest that you look around in your food community and find yourself a Gustav. He'll save you a lot of money. And he'll introduce you to some of the most fabulous culinary experiences you'll ever have.

Thanks to Gustav, my refrigerator now contains an impressive selection of grass-fed cheeses from local artisans and from around the world. With Gustav's permission, I've included some of his lessons here, in hopes that they will help you along your culinary journey, at least until you're able to find your own personal Gustav.

AMERICAN ARTISANAL CHEESE-MAKERS

It's no secret that America is a great cultural mosaic and that many of our cheese-making traditions come from other countries. In fact, the only cheeses that are truly original to this country are Jack cheese from California and Brick and Colby cheeses from Wisconsin.

In Europe, cheese-making is taken very seriously. A number of the finest European cheeses enjoy formal name-controlled status. In France, this is called A.O.C., or Appellation d'Origine Contrôlée. Directly reflective of a region's *terroir,* A.O.C. labeling means that the cheese-makers who are legally allowed to use certain cheese labels, such as Roquefort or Parmesan-Reggiano, must comply with a number of requirements regarding how and where a cheese is produced. An A.O.C. label indicates that a cheese comes from a specific geographic area and that only certain breeds of livestock provide the milk. It also specifies how the cheese was produced and aged, the exact size and shape of the cheese, and of course, the flavor attributes.

When it comes to American artisanal cheese, although the makers may adhere to certain European traditions, they are often unable to use the A.O.C. label. Instead, they come up with their own names, based on where the cheeses were made, such as Great Hill Blue, from Marion, Massachusetts; Pt Reyes Original Blue, from Point Reyes, California; Northland Sheep Dairy's Bergère Bleue, from New York; or Bayley Hazen Blue, from Jasper Hill Farm in Vermont. It is the range of regional characteristics that makes each of these cheeses unique, despite the fact that none have formal name-controlled status.

Even though North America's cheese reputation is generally equated with processed "cheese food," the area is currently in the midst of a fast-growing cheese revolution. Artisanal cheese-makers are popping up all across the United States and Canada. These cheeses are rarely found in supermarkets. Seek out these cheese-makers just as you would pastured meat farmers: look in local food directories, visit farmers' markets, ask around. If there are artisanal cheese-makers in your area, you won't have to look too far before you find someone bragging about them. If you're fortunate enough to live near a good gourmet cheese market in your community, be sure to pay a visit and check out the origins of the cheeses. Today's self-respecting cheesemongers can no longer dismiss the glorious cheeses that are now made within the U.S. borders.

GUSTAV'S TIPS FOR SELECTING CHEESE

Under Gustav's careful tutelage, I learned about the numerous issues to consider when selecting cheese. These include overall appearance, scent, taste, and "mouth-feel." Equally important are the history and culture of the cheese-makers; the *terroir,* or unique flavor characteristics owing to the region of the cheese and even how happy the animals were at milking time. But, standing in front of the cheese counter, I had a difficult time remembering everything I had learned. So now I rely on the acronym PHEET (easy to remember when you're confronted with especially smelly cheeses), which stands for the four primary considerations when buying cheese: PHysical characteristics, Ethnicity, Ethics, and *Terroir.*

Physical Characteristics. Before buying cheese, check the condition of the rind. A cracked rind can indicate that the cheese hasn't been aged properly. Sampling is next. When sampling, first smell the cheese. Although some cheeses taste very different from what their scent suggests, what you smell is an important part of the flavors you experience. Bite into the cheese with your front teeth. Let it linger and soften on your tongue. Notice how it feels on the sides of your tongue, the upper palate, and then the back of your tongue. Each of these areas of your mouth perceives taste differently. When you taste cheese, this mouth-feel is critically important. Is the cheese chalky and fragmented, as many goat cheeses should be? Can you detect crystallization (caused by amino acids that give particular cheeses their unique texture), as you would with a good gouda or Parmesan-Reggiano? Naturally, the desirability of a cheese's unique flavor and texture is entirely subjective. What matters is not what the food critics or local epicureans say, but how it tastes to *you.*

Ethnicity. Most fine cheeses come with a story, reflecting the history and the culture of the people who produced it. All cheeses—whether a British cheddar, a locally made chèvre, or a Spanish sheep's milk cheese—are essentially made from only three ingredients: milk, rennet, and culture. Everything else that makes the cheese unique is the result of the ingenuity and resourcefulness of the people who made it. Years ago, for example, the Swiss developed cheese that could be made in large, 80- to 100-pound wheels that would help them survive long periods when they were isolated by harsh winter weather and avalanches. In the warm Mediterranean, where refrigeration was once a problem, many cheeses are still eaten fresh without aging, and they don't require refrigeration.

One of Gustav's favorite delicacies is a mountain cheese from Switzerland. In his words, this cheese "*transcends* its government-subsidized cousin, Gruyere." L'Etivaz, as it is called, has for ages been produced in the town of L'Etivaz. During the 1930s, as industrial agricultural practices and subsidy policies became more widespread throughout

Europe, seventy-six families from this community banded together, determined to continue using only their traditional methods for cheese-making. They refused to participate in subsidy programs and forbade mechanization (and the use of chemicals) of any kind. They also refused to use any milk that came from outside their immediate area. To this day, L'Etivaz, which continues to be an organic, raw, grass-fed cheese, is still cooked in copper kettles over wood fires and is produced only between May and October.[3]

Ethics. Gustav tells me he has customers who *insist* that they can detect, when they eat the cheese, how well the livestock were treated. Just as with meat, if the animals are mistreated or if they are agitated, they will release stress hormones that affect the quality of the milk. Whether it's possible to perceive such subtle nuances is hard to say, but simply knowing that animals have been treated well—that they lead calm lives and enjoy lush pasture and receive excellent care—may contribute to your dining experience. If you're buying a locally produced cheese, it's possible to find out how the animals are treated. With imported cheeses, you can at least ask if the animals are grass-fed or are raised according to organic standards.

Terroir. Terroir is a French word that describes the regional characteristics influencing the flavor and qualities of food and wine. *Terroir* can include the geology, geography, culinary traditions, vegetation, and even weather conditions of a specific region. The taste of a good single-malt whiskey is often described as reminiscent of the peaty ground of Scotland. You'll hear the same kind of comments about a genuine Bordeaux Supérieur appellation wine, which can come only from grapes grown on specific soils in the Bordeaux region of France. Gustav describes Brin d'Amour, a soft herb-crusted Corsican cheese made from the milk of sheep that graze on the tidal plains, in similar terms. Take one bite of this cheese, he'll say, and you'll taste the salt of the sea and the mineral content of the earth on which the sheep grazed.

The concept of *terroir* is a practical consideration when planning your cheese accompaniments. Foods from the same region, reflecting the same *terroir*, are likely to pair well. For example, a successful cheese course may include the simple pairing of a drop of genuine balsamic vinegar atop a shard of authentic Parmesan-Reggiano, both of which come from the Emiliano Romano section of Italy.

All the characteristics described here—taste, smell, texture, animal welfare, culture, and *terroir*—should be considered when selecting cheese. It makes the whole experience more fun. You'll develop a greater appreciation for cheese. And a dinner party where the food that is served has particular meaning makes for interesting conversation.

Cheese for Breakfast, Lunch, Dinner, and Dessert

I asked Gustav, the cheese guru, to describe for me the quintessential cheese course.

"Which one?" he asked. I was surprised. Isn't there only one? But according to Gustav, a cheese course can be served for breakfast or for lunch. It can be served as an appetizer or as a main course. Then there's the popular after-dinner cheese course, which shouldn't be confused with the dessert course. I was impressed.

For breakfast, try fresh fruit with cheese, but be sure to select a coffee-friendly variety, such as a Fontina or Gruyere. A good Fontina should be rather fruity and almost beefy. Italy's premier Fontina Val d'Aosta (a name-controlled cheese) would be the best-known variety, but Fontinas can also be found among a handful of U.S. artisanal cheese-makers. As for Gruyeres, there are several excellent brands, both domestic and European. Another option is a triple crème, which is a category of silky, buttery, soft-ripened cheeses that contain at least 75 percent butterfat. With any of these choices, it's best to pair them with crusty bread, either a high-quality baguette, a croissant, or a nut bread. Whatever you decide, make sure that the bread has a consistency different from that of the cheese. Eat them together, but don't *smear* the cheese onto the bread as you would with peanut butter and jelly. You want the cheese to maintain its integrity.

An ideal cheese-centered lunch would consist of a small salad—perhaps curly endive topped with a sharp vinaigrette made with champagne vinegar or white or red wine vinegar—accompanied by a selection of three cheeses of varying textures and flavors. Start with a silky Camembert, follow with a Gouda, and finish with a sharp blue. Add a wedge of crusty bread. Be sure to contrast the vinaigrette with the cheeses. You'll want to cut the butterfat with something acidic. Not only does it make the meal more interesting, but the vinegar also helps emulsify the cheese. Ideal beverages for such a feast would be a favorite beer or, if you're feeling celebratory, some champagne or other sparkling wine.

Any cheese course should involve a progression of flavors and a variety of textures. Start with a soft, silky cheese of a subtle flavor and then work up to the ones with the strongest flavors. In between, incorporate a more astringent cheese, such as a chèvre or a Parmesan-Reggiano. Both will leave your mouth clean, which will enhance the flavors of the cheeses that follow. The same caveats apply to a cheese appetizer, main course, or after-dinner selection. The primary difference between each is the portion size (small shards for appetizers and after-dinner selections, larger portions for a main course) and the accompaniments. Although some ultra-chic restaurants might serve a cheese course of fourteen or more varieties, in my opinion (and Gustav's), an ideal cheese course shouldn't exceed an assortment of five cheeses. A cheese course is a social and educational event. You want your guests to enjoy each other's company and still remember what they're eating, without having to take notes. Try serving a soft creamy brie or Camembert, followed by a Parmesan-Reggiano, then an aromatic washed-rind cheese, followed by a chèvre to cleanse the palate. Conclude with an intense blue cheese.

There are a number of wonderful accompaniments for cheese courses. Try a selection of rinsed olives with appetizer and dinner cheese courses. Cured meats add substance to a main course. Dried or fresh locally grown fruits, chutneys, or fruit pastes are perfect for after-dinner and dessert courses. Toasted nuts and hearty breads work with just about any cheese course. For the perfect dessert, try a wedge of triple crème, accompanied by a small amount of strawberries (in season) and a flute of champagne. You'll experience a wide variety of flavors and textures: smooth and silky cheeses; sweet, juicy, and slightly tart berries; and bubbly champagne.

WHAT'S UP WITH ORANGE CHEESE?

I've already confessed to a childhood romance with Velveeta, so I don't mind admitting that coupled with that, I'd always felt that cheese should be orange. Sometime in my teenage years, I was able to relinquish my orange cheese requirement, but one question always haunted me: Why did companies start making orange cheese? I found the answer in Steve Jenkin's *Cheese Primer*, an essential text should you decide to take up a steady cheese habit.

As Jenkin explains, long ago many cheeses naturally had an orange hue, owing to the fact that the animals were on a diet high in (can you guess?) grass. In an effort to restore this effect as cheese-making moved to industrial methods, cheese-makers added coloring agents, such as vegetable and fruit extracts, to the milk, along with a starter to create orange, green, and even red cheeses.

$\mathcal{A}$BOUT PASTEURIZATION

Numerous topics stir up controversy in the dairy world: Grain-fed or grass-fed? Organic or conventional? Hormones or hormone-free? But none seem to stir more passionate debate than the issue of pasteurization.

Invented by the French chemist Louis Pasteur in 1864, pasteurization is a process that uses heat to destroy potentially harmful microorganisms in milk. It's purportedly done to protect consumers from infections and diseases, such as tuberculosis and salmonella, and there is no question that there was a time, before modern sanitation, that it offered important, sometimes life-saving benefits. Some argue that pasteurization continues to be necessary to protect people—particularly immune-compromised individuals—from ingesting anything that might be harmful to them. Milk that has not been pasteurized is called *raw milk,* and cheese made from such milk is called *raw milk cheese.*

In many parts of the country, raw milk cannot be sold legally. Cheese made from raw milk, however, can be sold as long as it has been aged for a minimum of sixty days. Therefore, soft or fresh cheeses marketed in the United States are likely to be pasteurized. The legal issues that surround raw milk vary from state to state, so check your state laws to see what's legal, or visit the Web site www.realmilk.com.

I've long been a supporter of raw milk, and like many other raw-milk fans, I don't believe the benefits of pasteurization outweigh its adverse effects on milk's nutritional value. Raw milk—because it has not been subjected to high heat—retains both the lactic-producing bacteria that naturally fight pathogens and the enzymes that help our bodies absorb the nutrients naturally found in milk. In his book *The Untold Story of Milk,* Dr. Ron Schmid writes that pasteurization results in the loss of soluble calcium and phosphorus, many of the B vitamins (including B-6, thiamin, and folic acid), nearly all of the enzymes needed for proper digestion, and half of its original vitamin C content.

I do believe, however, that in an industrialized food system, milk products are more likely to suffer from sloppy handling practices. These products are also expected to travel long distances to market. Once pasteurized, milk can be stored for longer periods of time, which makes it easy to ship without spoiling. Under these circumstances, pasteurization may very well serve an important role in protecting public health. However, there's reason to believe that good animal husbandry, proper handling practices, and clean equipment do even more to ensure the safety of milk.

Still, it's not uncommon for gourmands to reject the notion of pasteurization as well. For them, pasteurization compromises the subtle flavor of dairy products. Sheep's milk cheeses, for example, can vary tremendously in flavor due to the different breeds, the different times of the year when the cheese is produced, the different pasture vegetations, and even the variations between the morning milking and the evening milking. All of these variables contribute to the flavor of a cheese, creating subtle nuances that may be lost in pasteurization.

The complete elimination of pasteurization policies, however, could pose serious health threats. Doing so would require extensive inspection and accountability practices that could be impossible to enforce and dangerous to expect. In fact, the health benefits of raw milk are occasionally called into question, in large part because most of the research was conducted in the 1930s and 1940s, before the mass industrialization of the American food supply. Fortunately, there are some pasteurization practices that minimize damage to the flavor and nutritional value of the milk. When pasteurized, milk should ideally be held at a lower temperature for a longer period of time, as opposed to the faster and less costly approach of heating it to high temperatures for less time. If the issue of pasteurization concerns you, you may want to avoid ultra-pasteurized products, a rapidly growing trend among some of the more popular brands of organic milk. Natural by Nature, the brand of grass-fed milk mentioned earlier, does not ultra-pasteurize its milk. Contrary to popular belief, ultra-pasteurization does not extend the shelf life of a carton of milk once it has been opened. Once exposed to air, all milk will spoil at the same rate.

I appreciate the arguments in favor of pasteurization; nevertheless, as I noted above, I prefer raw milk and cheese. I'll admit that I participate in the "raw milk underground," networking among like-minded farmers to buy fresh milk directly off the farm, from producers I know and trust. While the sale of raw milk is illegal in many states, it is legal in others. If you're interested in purchasing raw milk, please check with local farmers you know and trust, or visit the Web site mentioned earlier (www.realmilk.com). Here you will find comprehensive information about the benefits of raw milk, as well as state by state listings about the legal status, and places where you can acquire raw milk products.

$\mathcal{R}$ECIPES

LEMON-HONEY CRÈME BRÛLÉE 230

CINNAMON-ORANGE CHOCOLATE MOUSSE 231

PUMPKIN CHEESECAKE WITH A GINGERSNAP-WALNUT CRUST 232

VANILLA ICE CREAM 234

BITTERSWEET HOT FUDGE SAUCE 235

All recipes without attribution are from Shannon Hayes, Sap Bush Hollow Farm, West Fulton, New York.

Lemon-Honey Crème Brûlée

Here's a fresh twist on an old favorite. There's just enough lemon to make this dessert refreshing while maintaining a creamy, mildly sweet custard.

SHOWCASE

SERVES 6

3 cups heavy cream

½ cup honey

7 egg yolks

2 teaspoons lemon extract

2 teaspoons lemon zest

½ cup light brown sugar or white sugar

You will need six 6-ounce ovenproof ramekins and a large baking pan to make this dessert.

Preheat oven to 325°F.

Before beginning, bring a teapot full of water to a boil, and then turn off the heat. Combine the cream and the honey in a nonreactive medium saucepan; stir over moderate heat until the mixture simmers—do not boil. Turn the heat down to very low, and simmer uncovered for 10 minutes. Remove the saucepan from the heat, and cool for 5 minutes.

In a separate bowl, whisk the egg yolks until well blended. Slowly whisk in the cream-and-honey mixture. Stir in the lemon extract and lemon zest. Divide the custard among the six ramekins, and set the ramekins in a large baking pan. Carefully pour the water from the teapot into the pan until it comes halfway up the sides of the ramekins. Bake for 45 to 50 minutes or until the custards are set in the center. Remove the pan from the oven, and remove the ramekins from the pan. Let cool to room temperature, cover them with plastic wrap, and then place the ramekins in the refrigerator for 2 to 4 hours, or overnight.

About 2 hours *but no more than 4 hours* before serving, sprinkle the tops of the custards with the sugar. Place them about 2 inches below the heat source of a broiler until the sugar melts and browns, about 5 minutes. Be sure to rotate the ramekins frequently to ensure even browning. Refrigerate the ramekins until you are ready to serve.

Cinnamon-Orange Chocolate Mousse

This is a serious mousse for serious chocoholics. The hints of cinnamon and orange brighten the flavor and make it unforgettable.

SHOWCASE

SERVES 6

1 teaspoon unsweetened cocoa

3 teaspoons freshly ground cinnamon

4 large eggs

1 cup heavy cream

4 tablespoons honey

8 ounces semisweet chocolate, finely chopped

2 tablespoons Grand Marnier

¼ teaspoon salt

For the garnish:

1 cup whipped cream

6 thin slices of orange (each about ¼-inch thick)

Combine unsweetened cocoa and 1 teaspoon of the ground cinnamon; set aside.

Separate the eggs, reserve the yolks, and refrigerate the whites. In a medium saucepan, whisk together the yolks, cream, and 2 tablespoons of the honey. Stir the mixture over medium-low heat until it thickens enough to coat a spoon, about 10 minutes. Turn off the heat, and stir in the chocolate. Continue to stir until the chocolate has melted and is well blended with the cream and egg yolks. Mix in Grand Marnier, the remaining 2 teaspoons of cinnamon, and salt. Transfer the mixture to a large bowl, and set aside to cool.

Whisk together the egg whites and the remaining 2 tablespoons of honey until well blended; beat until stiff peaks form. Slowly fold the whites into the chocolate mixture.

Divide the mousse into six (6-ounce) ramekins or goblets. Refrigerate for 4 to 6 hours, or overnight, allowing the mousse to set. When ready to serve, top each serving of mousse with a dollop of whipped cream, a dusting of the cocoa-cinnamon mixture, and an orange slice.

Pumpkin Cheesecake
with a Gingersnap-Walnut Crust

Imagine the best pumpkin pie you've ever had and the ultimate cheesecake, and you'll know what to expect from this dessert. Serve it as an autumn treat, or dazzle your family on Thanksgiving.

SHOWCASE • MINIMUM PREPARATION

SERVES 12 TO 16

For the crust:

2 cups ground gingersnaps

½ cup ground walnuts

½ cup melted unsalted butter

Preheat oven to 350°F.

Combine the ground gingersnaps and walnuts; mix thoroughly, and blend in the melted butter. Gently press the mixture into the bottom of a 9-inch springform pan; bake for 10 minutes or until lightly browned. Remove the pan from the oven, and allow the crust to cool while you make the filling.

For the filling:

2 pounds cream cheese, room temperature

1 ½ cups pure maple syrup

3 eggs

2 cups mashed canned pumpkin

2 tablespoons bourbon

1 tablespoon cinnamon

½ teaspoon ground ginger

1 teaspoon freshly grated nutmeg

½ teaspoon freshly ground allspice

¼ teaspoon freshly ground cloves

1 cup heavy cream, chilled

1 cup whipped cream for garnish

Using a large mixer, blend the cream cheese and maple syrup until smooth. Beat in the eggs, one at a time. Fold in the pumpkin and the remaining ingredients (except the whipped cream), and mix until well blended. Pour the filling into the crust; bake for 1 ½ hours, or just until the cake sets in the middle. Allow the cake to rest at room temperature for 1 hour; when completely cool, cover with plastic wrap, and refrigerate for 4 hours, or overnight, before serving. Serve each slice with a generous dollop of whipped cream.

SERVING AND STORING CHEESE

Fine, grass-fed cheese can be costly. Although the price is justifiable when you consider the quality of the milk and the craftsmanship that goes into making these cheeses, you will want to make sure that you maximize your enjoyment.

When serving cheese, take it out of the refrigerator, leave it wrapped in its original packaging, and allow it to come to room temperature. If you're serving a selection of cheeses in a casual setting, it's perfectly acceptable to lay them out on a cheese board. Set a few cheeses on a marble slab in the middle of the table and allow your guests to chip away at them. Be sure to provide a separate cutting utensil for each cheese.

For more formal dining, present each guest with his or her own plate containing a selection of cheeses. Servings should be small shards (unless it's a main course), and the cheeses should be evenly spaced around the perimeter of the plate in the order in which they should be eaten (milder cheeses are eaten first, stronger cheeses last). If you like, add a few accompaniments in the spaces between the shards, such as toasted nuts, olives (unless it's a dessert course), or fruit. A formal cheese course should be eaten with a knife and fork, accompanied by only a small amount of crusty bread and a good bottle of wine.

It is acceptable (and even expected) that you show off for your guests when you present your cheese course by telling them about the PHEET (PHysical characteristics, Ethnicity, Ethics, *Terroir)*. Describe the physical characteristics, mention the people and the culture that produced it, tell how the animals were kept, and divulge a bit about the region. They'll be very impressed. It's also fine to clue them in as to the order in which to try the cheeses.

The rinds on many cheeses can be trimmed away, but soft-ripened rinds (such as those found on brie) can be eaten. When you have finished serving, package each cheese in fresh wrapping (plastic wrap, wax paper, or foil are all acceptable). Even though this grates against my environmental sensibilities, fresh packaging is the best way to ensure that the cheeses are properly sealed. Reused materials will not seal properly.

When buying cheese, you should check that the interior is free of mold and discoloration (with the exception of cheeses in which mold is part of the cheese experience, such as a blue cheese or a Stilton). To ensure the best quality, buy the smallest-possible amount for what you will need. Eat your cheese as soon as possible. Hard cheeses generally last about a month, and soft cheeses will last a few weeks. Do not freeze cheese: the quality deteriorates considerably. When storing cheeses in your refrigerator, keep them in the vegetable drawer.

Vanilla Ice Cream

This recipe, reprinted here with permission, comes from Sally Fallon's book Nourishing Traditions: The Cookbook That Challenges Politically Correct Nutrition and the Diet Dictocrats.[4] *It calls for raw eggs and raw cream, so if you have concerns about using either, you may not want to prepare it. However, if you have access to good pastured eggs and raw cream, this recipe is unbelievably delicious—it's the best vanilla ice cream I've ever eaten. It is also incredibly easy to prepare.*

MAKES 1 QUART

3 egg yolks

½ cup pure maple syrup

1 tablespoon vanilla extract

1 tablespoon arrowroot

3 cups heavy cream, preferably raw, not ultra-pasteurized

Beat egg yolks, and blend in remaining ingredients. Pour mixture into an ice cream maker, and process according to the manufacturer's instructions. For easier serving, transfer ice cream to a shallow plastic container, cover, and store in the freezer.

Note: Sally's recipe calls for 1 tablespoon of vanilla extract, but I prefer to use 3 tablespoons.

Bittersweet Hot Fudge Sauce

This is a beautiful fudge sauce. Unlike the overly sweet (and very expensive) varieties you might find in the grocery store, it has a slightly bitter taste that pairs well with sweet ice cream. This sauce poured over the Vanilla Ice Cream (see page 234) is one of my favorite desserts.

IN A HURRY • MINIMUM PREPARATION

SERVES 4 TO 6 (MAKES ABOUT 1 ½ CUPS SAUCE)

4 tablespoons unsalted butter

½ teaspoon salt

½ cup unsweetened cocoa

½ cup dark brown sugar

1 cup heavy cream or half and half

1 tablespoon vanilla extract

In a heavy skillet, melt the butter over medium heat. Mix in the salt and cocoa, add the brown sugar, and stir thoroughly. Whisk rapidly for about 30 seconds. Add the heavy cream or half-and-half. Whisk for an additional 1 to 2 minutes, until the mixture bubbles and thickens. Stir in the vanilla extract, allow the mixture to cool slightly, and serve over ice cream.

CHAPTER SEVEN

FINDING AND WORKING WITH YOUR FARMER

It's easier than finding a needle in a haystack.

Not long ago, before our food system became industrialized, most nonfarming Americans still had close ties with agriculture. In those days, finding a farmer who could provide fresh food was not a difficult or unusual task. If the grass-fed movement—aided by the sustainable-farming and sustainable-cuisine movements—is successful, direct connections between farmers and consumers will become the norm once more.

Having a successful farmer-consumer relationship requires some effort, but the payoff is worth the trouble. The rise in the number of farmers' markets throughout the country means that finding fresh food is easier now than at any time in the past twenty years or more. But even though some farmers' markets are adding grass-based farmers and some health-food stores and co-ops are including these products in their inventories, you may still need to find a farmer for your grass-fed meat. For the most part, grass-fed meat cannot be found in typical grocery stores. In fact, many consumers are finding that the best selection, the best prices, and the best assurance of quality meat result from meeting the farmer face-to-face and getting to know the farmer's operation.

If you don't already know a farmer in your area, here are a few tips to help you find one:

1. *Turn to the back of this book*. Farmers from all over the country contributed recipes to this volume and would welcome receiving a call from you. Although the list is not a comprehensive directory, many states and provinces are represented, so this is an easy place to start. Be sure to start with a farmer in your region. Supporting local agriculture is an important step toward preserving local food systems. Small-scale family farms make innumerable contributions to local economies and the quality of life in communities.

2. *Do a search on the Web*. The most comprehensive list of farms marketing grass-fed meat can be found on Jo Robinson's Eat Wild Web site at www.eatwild.com. This site also provides a wealth of up-to-date research information about conventionally grown and pasture-raised products. The following Web sites are also worth exploring: www.apppa.org, www.eatwellguide.org, www.greatbeef.com, and www.localharvest.org. Or search online for regional sites such as www.farmtotable.org, www.csuchico.edu/agr/grsfdbef, and www.futureharvestcasa.org. These sites provide directories to farmers using sustainable growing practices, as well as information on finding farmers' markets, restaurants, food co-ops, and health food stores featuring local, sustainably produced foods. The Farm To Table Web site also features recipes and menus for foods in season.

3. *Contact your regional organic or sustainable farmers' association*. Not all grass-fed meat producers have chosen to be certified as "organic," but many still participate with these farming associations. Generally, the directors and employees who work with these organizations know which farms are producing specific products in the area. Many of them may also be willing to give advice about which businesses are the most reputable.

4. *Pay a visit to a farmers' market or farm stand in your area*. Even if you don't find meat for sale, regional farmers are often in close contact with one another. Ask farmers in your area if they know where you can find grass-fed meat and dairy products.

5. *Check your local health food or natural-foods store*. These days, many health food stores carry pasture-raised products. If not, you may want to suggest that they do.

Finally, if you're unable to find a local source for grass-fed meat, some farms and food purveyors will ship. Check the farms listed in the back of this book; others can be found online.

QUESTIONS TO ASK

The best way to know if your food is grown in a sustainable, healthful fashion is to visit the farm and have a look around. Each chapter of this book gives some suggestions about what you should look for when evaluating different types of farms, but you should always trust your instincts. Some of the things you see on a farm may not be picture-perfect; but if the animals look healthy and you like the farmers, it's probably a good place to do business.

Unfortunately, it's not always possible to see a farm for yourself. You may live in an urban area. Your local farm may not be set up to handle visitors. Or you may simply be too busy to visit. But if you do manage a visit or are able to talk to the farmer by phone, here are some questions to get you started:

1. *"How do you market your animals?"* Farmers will tell you either that they sell their animals by wholes, halves, combination packs, and quarters (for beef) or that they sell retail cuts. Buying wholes, halves, combination packs, and quarters is like buying the meat wholesale. You would be purchasing a large quantity of a particular type of meat. Descriptions of the types of cuts you might receive can be found later in this chapter. Buying retail cuts means that you are buying the meat just as you might in the store. Rather than purchasing an entire half an animal, you can buy as little as you want and just the cuts you want. Retail cuts are usually priced higher, but if you like to eat only certain cuts, this is the better way to go.

2. *"Where can I buy your meat?"* Many farmers sell their meat directly off the farm, but they often also go to farmers' markets. Find out the hours that you can go to the farm to buy or the dates and times of the farmers' markets. Also, if the farm is far away, the farmer might offer products through a health food store in your area. Occasionally, if a farmer has a number of customers in one geographic area (or if you order a large-enough quantity of meat or offer to pay a delivery fee), he or she can arrange for a delivery.

3. *"How are your animals fed?"* For grass-fed meat, the first response should be that the animals are out on pasture, but remember: not all farm animals are ruminants; some cannot live on grass alone. Pigs and poultry need to be supplemented with grain. Also, many parts of North America do not have grass year-round. If it is winter or there is a drought, farmers may need to feed the animals hay and grain. If you will eat only those animals that have been harvested off grass, be sure to tell the farmer this so that you won't be sold something you don't want.

4. *"How are your animals processed?"* Again, you should be looking for efforts the farmer has made to keep the animals calm and comfortable. Travel should be limited to the extent possible; farmers should be arranging for livestock delivery to slaughterhouses at a time when the animals can settle down and not be overstressed. The animals should be herded onto trucks quietly. In some states, farmers are even able to process certain animals at home.

WELCOME VISITORS

Here's a little secret: every farmer has favorite customers, which means that every farmer also has less-than-favorite customers. As in any other business, if you achieve the farmer's favored status, perks can be numerous; farmers will often bend over backward for you. And fortunately, you need not be a member of a prestigious country club or present the "right" business card to get preferential treatment. The path toward the bright side of farmer favoritism is easy to follow:

1. *If you're a customer (or want to be), show up when you're supposed to show up.* Farmers lead incredibly busy lives. During the spring, summer, and fall, many will put in twelve-hour (and sometimes even longer) days. In addition to selling you meat, they must build fences, maintain buildings and machinery, tend to the livestock, process meat, pack orders, and then do all the arduous desk work that any business requires. I know many farm families that are not able to sit down to a meal until well after nine at night in the summer. Although they theoretically work from home, when the grass is green and growing, farmers are rarely in their homes—they are usually working in the fields, making deliveries, or running errands. Thus, if the farm is open during certain hours, it's best to go during that time—not a few minutes before or a few minutes after. Farmers may not lock the doors at closing time (as your favorite department store would), but if you show up early or late, you are typically interrupting their chores, a sale setup, or dinner or lunch with their family. If you cannot get to a farm during the appointed sale hours, most farmers will be happy to arrange an appointment. Again, however, punctuality is a must. Farmers will have to stop work for your arrival, and if you're late, they'll be behind for the remainder of the day.

2. *Keep your dogs in the car, or leave them at home.* A farm seems like a wonderful place to bring Fido for a romp, but doing so is actually dangerous. Many farms have guardian livestock (such as dogs, llamas, or donkeys) that are comfortable with people but that are trained to defend their flocks from foreign dogs. Also, although Fido may seem mild

and gentle at home, all dogs are unpredictable. At Sap Bush Hollow, we call them "the chicken killers." Despite their wonderful personalities, many dogs are not used to livestock and some have chase-and-kill instincts that kick in the minute they see farm animals. If you must bring your dog and you need to let it out for a minute, be sure to talk to the farmer first and to use a leash.

3. *Keep a close eye on your children.* Some of your children's fondest memories will probably be of trips out to the farm with you. It's a wonderful idea to bring them along. I can't think of a better way to help a child understand his or her connections to the earth, to the food we eat, and to the broader community. But remember: the farm is not a playground. Never leave children unattended. The hazards include equipment, fences (often electrified), open water, pets, livestock, tools, electrical outlets, chemicals, other vehicles coming and going, woodpiles, knives, guns, and unstable buildings. If you want to bring your child to see the livestock, ask the farmer first. The farmer will almost certainly agree but will want to be prepared so that your visit is safe and enjoyable.

4. *Understand the costs.* Farming is a wonderful way of life, but it is not a highly lucrative venture. Farmers are some of the lowest-paid people in our economy. By selling direct to consumers, many farmers stand a chance of earning the money they need to live while still keeping the livestock in an environmentally sustainable system. However, because they're not participating in a large commodity market or benefiting from our nation's cheap-food policies, the meat will cost more than what you would buy in the grocery store. It will cost more because you're getting more. You're getting healthier food, grown in accordance with a specific set of values. The price the farmer asks enables him or her to continue to steward the land responsibly, and the money you pay goes back directly into your local economy.

5. *Take the time to get to know the farmer.* The sustainable agriculture and grass-fed movements are about healthy, environmentally friendly food, but they're also about making connections, developing friendships, and building community. The relationships that develop between farmers and customers can be lifelong and rewarding.

ORDERING WHOLE OR HALF CARCASSES

For a number of practical reasons, grass-fed meats cost more than conventionally raised, store-bought meats. But if you're one of the growing number of consumers who are drawn to the health, environmental, and animal-welfare benefits of pasture-raised food, you'll find it well worth the price. One way to make grass-fed meats more affordable is to invest in a large freezer and buy whole and half animals. In addition to being less expensive than purchasing retail cuts (buying just one or two steaks or roasts as you need them), you can reduce the number of trips you make to the farm or farmers' market, and you can have the meat cut to your specifications.

To make this process easier, this chapter lists some simple cutting instructions and also basic tips for how the wholesale buying practice works. Please note, however, that there are a number of different ways that carcasses can be cut up. The suggested cutting instructions below are just that—*suggestions*. They include a variety of common cutting options. If you want to have something different, ask your farmer or butcher.

When you decide to purchase meat this way, there are a few important questions you should be prepared to answer:

1. Do you want the bones? Bones make for tasty and nutritious treats for dogs. They can also be used to make soup stock.

2. Would you like any of the organ meats? Many people consider organ meats a delicacy. Others use organ meats for pet food.

3. What size would you like your roasts to be? The smaller the roasts are cut, the more of them you'll have, but the fewer people each roast will feed. In general, roasts serve about two to three people per pound. Pot roasts typically serve two people per pound. A standing rib roast of beef will serve about two people per rib.

4. How would you like your stew and ground meat packaged? The most common options are 1-pound, 1½-pound, and 2-pound packages.

5. What percentage of fat-to-lean meat would you like for your ground beef? Although many people opt for the leanest ground beef possible (90% or more lean meat), this can make for dry meat. For the perfect burger, the ideal lean-to-fat ratio is 80% lean to 20% fat or 85% lean to 15% fat. Remember, fat from grass-fed meat is not a bad thing. It is a rich source of omega-3 fatty acids and conjugated linoleic acid, both regarded as "good fats" or "heart-healthy" fats.

6. How would you like your steaks or chops packaged? The most common choices are one, two, three, or four steaks or chops per package.

7. How thick would you like your steaks or chops cut? The range can be anywhere from ½ inch to 1½ inches. To ensure juiciness with these lean meats, I recommend no less than 1 inch thick.

CUTTING SUGGESTIONS FOR BEEF (AND BISON)

The following are suggested options for cutting a side of beef, which constitutes one-half of a beef carcass and includes one hindquarter and one front quarter. The side of beef is divided into eight primal sections: four from the front quarter (chuck, rib, plate, and foreshank) and four from the hindquarter (flank, round, sirloin, and short loin).

Remember that the size of each carcass varies depending on the breed and conformation of the steer. Also, the size of the roasts and the thickness of the steaks will be your decision. Thus, it's impossible to provide an exact inventory of the size and number of each cut you'll receive. Please be aware that the figures below are only estimates. There is tremendous variation in yields owing to differences in breeds, as well as diet. Since they tend to be leaner, grassfed animals may have lower percentages.

Wholesale beef is usually purchased in one of four ways:

1. *Whole beef carcass.* This may require up to 15 cubic feet of freezer space. Although a live beef animal may weigh upward of 1,000 pounds, the estimated meat yields will be only about 50 percent of that weight (about 70 percent of hanging weight). This figure varies considerably depending on how you have the carcass cut. For example, if you choose primarily boneless cuts, the final weight will be significantly less. To determine the cutting instructions, simply double the amount of cuts you see listed here.

2. *Side of beef.* Again, this is one-half of the beef carcass and includes cuts from each of the eight primal sections, which are listed below. Plan on having 7.5 cubic feet of freezer space to accommodate the meat. The estimated yields would be about 25 percent of the live weight (about 35 percent of hanging weight).

3. *Quarter beef.* Some farmers will give you the option of purchasing a front quarter or hindquarter of the carcass. If you find that you use only cuts from certain primal sections, then this is a good option. However, be forewarned that many farmers do not like to sell beef in this fashion. The hindquarter is generally more popular than the front, and if too many people order only hindquarters, the farmer is left trying to market the less-popular front-quarter cuts. Plan on having 3 to 4 cubic feet of freezer space to accommodate the meat. A front quarter of beef will weigh about 12.5 percent of the live weight (17.5 percent of the hanging weight). A hindquarter will weigh roughly 12.5 percent of the live weight (17.5 percent of the hanging weight).

4. *Split half.* Contrary to the name, this is actually a quarter of a carcass. This is often a popular way to buy meat because it gives the buyer most of the variety that comes with a side of beef and enables the farmer to sell the whole carcass with ease. Split halves include a selection of cuts from all the different primal sections. Plan on getting about half of the different cuts you see listed below. However, because the farmer must divide the primal sections between you and other customers, you may have to be flexible about the cutting options. If you still want a split half but want more control over how the primal sections are divided, try finding another family to go in with you on a side of beef, and decide among yourselves how the different cuts should be made. Allow 3 to 4 cubic feet of freezer space. The meat will weigh roughly 12.5 percent of the animal's live weight (about 17.5 percent of hanging weight).

SOME GENERAL EXPLANATIONS AND DEFINITIONS

Live Weight: The amount an animal weighs while still alive, just before slaughter.

Hanging Weight: The weight of the carcass after slaughter and dressing, before it has been cut. This weight does not include things such as the blood, hide, head, or innards.

Required Freezer Space: Plan on allowing 1 cubic foot of freezer space for 35 pounds of meat.

The price of beef is typically determined by the hanging weight. Hanging weights are generally 55 percent to 60 percent of the live weight of the animals. Your farmer will usually charge you a price per pound based on the hanging weight, and then you are responsible for paying the butcher fees, which often include a kill fee and a cutting-and-wrapping fee. Sometimes, to make things simpler, the farmer will charge you a higher price per pound, which incorporates all the other fees. Occasionally, farmers charge a transportation fee (to have the animal transported for slaughter) and a delivery fee (if he or she must bring the meat to your home). Be sure to clarify these different costs with your farmer before you agree to the purchase.

FRONT QUARTER PRIMAL SECTIONS AND RETAIL CUTS

CHUCK: *The chuck comes from the shoulder of the beef cow. There are three primary options for processing the chuck.*

Option 1: Steaks and roasts

- Cross rib pot roast (a type of boneless or bone-in chuck roast)
- Chuck blade roasts or steaks (Roasts will be thicker; steaks will be thinner.)
- Arm roasts or steaks
- Ground beef and stew beef

Option 2: Ground beef

- All of the meat in the chuck can be made into ground beef.

Option 3: Ground beef and stew beef

- Half of the chuck meat is cut into cubes for beef stew, and the other half is ground.

FORESHANK/BRISKET: *The foreshank is the front leg of the carcass.*

Option 1: Shank cross cuts and ground beef

- Shank cross cuts (These make the best beef stews and can also be used for osso buco.)
- Ground beef

PLATE: *The plate lies just below the rib primal section.*

Option 1: Steaks and ribs

- Skirt steaks or skirt steak rolls (pinwheel steaks) or fajita strips
- Short ribs
- Stew beef and/or ground beef

Option 2: Ground beef and stew beef

- Part of the meat from the plate can be processed into stew beef cubes, and the remainder can be made into ground beef. Alternatively, all of the meat from the plate can be ground.

RIB: *The primal section labeled "rib" lies just behind the chuck, on the upper half of the carcass.*

Option 1: Short ribs and standing rib roast

- Short ribs
- One 7-bone standing rib roast, or two standing rib roasts (one 3-bone and one 4-bone)

Option 2: Short ribs and steaks

- Short ribs
- Approximately seven rib steaks (depending on the thickness), or boneless rib steaks, or Delmonico (rib eye) steaks. *Be aware that typically steaks from the rib section primal are cut only from the smallest end of the rib, where the meat is most tender. So although you can order seven steaks from this primal section, some of the larger ones will be a tad bit chewier.*

Option 3: Short ribs, standing rib, and steaks

- Short ribs
- One 3-bone or one 4-bone standing rib roast
- Three or four rib steaks, or boneless rib steaks, or Delmonico (rib eye) steaks

HINDQUARTER PRIMAL SECTIONS AND RETAIL CUTS

FLANK: *The flank lies behind the plate and is the abdomen.*

Option 1: Steaks and ground beef

- One flank steak (This was the original London broil, but today, London broil refers to any lean, thick steak from the round or sirloin; it usually does not refer to the flank steak.)

- One hanger steak (*Important!* There is only one hanger steak per animal, so if you are buying one side of beef and want the hanger steak, you may have to fight with the person buying the other side. It is a very delicious, albeit somewhat chewy, cut.)

- Ground beef

Option 2: Ground beef

- All of the meat from the flank can be ground.

ROUND: *The round comprises the hind leg of the carcass.*

- Tip roasts (round tip) or tip steaks (round tip steak) or half roasts and half steaks
  Note: Tip roasts are the most tender cut from the round.

- Top round roasts (which are almost as tender as the sirloin tip), or top round steaks (London broil), or half top round roasts and half top round steaks

- Eye round roast

- Bottom round roasts, or minute steaks (cube steaks), or sandwich steaks, or shaved steaks (paper-thin-sliced steaks that can be fried in less than one minute), or half bottom round roasts and half minute or sandwich or shaved steaks

- Ground beef

- Boneless rolled rump roast

SHORT LOIN: *This is the most popular cut of beef, containing the most tender meat. It is located between the rib and the sirloin, on the top half of the carcass.*

Option 1: Porterhouse selections

- Porterhouse steaks

- T-bone steaks

  Note: Assuming the steaks are cut 1-inch thick, there should be about sixteen steaks total.

Option 2: Tenderloin roast or fillets and Top loin steaks

- One whole beef tenderloin or fillet steaks

- All top loin steaks (NY Strip or Kansas City steaks)

SIRLOIN: *The sirloin is located just in front of the round.*

Option 1: Steaks and Roasts

- Sirloin roasts, or all sirloin steaks, or half sirloin roasts and half sirloin steaks

Option 2: Tri-tip, kabobs, and steaks

- One tri-tip roast or steaks

- Kabobs or ground beef

- Sirloin steaks

CUTTING SUGGESTIONS FOR VEAL

Below are suggested instructions for cutting a side of veal. They are divided according to seven wholesale cuts: four from the front quarter (chuck, breast, shank, and rib) and three from the hindsaddle (flank, loin, and leg). Wholesale veal calves are typically sold as halves (sides) or wholes, and the pricing procedure is the same as for beef. Hanging weight is typically 55 percent of the live weight, and the yields of meat (including organ meats and bones) should be about 70 percent of the hanging weight.

Remember, if you are purchasing a whole veal calf, double the number of cuts you see here. Due to variations in age and size at harvest, it is not possible to provide exact information as to the size and numbers of cuts.

FRONT QUARTER

BREAST: *The breast lies just behind the foreshank.*

Option 1: Whole breast (Either bone-in or boneless)

Option 2: Brisket, ribs, and steaks

- Brisket
- Short ribs
- Skirt steaks

CHUCK: *Also called the shoulder, the chuck comes from the very front of the carcass and includes the neck.*

Option 1: Arm and blade roasts and steaks

- Chuck arm roasts or steaks
- Chuck blade roasts or steaks
- Stew meat (cubes) (also used for "city chicken")

Option 2: Stew or ground meat and arm roasts or steaks

- Chuck arm roasts or steaks
- Stew meat or ground meat

Option 3: Stew or ground meat and blade roasts or steaks

- Chuck blade roasts or steaks
- Stew meat or ground meat

Option 4: Boneless roasts

- Boneless shoulder roasts
- Stew meat or ground meat

Option 5: All stew meat or all ground meat

- All of the meat from the shoulder is cut into cubes for stewing, or it is all ground.

FORESHANK: *This is the front leg of the carcass.*

Option 1: Whole shank

Option 2: Cross-cut shanks (used in osso buco)

Option 3: Ground veal

RIB: *The rib is located behind the shoulder and above the breast, on the top of the carcass.*

Option 1: Roasts and ribs

- One 7-bone rib roast, or one 3-bone rib roast and one 4-bone rib roast
- Short ribs

Option 2: Chops and ribs

- Rib chops
- Short ribs

Option 3: Roast and chops

- One 3- or 4-bone rib roast
- 3 to 4 rib chops
- Short ribs

HINDSADDLE

FLANK: *The flank lies behind the breast on the bottom of the carcass.*

Option 1: Ground veal

Option 2: Stew meat

LEG: *The leg includes the round and sirloin and is located in the back of the carcass.*

Option 1: Ground veal and cube steaks

- Ground veal
- Cube steaks
- Cutlets

Option 2: Roasts and cutlets

- Sirloin roast
- Sirloin chops
- Rump roast, either bone-in or boneless and tied
- Cutlets
- Heal of round pot roast
- Cross-cut shanks (for osso buco)

LOIN: *The loin lies above the flank on the top of the carcass.*

Option 1: Loin chops

CUTTING SUGGESTIONS FOR VENISON

These cutting instructions apply to venison, elk, moose, or antelope (pronghorn). Since the sizes of these animals vary greatly, the number of roasts and steaks will vary as well.

BREAST

Option 1: Ground venison

- All of the meat is ground for ground venison or sausage.

Option 2: Stew meat

- All of the meat is cut into cubes for stew meat.

LEG

Option 1: Roasts

- Round roasts
- Heel of round pot roast

Option 2: Steaks

- Round steaks
- Heel of round pot roast

Option 3: Steaks and roast

- Round roast
- Round steaks
- Heel of round pot roast or ground venison

LOIN

Option 1: Loin chops

- The loin is divided into loin chops. You choose the thickness (1-inch is recommended).

Option 2: Loin roast

- The loin is boned out to create a boneless tenderloin roast or "backstrap."

NECK

Option 1: Slices and roasts

- Neck pot roast
- Neck slices (sometimes called "chops")

Option 2: Ground venison

- All of the meat from the neck can be ground. If you like, your butcher can make some of this ground meat into sausage, although he may want to blend it with ground pork in order to allow for adequate amounts of fat.

Option 3: Stew meat

- All of the meat from the neck is cut into cubes for stew meat.

RIB

Option 1: Roasts and ribs

- One 7-bone rib roast, or one 3-bone rib roast and one 4-bone rib roast
- Short ribs

Option 2: Rib chops and short ribs

- Seven rib chops
- Short ribs

Option 3: Rib chops and rib roasts

- One 3- or 4-bone rib roast
- 3 to 4 rib chops
- Short ribs

SHOULDER

Option 1: Roasts

- Boneless rolled shoulder roasts
- Arm pot roasts

Option 2: Stew meat

- All of the meat from the shoulder is cut into cubes for stew meat.

Option 3: Roasts and stew meat

- Either boneless rolled shoulder roasts or arm pot roasts
- Stew meat

SHANKS (FRONT AND HIND)*

* Because there are two shanks, two of the options below may be selected.

Option 1: Stew meat

- All of the meat is cut into cubes for stew meat.

Option 2: Ground meat

- All of the meat is ground for ground venison or sausage.

Option 3: Whole shank

- The shanks are left whole for braising.

Option 4: Cross cut shanks

- The shank is cut cross-wise for use in stews or osso buco.

SIRLOIN

Option 1: Sirloin roasts and cutlets or kabobs

CUTTING SUGGESTIONS FOR LAMB AND GOAT

Whereas beef, bison, venison, and veal carcasses are typically split in half, goat and lamb carcasses are generally left whole. However, to avoid confusion, the cutting options listed below are for a half-carcass. The bone structure and the muscle position of goat carcasses and lamb carcasses are quite similar, so only one cutting list is described for both types of animals.

If you are buying a freezer lamb or goat, chances are you will be purchasing the entire animal, since it is quite small. Thus remember that you can choose two options from each of the primal sections listed. Hanging yields for lambs are typically 45 to 55 percent of live weight, and the typical meat yields are usually 40 to 45 percent of live weight. Hanging yields for goats vary greatly, but 45 percent is average. As with beef, prices are usually determined by the hanging weight of the carcass, plus additional fees for killing, wrapping, cutting, and transporting.

FORESADDLE PRIMAL SECTIONS AND RETAIL CUTS

BREAST: *The breast lies beneath the ribs.*

Option 1: Breast of lamb and riblets

Option 2: Boneless rolled breast and riblets

NECK

Option 1: Neck slices

Option 2: Ground lamb

RIB (OR HOTEL RACK): *The rib section lies along the top of the animal, just behind the shoulder.*

Option 1: Rack of lamb

- One rib roast (or rack of lamb), containing 6 to 8 ribs

Option 2: Rib chops

SHANKS: *There are four shanks per animal, two from the front and two from the rear. Thus, you can specify how you would like each of the four leg shanks cut.*

Option 1: Whole shanks

Option 2: Cross cut shanks

Option 3: Ground lamb

SHOULDER: *The shoulder is the top front of the lamb or goat.*

Option 1: Chops

- Shoulder blade chops
- Shoulder arm chops

Option 2: Saratoga chops

- Boneless Saratoga chops
- Stew meat or kabobs

Option 3: 1 Boneless square-cut shoulder roast

Option 4: Rolled boneless shoulder roast

Option 5: Cubed meat and ground lamb

- Stew meat or kebabs
- Ground lamb

HINDSADDLE PRIMAL SECTIONS AND RETAIL CUTS

FLANK: *The flank is just beneath the loin.*

Option 1: Ground lamb

Option 2: Rolled and pinned flank roast

LEG: *The leg comprises the rear of the carcass.*

Option 1: Sirloin chops, steaks, and ground lamb

- Ground lamb
- Sirloin chops or one sirloin roast
- Leg steaks
- Kabobs

Option 2: Leg roast

- Ground lamb
- Sirloin chops or one sirloin roast
- One whole leg of lamb, or two half legs (a sirloin half and a shank half)

Option 3: Butterflied roasts

- Ground lamb
- Butterflied (boneless) whole leg, or two boneless half legs

Option 4: Half leg and kabobs

- Ground lamb
- Sirloin half leg (bone-in or boneless)
- Kabobs

Option 5: Ground lamb and kabobs

- Ground lamb
- Kabobs

LOIN: *The loin lies on the top part of the carcass, just behind the rack.*

Option 1: Double loin chops

Option 2: Two loin roasts

Option 3: Single loin chops

CUTTING SUGGESTIONS FOR PORK

Like beef, pork carcasses are typically split in half. Farmers will often sell pork in halves or wholes, with the prices based on hanging weight and any other necessary fees. Typical hanging yields for pork are 70 to 75 percent of live weight (less if the animal has been skinned), and the actual meat yields are 55 to 60 percent of the live weight.

Specifying cutting suggestions for pork has been a challenge because of the extensive variety of cuts possible. The suggestions outlined below contain some of the more popular cutting options, but they are by no means exhaustive. If there is a particular cut that you are interested in, your farmer will most likely be able to make the appropriate arrangements for you.

A lot of trim is cut from a hog carcass during processing. Thus, if you opt to have some additional meat ground, you can also choose to have sausage made. The types of sausages available will depend on the butcher's recipes but could include sweet Italian, hot Italian, or breakfast sausages, in a choice of bulk packages or links, as well as hot dogs, chorizo, and any number of regional specialties the butcher has mastered. As you peruse the list of cutting options below, keep in mind that in addition to the cuts mentioned, you will also be able to order from a selection of sausages.

The suggested cutting instructions are for half of a hog, and they are divided into six primal-section categories. Remember that if you are ordering a whole hog, you will be able to select from two of each of the categories.

LEG: *The hind leg produces the largest (and, in my opinion, the best-tasting) roasts from the pig. You can have them cut down to a size that suits you.*

Option 1: Giant roast

- One giant fresh or cured ham, upward of 16 pounds
- Ham hocks, fresh or cured

Option 2: Large roasts

- Two fresh or cured hams, about 6 to 8 pounds each
- Ham hocks, fresh or cured

Option 3: Small roasts

- Several smoked or cured ham roasts cut to a specified size, at 2, 3, or 4 pounds each
- Ham hocks, fresh or cured

Option 4: Steaks and roasts

- Ham steaks or slices, fresh or cured, about 1 pound each
- One large or a few small fresh or cured ham roasts
- Ham hocks, fresh or cured

LOIN: *The loin lies above the pork belly, on the top half of the pig. The most prized meat comes from this cut, and there are many options for how this primal section can be broken down into retail cuts. Some of the more popular ones are listed below.*

Option 1: Chops

- Fresh or cured backfat
- Blade chops
- Rib chops
- Loin chops
- Sirloin chops

Option 2: Country-style ribs and roasts

- Fresh or cured backfat
- Country-style ribs
- Sirloin roast
- Center loin roast, bone-in (rib roast) or boneless

Option 3: All roasts

- Fresh or cured backfat
- Sirloin roast
- Center loin roast, bone-in (aka rib roast) or boneless
- Blade loin roast

Option 4: Chops and roasts

- Fresh or cured backfat
- Blade chops
- Rib chops
- Loin roast

Option 5: Tenderloin and roasts

- Fresh or cured backfat
- Tenderloin roast or medallions
- Loin roast
- Country-style ribs
- Sirloin roast

NECK AND JOWLS

Option 1: Smoked neck bones for soups and jowl bacon

Option 2: Sparerib-style neck bones (fresh, not smoked) and sausage

SHOULDER, BOSTON BUTT: *Also known as Blade Boston or Boston Shoulder, the Boston butt is the top half of the pork shoulder. It sits directly behind the neck of the carcass.*

Option 1: Blade steaks or shoulder blade steaks

Option 2: Blade Boston roast, fresh or smoked

Option 3: Boneless blade Boston roast, fresh or smoked

Option 4: Ground pork, sausage, or hot dogs

SHOULDER, PICNIC: *The picnic shoulder is the lower half of the pork shoulder. It lies directly below the Boston butt and includes the front leg of the pig (hock).*

Option 1: Hock, steaks, and roasts

- Hock, fresh or smoked
- Arm steaks or shoulder steaks
- Two arm roasts

Option 2: Ground pork, sausage, or hot dogs

- The meat from the picnic shoulder can be ground for sausages.

Option 3: Roasts and hocks

- Whole picnic shoulder roast, fresh or smoked
- Hock, fresh or smoked

SPARERIBS AND BELLY: *This is the lower half of the carcass, between the picnic shoulder and ham.*

Option 1: Spareribs and bacon

Option 2: Spareribs and fresh pork belly

Option 3: Spareribs and salt pork

$\mathcal{R}$UBS, PASTES, AND MARINADES

One of the best ways to complement the amazing flavor of grass-fed meats is by applying an herb or spice rub, or paste, before cooking the meat. When roasting, frying, or grilling, this creates a wonderful savory crust on the outside of the meat. Although you might find your-self habitually snacking on this crust as you carve your evening feast, try not to eat it all, or your family and guests will have to bar you from the kitchen in order to protect their dinner.

The most important ingredient in all of these rubs and pastes is the salt. Salt, when applied to meat before cooking, blends with the melting fats and sugars, contributing to the overall flavor profile of the meat (by contrast, when it is added after cooking, it just makes the meat taste salty). Feel free to experiment with your own versions of the rubs and pastes listed here, but always be sure to include the salt!

RUBS

To make a rub, choose a recipe below. Combine all the ingredients in a small bowl. Mix thoroughly. Store any remaining rub in an air-tight container for later use.

BARBECUE SPICE RUB

Can be used to season pork, beef, or chicken.

½ cup chili powder

3 tablespoons freshly ground black pepper

4 tablespoons sugar

3 tablespoons coarse salt

2 tablespoons paprika

BASIC HERB RUB

This will work on pork or beef. This rub is best made in a food processor.

3 cloves garlic

1 tablespoon coarse salt

2 teaspoons freshly ground black pepper

1 tablespoon dried rosemary, finely chopped

2 teaspoons dried thyme

CARDAMOM-CINNAMON RUB

Ideal for lamb, this recipe is best if you are able to freshly grind the cardamom, cinnamon, and cloves, but it will also work well if you have only pre-ground spices on hand.

½ teaspoon ground cardamom

½ teaspoon ground cinnamon

¼ teaspoon ground cloves

½ teaspoon cayenne pepper

1 teaspoon coarse salt

CHICKEN HERB RUB

I like to prepare the mixture in large quantities, and then I store it in my kitchen cupboard. Whenever I roast a chicken, I combine 2 tablespoons of these mixed herbs with 1 clove of chopped garlic and ¼ cup of olive oil and rub it all into the meat and the skin of the bird before roasting.

1 tablespoon coarse salt

1 tablespoon freshly ground black pepper

1 tablespoon dried thyme

2 tablespoons dried oregano

CUMIN-CINNAMON RUB

This recipe makes a large quantity of rub, which can be stored in an airtight container for later use. It is ideal for beef steaks.

1½ tablespoons chili powder

1½ tablespoons ground cumin

1 tablespoon ground coriander

1½ tablespoons coarse salt

1 teaspoon sugar

1 teaspoon freshly ground black pepper

1½ teaspoons ground cinnamon

½ teaspoon cayenne pepper

GARLIC-HERB RUB

This herb rub will work on pork, lamb, veal, venison, goat, or beef. I like to make a double or triple batch and keep it on hand for a quick, convenient meat seasoning. I find it a very handy seasoning mix to take along when we're camping.

1 tablespoon dried thyme

1 tablespoon dried rosemary

2 tablespoons dried oregano

1 teaspoon ground fennel

2 teaspoons garlic powder

1½ tablespoons coarse salt

2 teaspoons freshly ground black pepper

GARLIC-ROSEMARY RUB

This will work well with pork, beef, and lamb.

2 tablespoons dried rosemary

1½ tablespoons coarse salt

1 clove garlic, minced

2 teaspoons freshly ground black pepper

GARLIC, SALT, AND PEPPER RUB

Use this classic blend on beef, lamb, pork, or poultry. You simply can't go wrong.

½ teaspoon garlic powder

2 teaspoons coarse salt

1 teaspoon freshly ground black pepper

MOROCCAN SPICE RUB

A terrific recipe to use when you tire of seasoning your pork with herbs and long for something a little more spicy and exotic.

2 tablespoons ground nutmeg

1 tablespoon coarse salt

1 tablespoon ground ginger

2 teaspoons freshly ground black pepper

2 teaspoons ground mace

1 teaspoon ground cinnamon

2 teaspoons ground allspice

MUSTARD SAGE RUB

Here's a fabulous seasoning blend to show off a tasty cut of grass-fed pork.

1 tablespoon dried sage, crumbled

2 teaspoons dried thyme

1 tablespoon powdered mustard

1 tablespoon coarse salt

1½ teaspoons freshly ground black pepper

OREGANO-SALT RUB

This is another "one rub fits all" blend. It works with beef, pork, lamb, and poultry.

1 teaspoon dried rosemary, finely chopped

2 tablespoons dried oregano

2 teaspoons coarse salt

1 teaspoon freshly ground black pepper

SAGE AND THYME PORK RUB

This is a terrific blend for slow-cooked pork roasts. It is best made in a food processor.

¼ cup dried sage

2 tablespoons dried thyme

1 tablespoon dried oregano

2 tablespoons coarse salt

1 tablespoon freshly ground black pepper

4 cloves garlic

PASTES

To make a paste, choose a recipe below. Combine all the ingredients in a food processor. Mix thoroughly. Store any leftover paste in an air-tight container.

CURRY PASTE

I find this curry paste much tastier than the canned paste available in stores. Use it on lamb.

4 tablespoons curry of your choice
(I use muchi—hot—curry)

1½ teaspoons sea salt

2 teaspoons freshly ground black pepper

2 cloves garlic

⅓ cup olive oil

MUSTARD-ROSEMARY GARLIC PASTE

While I prefer to use this paste on lamb ribs, it will also work on chops and legs.

1 tablespoon olive oil

1 tablespoon Dijon mustard

2 teaspoons dried rosemary

2 teaspoons coarse salt

1 teaspoon freshly ground black pepper

1 clove garlic, crushed

ROSEMARY, THYME, AND MUSTARD PASTE

This is the ideal coating for a roasted leg of lamb.

2 cloves garlic, minced

1 tablespoon coarse salt

2 teaspoons freshly ground black pepper

1 tablespoon dried rosemary, crumbled

2 teaspoons dried thyme

½ teaspoon dried mustard

6 tablespoons olive oil

MARINADES

ANCHO-CHIPOTLE MARINADE

The smoke just might blow out your ears when you marinate your pork chops this way, but your taste buds will thank you.

1 large dried ancho chili, seeds removed

2 cups boiling water

1 7-ounce can chipotle peppers
   in adobo sauce

1 teaspoon freshly ground cumin

1 teaspoon dried oregano, crumbled

1 clove garlic, minced

1 teaspoon coarse salt

1 teaspoon freshly ground black pepper

2 tablespoons cider vinegar

½ cup apple cider

Cover the ancho chili with boiling water, and let sit for 30 minutes; remove the pepper, set aside, and reserve ¼ cup of the water. Place the ancho chili, chipotle peppers, and the reserved water in a food processor. Add the cumin, oregano, garlic, salt, pepper, vinegar, and apple cider; purée until smooth.

SPICY YOGURT MARINADE

This is a delicious way to spice up lamb shoulder or leg chops, especially if you're going to cook them over the grill. It would also work well for a grilled butterflied leg of lamb (although you'd need to double or quadruple the volume).

¼ cup plain yogurt

1 teaspoon grated fresh ginger root

2 teaspoons fresh lemon juice

1 teaspoon freshly ground cumin

1 teaspoon freshly ground coriander

¼ teaspoon freshly ground nutmeg

½ teaspoon turmeric

⅛ teaspoon cayenne pepper

½ teaspoon freshly ground cinnamon

2 cloves minced garlic

Whisk all the ingredients together until smooth and well blended.

Annotated Bibliography

I wish I could say that all the brilliant ideas in this book were mine, but there were a number of other writers and cooks who helped to make it happen. The resources listed below are valuable for anyone interested in learning more about how to prepare meat properly or how to adopt a more sustainable, healthy diet. These are some of my favorite books, and I recommend them highly.

Aidells, Bruce, and Denis Kelly. *The Complete Meat Cookbook: A Juicy and Authoritative Guide to Selecting, Seasoning, and Cooking Today's Beef, Pork, Lamb, and Veal.* New York: Houghton Mifflin, 1998.

This is an entertaining and comprehensive guide to preparing a wide array of meats. I learned to cook meat from Aidells and Kelly—they provide much helpful information for both beginning and seasoned cooks.

Editors of *Cook's Illustrated* Magazine. *Best Recipe: Grilling and Barbecue.* Brookline, Mass.: Boston Common Press, 2001.

This helpful book demystifies grilling. The recipes and techniques are well-tested and fool-proof.

———. *The Cook's Illustrated Complete Book of Poultry.* New York: Clarkson Potter, 1999.

A comprehensive, well-illustrated guide to poultry, this book includes chapters on chicken, turkey, geese, duck, quail, squab, and pheasant.

Fallon, Sally, with Mary G. Enig. *Nourishing Traditions: The Cookbook That Challenges Politically Correct Nutrition and the Diet Dictocrats.* Washington, D.C.: New Trends Publishing, 1999.

You will never eat the same way again after you peruse this well-researched cookbook. Fallon and Enig pair the culinary customs of ancient people with current research on human nutrition to offer a way of eating that is both environmentally sustainable and highly nutritious.

Robinson, Jo. *Pasture Perfect: The Far-Reaching Benefits of Choosing Meat, Eggs, and Dairy Products from Grass-Fed Animals.* Vashon, Wash.: Eatwild, 2004.

A sequel to Why Grassfed is Best, Jo Robinson chronicles the most recent scientific research about grass-based and conventional farming. Includes recipes.

———. *Why Grassfed Is Best! The Surprising Benefits of Grassfed Meat, Eggs, and Dairy Products.* Vashon, Wash.: Vashon Island Press, 2000.

Jo's thorough research and clear, easy-to-understand writing explain the many benefits of grass-fed meat. This is a very handy reference, as well as a wonderful gift for someone interested in learning more about grass-fed products. Jo also maintains a Web site featuring the most up-to-date information on this subject: <http://www.eatwild.com/>.

Notes:

CHAPTER ONE: GRASS-FED 101

1. F. Diez-Gonzalez et al., "Grain-feeding and the Dissemination of Acid-resistant Escherichia Coli from Cattle," *Science* 281 (1998): 1666.

2. J. B. Russell, F. Diez-Gonzalez, and G. N. Jarvis, "Potential Effect of Cattle Diets on the Transmission of Pathogenic Escherichi Coli to Humans," *Microbes Infect* 2, no. 1 (2000): 45–53.

3. Iowa State University Extension, "Livestock Confinement Dust and Gases," *National Dairy Database*, June 1992; B. M. Larsson et al., "Airway Responses in Naïve Subjects to Exposure in Poultry Houses," *American Journal of Industrial Medicine* 35 (1999): 142–49; P. D. Morris, S.W. Lenhart, et al., "Respiratory Symptoms and Pulmonary Function in Chicken Catchers in Poultry Confinement Units," *American Journal*

of *Industrial Medicine* 19(1991): 195–204; J. B. Kliebenstein et al., "A Survey of Swine Production Health Problems and Health Maintenance Expenditures," *Preventive Veterinary Medicine* 1 (1983): 357–69; A. Beetz, "Grass-Based and Seasonal Dairying: Livestock Production Guide," *ATTRA*, December 1998, <http://attra.ncat.org/attra-pub/PDF/grassbase.pdf> (accessed May 1, 2004); D. Herenda and O. Jakel, "Poultry Abattoir Survey of Carcass Condemnation for Standard, Vegetarian, and Free Range Chickens," *Canadian Veterinary Journal* 35, no. 5 (1994): 293–96; T. Gatz-Lambert, "Subacute Acidosis: An Often Unobserved Thief," *Feedlot* 8, no. 3 (2000); B. A. Gardner et al., "Health of Finishing Steers: Effects on Performance, Carcass Traits, and Meat Tenderness," *Journal of Animal Science* 77 (1999): 3168–75.

4. Bruce Aidells and Denis Kelly, *The Complete Meat Cookbook: A Juicy and Authoritative Guide to Selecting, Seasoning, and Cooking Today's Beef, Pork, Lamb, and Veal* (New York: Houghton Mifflin, 1998).

CHAPTER TWO: BEEF, BISON, VENISON, AND VEAL

1. M. Burros, "The Greening of the Herd," *New York Times*, May 29, 2002.

CHAPTER THREE: LAMB AND GOAT

1. C. V. Ross, *Sheep Production and Management* (Englewood Cliffs, N.J.: Prentice Hall, 1989).

2. John R. Romans et al., *The Meat We Eat*, 14th ed. (Danville, Ill.: Interstate Publishers, 2001).

3. S. Gelaye and E. A. Amoah, *Chevon and Its Production*, Agricultural Research Station, Fort Valley State University, Fort Valley, Georgia, <http://www.aginfo.fvsu.edu/html/publications/GoatCenter/gelaye2.htm> (accessed May 21, 2004).

4. James R. Gillesple, *Animal Science* (Albany, N.Y.: Delmar Publishers, 1998).

CHAPTER FOUR: PORK

1. Sustainable Agriculture Network, *Profitable Pork: Alternative Strategies for Hog Producers* (Burlington, Vt.: Sustainable Agriculture Research and Education Program, 2001), <http://www.sare.org/publications/hogs.htm> (accessed May 24, 2004).

2. Lynn Cowan, "On Another Virginia Farm: 'The Other White Meat,' " *Washington Post*, May 30, 2001.

3. Editors of *Cook's Illustrated* Magazine, *Best Recipe: Grilling and Barbecue* (Brookline, Mass.: Boston Common Press, 2001).

CHAPTER FIVE: POULTRY AND RABBITS

1. Joel Salatin, *Pastured Poultry Profits* (Swoope, Va.: Polyface Incorporated, 1993).

CHAPTER SIX: DAIRY AND DESSERTS

1. A. Aro, S. Mannisto, I. Salminen, M. L. Ovaskainen, V. Kataja, and M. Uusitupa, "Inverse Association between Dietary and Serum Conjugated Linoleic Acid and Risk of Breast Cancer in Postmenopausal Women," *Nutrition and Cancer* 38, no. 2 (2000): 151-57.

2. S. K. Jensen, A. K. Johannsen, et al., "Quantitative Secretion and Maximal Secretion Capacity of Retinol, Beta-Carotene and Alpha-Tocopherol into Cows' Milk," *Journal of Dairy Research* 66, no. 4 (199): 511-22.

3. Ari Weinzweig, *Zingerman's Guide to Good Eating: How to Choose the Best Bread, Cheeses, Olive Oil, Pasta, Chocolate, and Much More* (New York: Houghton Mifflin, 2003).

4. Sally Fallon and Mary G. Enig, *Nourishing Traditions: The Cookbook That Challenges Politically Correct Nutrition and the Diet Dictocrats* (Washington, D.C.: New Trends Publishing, 1999), 550.

PARTICIPATING FARMERS

I owe a multitude of thanks to all of the farmers—throughout the United States and Canada—who helped to make this book possible. They are listed here by state. In addition to the products listed here, many of these and other pasture-based farmers sell items such as seasonal produce, honey, and wool so be sure to ask what other farm products they have available.

ARKANSAS

Heifer Creek Highlands
Joyce and Morgan Hetrick
288 Heifer Creek Road
Springfield, AR 72157
(501) 354-5025
joyce@heifercreek.com
Beef: Wholes, halves, retail cuts

COLORADO

Lasater Grasslands Beef
Tom and Dale Lasater
Matheson, CO 80830
(719) 541-2855
www.lgbeef.com
Beef: Retail cuts

**Oswald Cattle Company/
Back Country Beef**
Nancy and Steve Oswald
PO Box 304
Cotopaxi, CO 81223
(719) 942-4361
steveo@bwn.net
www.backcountrybeef.com
Beef: Wholes, halves, quarters, packages, retail cuts

ILLINOIS

Joy of Illinois Farm
Les and Penny Gioja
1689 CR 400E
Champaign, IL 61822
(217) 863-2758
Veal, lamb, goat, chickens, turkeys, ducks, geese, eggs: Halves, wholes

INDIANA

Grazey Acres
Jerry and Stacey Muncie
4014 W Lower Bloomington Road
Cory, IN 47846
(812) 864-2344
Pastured chicken, turkey, eggs, pork: Wholes

The Organic Grass Farm
Melvin and Suvilla Fisher
RR 2 Box 244-A
Rockville, IN 47872
(765) 569-5107
Turkey, chicken, beef, eggs, duck, rabbit: Wholes, halves, retail cuts

IOWA

Malabar Farm
Loren A. Olson, M.D.
3032 Settlers Trail
St. Charles, IA 50240
(641) 765-4356
mbrbelt@netins.net
Beef, lamb: Wholes, halves, split quarters, mixed packages

Tall Grass Bison
Bob Jackson
1858 220th Street
Promise City, IA 52583
(641) 874-5794
tgbison@lisco.net
www.tallgrassbison.com and
www.dietforthesoul.com
Bison

MASSACHUSETTS

Sojourner Sheep
Diane Roeder
502 N Farms Road
Northampton, MA 01062
(413)586-4822
diane@sojournersheep.com
www.sojournersheep.com
Lamb: Wholes, halves, retail cuts

MICHIGAN

Oak Moon Farm
Jack and Martha Knorek
22544 20 Mile Road
Olivet, MI 49076
(616) 781-3415
www.oakmoonfarm.com
Beef, lamb, goat, pork, poultry: Wholes, halves, quarters

MINNESOTA

Liberty Land and Livestock
Connie Karstens and Doug Rathke
61231 MN Hwy 7
Hutchinson, MN 55350
(320) 587-6094
connie@ourfarmtoyou.com
www.ourfarmtoyou.com
Lamb, beef, chicken, turkeys, eggs: Wholes, halves, quarters, retail cuts

Pastures A'Plenty
Jim, LeeAnn, Josh, Cindy, Andrew, Kirsten and Jacob VanDerPol
4075 and 4077 110th Avenue NE
Kerkhoven, MN 56252
(320) 367-2061
www.prairiefare.com
Pork, lamb, chicken: Wholes, halves, quarters, retail cuts

MISSOURI

Roth's Greener Pastures
David and Sheila Roth
11480 Panchot Lane
Ste. Genevieve, MO 63670
(573) 883-7810
dsroth@brick.net
Chicken, turkey, pork, beef: Wholes, halves, quarters, retail cuts

MONTANA

4K Ranch
Ellie and Jim Krise
HC 45 Box 4850
Terry, MT 59349
(406) 232-3436
krise@midrivers.com
Beef

Thirteen Mile Farm
Becky Weed and David Tyler
13000 Springhill Road
Belgrade, MT 59714
(406) 388-4945
www.lambandwool.com
Lamb: Wholes, halves, retail cuts

NEW HAMPSHIRE

Rocky Meadow Farm
Marcia and Wayne LeClair
201 Udall Road
Francestown, NH 03043
(603) 547-6464
wleclair@attglobal.net
*Beef: Wholes, halves, 30#
combination pack*

NEW YORK

Early Morning Organic Farm
Anton Burkett and Laurie Pattington
9658 State Route 90
Genoa, NY 13071
(315) 364-6941
earlymorn@baldcom.net
*Chicken, pork, turkeys, eggs, lamb:
Primarily retail cuts, wholes and
halves by prior arrangement*

Fallow Hollow Deer Farm
Brian and Martha Goodsell
125 Williams Road
Candor, NY 13743
(607) 659-4635
info@fallowhollow.com
www.fallowhollow.com
*Venison, poultry, rabbits, veal, beef,
goat, lamb*

Flying Pigs Farm
Jennifer Small and Mike Yezzi
Shushan, NY 12873
(518) 854-3844
orders@flyingpigsfarm.com
www.flyingpigsfarm.com
Pork, poultry, eggs

Free Bird Farm
Ken Fruehstorfer and
Maryellen Driscoll
497 McKinley Road
Palatine Bridge, NY 13428
(518) 673-8822
pigweeds@telenet.net
Poultry, eggs: Wholes

Freeman Homestead
Rae Ellen and Keith Freeman
8301 Kelly Hill Road
Stockton, NY 14784
(716) 672-8022
freemanhomestead@hotmail.com
*Pastured broilers, turkeys, stewing
hens, ducks, geese, grassfed beef,
lamb, rabbit pork: Wholes, halves and
frozen retails cuts*

Heather Ridge Farm
Carol Clement and John Harrison
989 Broome Center Road
Preston Hollow, NY 12469
(518) 239-6234 or (518) 239-8319
heatherridgefarm@aol.com
*Pork, beef, chicken, eggs: Wholes,
halves, quarters, retail cuts*

Kingbird Farm
Karma and Michael Glos
9398 West Creek Road
Berkshire, NY 13736
(607) 657-2860
karma@kingbirdfarm.com
www.kingbirdfarm.com
*Pork, beef, veal, poultry: Pork
halves, chickens, and pork, beef and
veal retail cuts*

Sap Bush Hollow
Jim, Adele and Shannon Hayes and
Bob Hooper
1314 West Fulton Road
Warnerville, NY 12187
(518) 827-7595
sapbush@midtel.net
www.sapbushhollowfarm.com
*Lamb, beef, pork, turkey, chickens,
geese, eggs: Wholes, halves,
retail cuts*

Skate Creek Farm
Amy Kenyon
1496 County Hwy 12
East Meredith, NY 13757
(607) 278-5602
akenyon@catskill.net
www.skatecreekfarm.com
*Poultry, veal, lamb, pork: Wholes,
halves, retail cuts*

Stone & Thistle Farm
Tom and Denise Warren
1211 Kelso Road
East Meredith, NY 13757
(607) 278-5773 (607) 278-6914(fax)
warren@catskill.net
www.stoneandthistlefarm.com
*Goat, lamb, pork, beef, chicken,
turkey, rabbits, raw goat milk:
Wholes, halves, quarters,
retail cuts*

Sunnyside Farm
Pam and Rob Moore
2083 Moore Hill Road
Nichols, NY 13812
(607) 699-7968
*Raw milk cheese, beef, veal, pork,
eggs: Wholes, halves, retail cuts*

Sweet Grass Farm
Wendy Gornick
5537 Cooper Street
Vernon, NY 13476
(315) 829-5437
wgornick@borg.com
*Beef, veal, lamb, pork, chicken,
turkey, ducks, and brown eggs:
Wholes, halves, and quarters,
combination packs, retail cuts*

Sweet Tree Farm
Judy Pangman and Frank Johnson
138 Karker Road
PO Box 88
Carlisle, NY 12301
(518) 234-7422
sweetree@telenet.net
*Beef, pork, eggs: Wholes, halves,
quarters, retail cuts*

Willow Wood Farm
Judy and Bill Beckman
26 Graves Road
Mechanicville, NY 12118
(518) 664-0750
Chicken, turkey: Wholes

Zu Zu's Petals
Pam Millar
439 Dawson Hill
Spencer, NY 14883
(607) 589-4762
zuzuspetalsfarm@calrityconnect.com
*Poultry, eggs, lamb, beef: Wholes,
halves, quarters, retail cuts*

OREGON

River Run Farm
Jim and Ellen Girt
19224 Swedetown Road
Clatskanie, OR 97016
(503) 728-4561
info@riverrunfarm.com
www.riverrunfarm.com
Beef: Retail cuts

PENNSYLVANIA

Forks Farm
John, Todd, Emily, Anna and
Molly Hopkins
299 Covered Bridge Road
Orangeville, PA 17859
(570) 683-5820
forks@epix.net
*Beef, lamb, pork, chicken, turkey,
eggs: Wholes, halves, quarters, retail
cuts*

TEXAS

Burgundy Pasture Beef
Jon and Wendy Taggart
324 HCR 4103
Grandview, TX 76050
(817) 866-2028
taggart@exprestel.net
www.burgundypasturebeef.com
Beef: Wholes, halves, retail cuts

Lovejoy Farm
George and Henri Lovejoy
465 County Road 3635
Clifton, TX 76634
(254) 622-8836
lovejoy@txun.net
Beef

VERMONT

Westhaven Farm
Lucien and Elaine Hinkle
1724 Sanders Road
Bethel, VT 5032
(802) 234-5653
wsthaven@aol.com
www.westhavenfarm.com
Beefalo, beef: Quarters, halves, or retail cuts

VIRGINIA

Smith Meadows
Forrest and Nancy Pritchard
568 Smithfield Lane
Berryville, VA 22611
(540) 955-4389
info@smithfieldfarm.com
www.smithfieldfarm.com
Beef, veal, goat, pork, chicken, eggs: Wholes, halves & retail cuts

Touchstone Farm
Alan Zuschlag
140 Touchstone Lane
Amissville, VA 20106
(540) 937-6124
info@touchstonefarm.org
www.touchstonefarm.org
Lamb, goose: Wholes or halves, custom cut to customer specifications

WASHINGTON

Earth Cycle Farm
H and Seth Williams
55203 Sobek Road E.
Edwall, WA 99008
(509) 236-2265
earthcyc@ior.com
Beef: Wholes, halves, quarters, split halves

The Rock Garden
Skip and Christy Hensler
952 Viet Road
Newport, WA 99156-9325
(509) 447-4143
hensler@povn.com
www.povn.com/rock/
Lamb, eggs: Wholes, halves, retail cuts

WISCONSIN

Honey Creek Farm
Jim and Ginger Quick
W1532 Bluffton Road
Green Lake, WI 54941
(920) 294-6896
honeycreekfarm@centurytel.net
Beef, chickens, eggs: Wholes, halves, split sides, retail cuts

Kaehler's Mill Farm
Kay and Steve Castner
8707 Kaehler's Mill Road
Cedarburg, WI 53012
(262) 377-5002
kjcastner@americangalloway.com
www.kaysfarm.com
Beef: 25# combination packs

Northstar Bison
Lee and Mary Graese
1936 28th Avenue
Rice Lake, WI 54868
(715) 234-1496, (888) 295-6332
bison@centurytel.net
www.northstarbison.com
Bison: Halves and retail cuts

Sweetland Farm
Karen Bumann & David Schmidt
E3649 550th Avenue
Menomonie, WI 54751
(715) 232-8785
sweetlnd@wwt.net
www.sweetlandfarm.com
Eggs, chicken, beef, cheese: Wholes, halves, quarters and retail cuts

WYOMING

Cameron Ranch
Sara and Pete Cameron
7325 Riverview Road
Riverton, WY 82501
(307) 856-6057
www.cameronranch.com
Beef, lamb: Wholes, halves, quarters

CANADA

Muriel Creek Cattle Co.
Greg and Tina Sawchuk
PO Box 321
Ardmore, Alberta T0A 0B0
(780) 812-2561
bunkyfam@telusplanet.net
Beef, pork, poultry: Wholes, halves, retail cuts

Bar 7 Ranch
Dave and Pat Griffith and Tom and Dana Fehr
PO Box 1942
Vanderhoof, BC V0J 3A0
(250) 567-2860
info@bar7ranch.ca
www.bar7ranch.ca
Beef, pork, chicken, turkey, goat: Wholes, halves, quarters, combination packs (beef only)

Mother Nature's Beef
Riccardo Gorini
PO Box 34
Lake Francis, MB R0C 1T0
(866) 222-0822 or (204) 643-5594
leboeufmanitobain@wanadoo.fr
www.countryquarters.com/grass_fed.html
Beef: Wholes, halves, retail cuts

Daleview Farm
John and Karen Dale
Box 75
Meacham, SK S0K 2V0
(306) 944-4241
Poultry, pork, beef, elk: Wholes, halves, quarters, retail cuts (for elk)

Weber's Pasture Farm
Marvin and Amanda Weber
454 Side Road 10 North
RR #2 Dobbinton, Ont
NOH 1 L0
(519) 934-9906
Beef, lamb, poultry, eggs

INDEX

A

aging, of meat, 21
American Livestock Breeds Conservancy, 87
Angus (cattle), 15
antibiotics, and beef, 11–12
Appellation d'Origine Contrôlée (A.O.C.), 222
apples
    Apples and Calvados Sauce, 256
    Shoulder Chops with Cardamom, Apples, and Apricots, 103
apricots
    Shoulder Chops with Cardamom, Apples, and Apricots, 103
Armenian Lamb Shish Kabobs, ix, 111
Artichokes and Bacon, 163
Asian-Style Duck with Peanut Noodles, 210–11
Ayershire (cattle), 219

B

Backwoods Meat Pie, 42–43
bacon
    Artichokes and Bacon, 163
barbecue sauce
    Homemade Barbecue Sauce, ix, 153
Barbecue-Style Pork Ribs, 157
Basic Chicken Broth, 198
Basic Chicken Nuggets, 194
Bavarian Bread Dumplings, 122
beans
    Boston Baked Beans with Ham Hocks, 166–67
Béchamel Sauce, 57
beef, 11–19
    Backwoods Meat Pie, 42–43
    Beef Burgundy (Boeuf à la Bourguignone), 70
    Beef Stock, 78–79
    Beef Tongue, 55
    Best-Ever Beef Burgers, 49
    Boeuf à la Bourguignone (Beef Burgundy), 70
    Braised Beef with Rich Gravy and Rice, 72–73
    Bulgogi, 40
    Burgers, 48–49
    California Pot Roast, 54
    Chili Brew Beef Stew with Floating Biscuits, 74–75
    Classic Grilled Steaks, 38
    cooking methods for, 81
    cooking temperatures for, 9
    corn-fed, 11, 12
    Feta and Herb Stuffed Burgers, 49
    Fiesta Beef Casserole, 50
    Flambeau Roast, 53
    Flash-Roasted Beef, 29
    Garlic-Herb Steaks in a Bourbon Pan Sauce, 37
    Garlic-Tomato Short Ribs, 68–69
    Grilled Flank, Skirt, or Hanger Steak, 36
    ground, safety of, 8, 14
    harvest process, 18
    Linda's Sauerbraten, 60–61
    Luisella's Boiled Beef, 62–63
    Meatballs in Pineapple Sauce, 51
    Old-Fashioned Beef Stew, 71
    Polish Stuffed Beef Roll, 34–35
    quality of, 13–19
    Slow-Cooker Chili, 47
    Standing Rib Roast, 27
    Super-Slow-Roasted Beef, 30
    Super-Slow-Roasted Rosemary Crusted Chuck Steak, 39
    Teriyaki Short Ribs, 67
    Tom Clack's Deviled Kidneys, 123
    See also cattle; meat
Berkshires (pigs), 134
Best-Ever Burgers, 49
beta-carotene, 219
Biscuit Topping, 75
bison, 19
    Bison Sirloin Steak, 41
    cooking temperatures for, 9
Bittersweet Hot Fudge Sauce, 235
Boeuf à la Bourguignone (Beef Burgundy), 70
Boston Baked Beans with Ham Hocks, 166–67
bouillion, 197. See also broth; stock
Bourbon Pan Sauce, 37
Bowser, Tim, xv
Braised Beef with Rich Gravy and Rice, 72–73
Braised Lamb Shanks, 120–22
Braised Pork Heart, 168
Braised Rabbit with Mustard and Rosemary Sauce, 212
Brandied Pork Shoulder Chops with Apricots and Prunes, 164
Broiled Country Ham Steak, 150
Broiled Lamb Chops, 107
broth
    Giblet Broth, 205
    See also bouillon; stock
buffalo. See bison
Bulgogi, 40
Bumann, Karen (Sweetland Farm), 188, 262
burgers, 48-49
Burkett, Anton (Early Morning Organic Farm), 150, 261
Butterflied High-Roast Chicken with Crispy Potatoes, 192–93

C

cabbage
    Pennsylvania Red Cabbage, 121
California Pot Roast, 54
Cameron, Sara (Cameron Ranch), 60, 98
Cardamom-Cinnamon Rub, 254
Casciaro, Aleta (Earth Cycle Farm and Troedel Place), 51
casseroles
    Fiesta Beef Casserole, 50
    Lamb-Fennel Casserole, 124
    Mediterranean Goat Casserole, 104–5
Castner, Kay (Kaehler's Mill Farm), 127, 262
Castner, Steve and Kay (Kaehler's Mill Farm), 31, 262
cattle, breeds of, 15, 31, 134, 219. See also beef
Charolais (cattle), 15
cheese, 219–26. See also feta
Cheese Primer, The, 220
Cheviots (sheep), 84
Chevon (Goat) Hors d'oeuvre, 101
chicken, 171–77
    Basic Chicken Broth, 198
    Basic Chicken Nuggets, 194
    Butterflied High-Roast Chicken with Crispy Potatoes, 192–93
    Chicken Caramelized in Onions (Poulet aux Oignons), 191
    Chicken Fricassee, 172
    Chicken Fricassee with Wild Rice (or Without), 188–89
    Chicken Herb Rub, 254
    Chicken Liver Mousse (Terrine de Foies de Volaille), 202-3
    Chicken Nuggets, 194–95
    Chicken Pot Pie with Herbed Crust, 200–201
    Chicken with 40 Cloves of Garlic, 186–87
    cone-killed, 173
    cooking temperatures for, 9
    freshness of, 193
    Honey-Glazed Chicken, 185
    Kentucky Baked Chicken, 190
    Lemon Chicken Wings, 204
    Parmesan Chicken Nuggets, 195
    Pasta with Chicken and Squash, 196–97
    Poulet aux Oignons (Chicken Caramelized in Onions), 191

processing of, 173, 177
Shannon's Favorite Herb-Roasted Chicken, 182
Suvilla's Melt-on-your-Tongue Chicken, 183
Sweet-and-Sour Chicken, 184
Teriyaki Chicken Hearts, 199
Terrine de Foies de Volaille (Chicken Liver Mousse), 202–3
chili
Chili Brew Beef Stew with Floating Biscuits, 74–75
Slow-Cooker Chili, 47
chronic wasting disease, 44
chuck steak
Super-Slow-Roasted Rosemary-Crusted Chuck Steak, 39
chutney
Pear-raisin Chutney, ix, 158
Cinnamon-Orange Chocolate Mousse, 231
Clack, Tom, 123
Classic Grilled Steaks, 38
Classic Pulled Pork, ix, 152–53
Clement, Carol (Heather Ridge Farm), 154, 261
Clun Forest sheep, 87–88
Community Involved in Sustaining Agriculture (CISA), 88
Complete Meat Cookbook, The, 67
Conjugated Linoleic Acid (CLA), xv, 219, 242
cooking methods, 6-7, 81, 131, 169
Coopworth (sheep), 88
cornbread
Mexican Cornbread, 52
Cowan, Lynn, 134
cows. See beef; cattle
Curried Goat, 126
Curry Paste, 256
cutting suggestions
for beef and bison, 243–45
for lamb and goats, 248–49
for pork, 250–51
for veal, 246–47
for venison, 247–48

D
dairy, 219–27
desserts
Bittersweet Hot Fudge Sauce, 235
Cinnamon-Orange Chocolate Mousse, 231
Lemon-Honey Crème Brûlée, 230
Pumpkin Cheesecake with a Gingersnap-Walnut Crust, 232
Vanilla Ice Cream, 234
Devon (cattle), 15, 219–27

Doney's Eggnog, 216
Dorset (sheep), 88
Driscoll, Maryellen (Free Bird Farm), 12, 134, 192, 261
dry-aging, of meat, 21
dry-heat cooking, 6
duck
Asian-Style Duck with Peanut Noodles, 210–11
cooking temperatures for, 9
dumplings
Bavarian Bread Dumplings, 122

E
E.coli, 8, 14
Eatwild.com, xv, 238
eggs
Doney's Eggnog, 216
eggs from pastured hens, 215
Onion Pie, 214–15
Smoked Ham and Potato Frittata, 213
Ericson, Gustav, 26, 221

F
Fallon, Sally, 73, 197
farming
as a community affair, 174–76
with kids, 178–80
fatty acids, xv, 3, 15, 219, 242
feta
Feta and Herb Stuffed Burgers, 49
Lamb and Feta Sandwiches, 97
Fiesta Beef Casserole, 50
Fine Cooking, 12, 134
Finn (sheep), 88
Fisher, Melvin and Suvilla (The Organic Grass Farm), 174, 183, 260
Fisher, Suvilla (The Organic Grass Farm), 183, 260
Flambeau Roast, 53
Flash-Roasted Beef, 29
FoodRoutes Network, xv
Fournier, Marc (Sap Bush Hollow Farm), 56, 261
free-range
definition of, 2
meats, 172
Freeman Homestead Moussaka, 46
Freeman, Rae Ellen (Freeman Homestead), 46, 109, 185, 194, 196, 261
French Onion Soup, 80
Fresh Ham, 156–57

G
Galloway (cattle), 15, 31
Garlic-Herb Rub, 254
Garlic-Herb Steaks in a Bourbon Pan Sauce, 37

Garlic-Rosemary Rub, 255
Garlic, Salt, and Pepper Rub, 255
Garlic-Tomato Short Ribs, ix, 68–69
genetics, and beef quality, 15–16, 31
Giblet Broth, 205
Gingerbread Gravy, 61
Gingersnap-Walnut Crust, 232
Gioja, Penny (Joy of Illinois Farm), 184, 260
Glazed Ham in Maple-Raisin Sauce, 162–63
Glos, Karma and Michael (Kingbird Farm), 204, 261
Gloucestershire Old Spot (pigs), 134, 138
goat, 83-84, 219
Chevon (Goat) Hors d'oeuvre, 101
cooking methods for, 131
cooking temperatures for, 9
Curried Goat, 126
Mediterranean Goat Casserole, 104–5
Tom Clack's Deviled Kidneys, 123
Goodsell, Martha, 20
Goose, 9, 171
Roast Goose with Sherry and Oranges, 208–9
Gornick, Wendy (Sweet Grass Farm), 159, 261
Graese, Mary (Northstar Bison), 19, 41, 262
grass-fed
benefits of, 3-4
definition of, 2–3
for pets, 85
principles for cooking, 5–7
grass quality, and beef quality, 16–17
gravy
Gingerbread Gravy, 61
Gremolata, 77
Griffith, Dave and Pat (Bar 7 Ranch), 190, 262
Grilled Flank, Skirt, or Hanger Steak, 36
Grilled Lamb Loin, 108
Grilled Sirloin Chops in a Spicy Yogurt Marinade, 117
Grilled Veal Short Ribs, 66
ground meat, and E. coli, 8, 14
growth hormones, 12
guardians, for livestock, 90
Gyros, 112–13

H

ham
    Boston Baked Beans with Ham Hocks, 166–67
    Broiled Country Ham Steak, 150
    Fresh Ham, 156–57
    Glazed Ham in Maple-Raisin Sauce, 162–63
    Smoked Ham and Potato Frittata, 213
hamburgers, 48–49
Hampshire (sheep), 84
Harira (Moroccan Lamb Soup), 128
harvest process, 18–19
hash
    Venison Vegetable Hash, 43
Hayes, Sean (Sap Bush Hollow Farm), 202, 261
health benefits, of grass-fed meats, 3–4, 85
Hensler, Skip and Christy (The Rock Garden), 116, 262
Herb-Roasted Boneless Sirloin, 118
Herb-Roasted Turkey With Giblet Gravy, 205–7
herbs, 189
Hereford (pigs), 134
Hetrick, Joyce (Heifer Creek Highlands), 52, 260
Highland (cattle), 15
Hinkle, Lucien (Westhaven Farm), 70, 262
Homemade Barbecue Sauce, ix, 153
Honey-Ginger Brined Pork, 154–55
Honey-Glazed Chicken, 185
Honey-Glazed Pork Rib Roast with Apple-Walnut Stuffing, 160–61
Honey Roasted Pork Chops with Apples and Onions, 146

I

ice cream
    Vanilla Ice Cream, 234
Icelandic (sheep), 84

J

Jenkins, Steve, 220

K

Karstens, Connie (Liberty Land and Livestock), 102, 112, 114, 118, 124, 260
Kentucky Baked Chicken, 190
Kenyon, Amy (Skate Creek Farm), 33, 66, 261
Kerry Gold, 220
kidneys
    Tom Clack's Deviled Kidneys, 123
Knorek, Jack (Oak Moon Farm), 34, 40, 106, 110, 260

koftas
    Moroccan Lamb Koftas, 106

L

lactobacillus acidophilus, 173
lamb, 83-90
    Armenian Lamb Shish Kabobs, ix, 111
    Braised Lamb Shanks, 120–22
    Broiled Lamb Chops, 107
    cooking methods for, 131
    cooking temperatures for, 9
    cutting suggestions for, 248–49
    Grilled Lamb Loin, 108
    Grilled Sirloin Chops in a Spicy Yogurt Marinade, 117
    Gyros, 112–13
    Harira (Moroccan Lamb Soup), 128
    Herb-Roasted Boneless Sirloin, 118
    Lamb and Feta Sandwiches, 97
    Lamb Curry Pie, 98–99
    Lamb-Fennel Casserole, 124
    Lamb Riblets in Mustard-Rosemary Garlic Paste, 113
    Lamb Roast with Morel Gravy, 116
    Lamb Stew, 127
    Lamb-Stuffed Mushrooms, 102
    Moroccan Lamb Koftas, 106
    Moroccan Lamb Shish Kabobs, 111
    Pepper Soup, 130
    Rack of Lamb with Mint Crust, 114–15
    Rebekah's Coconut Curry Lamb, 125
    reheating, 107
    Roast Leg of Lamb, 115
    Shoulder Chops with Cardamom, Apples, and Apricots, 103
    Stewed Lamb Shanks, 119
    Sweet and Sour Lamb Chops, 109
    Thirteen Mile Lamb Dogs, 100
    Tom Clack's Deviled Kidneys, 123
    Turkish Lamb Shish Kabobs, 110
lard, 140
Large Blacks (pigs), 134, 138
Lasater, Tom and Dale (Lasater Grasslands Beef), 50, 260
LeClair, Marcia (Rocky Meadow Farm), 72, 260
Leicester (sheep), 88
Lemon Chicken Wings, 204
Lemon-Honey Crème Brûlée, 230
Linda's Sauerbraten, 60–61
liver
    Pork Liver and Apples, 165
livestock, guardians for, 90
Luchon Pork Pâté, 144–45
Luisella's Boiled Beef, 62–63

M

Maple- and Cider-Brined Pork with Creamed Leeks and Apples, 148–49
Maple-Braised Pork Sausages, 143
Maple-Raisin Sauce, 162–63
marbling, 15
marinades
    Ancho-Chipotle Marinade, 257
Masserini, Luisella, and Riccardo Gorini (Mother Nature's Beef), 62, 262
meat
    aged, 20–21
    cooking methods for, 6
    cooking temperatures for, 9
    grass-fed, benefits of, 3–4
    ground, 8, 14
    tenderness of, 13, 63
    See also beef
Meatballs in Pineapple Sauce, 51
Mediterranean Goat Casserole, 104–5
Mexican Cornbread, 52
Millar, Pam (Zu Zu's Petals), 147, 261
Mint Sauce, 115
Minted Cucumber Sauce, 112
moist-heat cooking, 6
Moore, Pam (Sunnyside Farm), 58, 261
Moroccan Lamb Koftas, 106
Moroccan Spice Rub, 255
Moroccan Spiced Pork Loin with Pear-Raisin Chutney, 158
Moroccan Lamb Shish Kabobs, 111
moussaka
    Freeman Homestead Moussaka, 46
Muncie, Stacey (Grazey Acres), 186, 198, 214, 260
mushrooms
    Lamb-Stuffed Mushrooms, 102
Mustard-Rosemary Garlic Paste, 256
Mustard Sage Rub, 255

N

National Organic Standards, 172, 220
Natural by Nature, 220
natural, definition of, 2
Natural Health for Dogs and Cats, 85
nitrites (in hams and bacon), 167
noodles
    Peanut Noodles, 211
Nourishing Traditions, 73, 197

O

Old-Fashioned Beef Stew, 71
omega-3 and omega-6 fatty acids, xv, 3, 15, 219, 242
Omega Diet, The, xv
onion
    French Onion Soup, 80
    Onion Pie, 214–15

Orange Pork Shoulder Roast, 159
Oregano-Salt Rub, 255
organic, definition of, 2, 172
Osso Buco, 76–77
Oswald, Nancy (Oswald Cattle
    Company), 54, 260

P
pancakes
    Potato Pancakes, 61
Pangman, Judy (Sweet Tree Farm), 148,
    261
Parmesan Chicken Nuggets, 195
Pasta with Chicken and Squash, 196–97
pastes
    Curry Paste, 256
    Mustard-Rosemary Garlic Paste, 256
    Rosemary, Thyme, and Mustard
        Paste, 256
pasteurization, 227–28
Pasture Perfect, xv, 219
pasture-raised meats. *See* grass-fed
pastured meats, 172
pâté
    Luchon Pork Pâté, 144–45
Peanut Noodles, 211
Pear-Raisin Chutney, ix, 158
Pennsylvania Red Cabbage, 121
Pepper Soup, 130
Peterson, Kacey and Kelly (River Run
    Farm), 49
pets, grass-fed foods for, 85
pies
    Backwoods Meat Pie, 42–43
    Lamb Curry Pie, 98–99
pigs, breeds, 134. *See also* pork
Pineapple Sauce, 51
Polish Stuffed Beef Roll, 34–35
Pollan, Michael, xv
pork, 144–40
    Artichokes and Bacon, 163
    Barbecue-Style Pork Ribs, 157
    Boston Baked Beans with Ham Hocks,
        166–67
    Braised Pork Heart, 168
    Brandied Pork Shoulder Chops with
        Apricots and Prunes, 164
    Broiled Country Ham Steak, 150
    Classic Pulled Pork, ix, 152–53
    cooking methods for, 169
    cooking temperatures for, 9
    cutting suggestions for, 250–51
    Fresh Ham, 156–57
    Glazed Ham in Maple-Raisin Sauce,
        162–63
    Honey-Ginger Brined Pork, 154–55
    Honey-Glazed Pork Rib Roast with
        Apple-Walnut Stuffing, 160–61

Honey Roasted Pork Chops with
    Apples and Onions, 146
Luchon Pork Pâté, 144–45
Maple- and Cider-Brined Pork with
    Creamed Leeks and Apples, 148–
    49
Maple-Braised Pork Sausages, 143
Moroccan Spiced Pork Loin with
    Pear-Raisin Chutney, ix, 158
Orange Pork Shoulder Roast, 159
Pork Liver and Apples, 165
Pork Sausages with Potatoes and
    Rosemary, 142
Pork Tenderloin Medallions Sautéed
    with Mushrooms and Potatoes,
    151
reheating, 107
Spicy Marinated Pork Chops, 147
Tom Clack's Deviled Kidneys, 123
Pot Roast
    California Pot Roast, 54
    tenderness of, 63
'Potato Pancakes, 61
poultry. *See* chicken; goose; turkey
Poulet aux Oignons (Chicken
    Caramelized in Onions), 172, 191
predators, protecting livestock from, 90
Pritchard, Nancy (Smith Meadows), 32,
    142, 213, 262
probiotics, 173
Pumpkin Cheesecake with a
    Gingersnap-Walnut Crust, 232

Q
Quick, Jim (Honey Creek Farm), 55, 262

R
Rabbit, 172
    Braised Rabbit with Mustard and
        Rosemary Sauce, 212
    cooking temperatures for, 9
Rack of Lamb with Mint Crust, 114–15
Raisin Sauce, 28
Rebekah's Coconut Curry Lamb, 125
Recombinant Bovine Growth Hormone
    (rBGH), 220
red cabbage
    Pennsylvania Red Cabbage, 121
reheating, lamb and pork, 107
ribs. *See* beef; pork; short ribs
Roast Goose with Sherry and Oranges,
    208–9
Roast Leg of Lamb, 115
roasts
    California Pot Roast, 54
    Flambeau Roast, 53
    Standing Rib Roast, 27
    tenderness of, 63
    Veal Pot Roast, 58–59

Robinson, Jo, xv, 219, 220, 238
Roeder, Diane (Sojourner Sheep Farm),
    86, 119, 260
Romney (sheep), 88
Rosemary, Thyme, and Mustard Paste,
    256
Roth, David and Sheila (Roth's Greener
    Pastures), 195, 260
rubs
    Barbecue Spice Rub, 253
    Basic Herb Rub, 253
    Cardamom-Cinnamon Rub, 254
    Chicken Herb Rub, 254
    Cumin-Cinnamon Rub, 254
    Garlic-Herb Rub, 254
    Garlic-Rosemary Rub, 255
    Garlic, Salt, and Pepper Rub, 255
    Moroccan Spice Rub, 255
    Mustard Sage Rub, 255
    Oregano-Salt Rub, 255
    Sage and Thyme Pork Rub, 256

S
Sage and Thyme Pork Rub, 256
salt, 145
sandwiches
    Lamb and Feta Sandwiches, 97
Sap Bush Hollow Farm, xiii, xvi, 241
sauces
    Apple and Calvados Sauce, 149
    Béchamel Sauce, 57
    Bittersweet Hot Fudge Sauce, 235
    Bourbon Pan Sauce, 37
    Homemade Barbecue Sauce, ix, 153
    Maple-Raisin Sauce, 162–63
    Mint Sauce, 115
    Minted Cucumber Sauce, 112
    Pineapple, 51
    Pineapple Sauce, 51
    Raisin Sauce, 28
sauerbraten
    Linda's Sauerbraten, 60–61
sausages
    Maple-Braised Pork Sausages, 143
    Pork Sausages with Potatoes and
        Rosemary, 142
Sawchuck, Tina (Muriel Creek Cattle
    Company), 49, 262
Schmid, Dr. Ron, 227
sea salt, 145
Shannon's Favorite Herb-Roasted
    Chicken, 182
Shaw, Denny, 6, 13
sheep, breeds of, 84–88. *See also* lamb
shish kabobs
    Armenian Lamb Shish Kabobs, ix, 111
    Moroccan Lamb Shish Kabobs, 111
    Turkish Lamb Shish Kabobs, 110

short ribs
    Garlic-Tomato Short Ribs, ix, 68–69
    Grilled Veal Short Ribs, 66
    Teriyaki Short Ribs, 67
Shoulder Chops with Cardamom,
    Apples, and Apricots, 103
Simmental (cattle), 15
skewering, techniques for meats and
    vegetables, 94
slaughterhouse conditions, 18–19
Slow-Cooker Chili, 47
Slow-Roasted Venison in Raisin Sauce,
    20, 28–29
Smoked Ham and Potato Frittata, 213
soups
    French Onion Soup, 80
    Harira (Moroccan Lamb Soup), 128
    Pepper Soup, 130
Spicy Marinated Pork Chops, 147
Spicy Yogurt Marinade, 257
Standing Rib Roast, 27
steaks
    Bison Sirloin Steak, 41
    Classic Grilled Steak, 38
    Garlic-Herb Steaks In a Bourbon Pan
      Sauce, 37
    Grilled Flank, Skirt, or Hanger Steak,
      36
    Super-Slow-Roasted Rosemary-
      Crusted Chuck Steak, 39
stew
    Chili Brew Beef Stew with Floating
      Biscuits, 74–75
    Lamb Stew, 127
    Old-Fashioned Beef Stew, 71
Stewed Lamb Shanks, 119
stock, 78-79, 197. See also bouillon
Stuffed Breast of Veal, 64–65
Suffolk (sheep), 84
Super-Slow-Roasted Beef, 30
Super-Slow-Roasted Rosemary-Crusted
    Chuck Steak, 39
super-slow roasting, 6
Suvilla's Melt-on-your-Tongue Chicken,
    172, 183
Sweet-and-Sour Chicken, 184
Sweet and Sour Lamb Chops, 109

T
Taggart, Jon and Wendy (Burgundy
    Pasture Beef), 53, 262
Tamworth (pigs), 134, 138
Tanner, Rebekah, 125
Teriyaki Chicken Hearts, 199
Teriyaki Short Ribs, 67
Terrine de Foies do Volaille (Chicken
    Liver Mousse), 202–3
Thirteen Mile Lamb Dogs, 100
Tom Clack's Deviled Kidneys, 123
tongue
    Beef Tongue, 55
    Tongue With Capers and Béchamel
      Sauce, 56–57
turkey
    estimated cooking times for, 217
    Herb Roasted Turkey With Giblet
      Gravy, 205–7
    heritage-breed, 187
    recommended cooking temperatures
      for, 9
    Turkish Lamb Shish Kabobs, 110

U
U.S. Department of Agriculture (USDA),
    8, 9, 14, 171
Untold Story of Milk, The, 227

V
Vacherin Mont d'Or, 220
VanDerPol, LeeAnn (Pastures A'Plenty),
    153, 260
Vanilla Ice Cream, 234
veal, 20–21, 32
    cooking temperatures for, 9
    cutting suggestions for, 246–47
    Grilled Veal Short Ribs, 66
    Osso Bucco, 76–77
    Stuffed Breast of Veal, 64–65
    Veal Chops, 33
    Veal Pot Roast, 58–59
    Veal Saltimbocca, 32
venison, 20
    cooking temperatures for, 9
    Freeman Homestead Moussaka, 46
    Slow-Roasted Venison in Raisin
      Sauce, 20, 28–29
    Venison Baked in Sour Cream, 45
    Venison Vegetable Hash, 43

W
Warner/Bratzler Scale (meat tenderness),
    13
Warren, Tom and Denise (Stone and
    Thistle Farm), 101, 261
Waters, Alice, xv
Weed, Becky (Thirteen Mile Farm), 100,
    260
wet-aging, of meat, 21
wet-heat cooking, 6
When Your Body Gets the Blues, xv
Why Grassfed is Best, 219
Williams, H. and Seth (Earth Cycle Farm
    and Troedel Place), 51, 262

Y
yogurt, for cooking grains and legumes,
    73

Z
Zuschlag, Alan, and Steve Burton
    (Touchstone Farm), 86, 120, 128, 262

Shannon Hayes has a Ph.D. from Cornell University in sustainable agriculture and community development. She is a partner with her family on Sap Bush Hollow Farm, a pasture-based farm in New York State. Her essays and articles on food, agriculture, and rural living have appeared in *Adirondack Life and Yankee Magazine* and on Northeast Public Radio. She lives with her husband and daughter in Warnerville, New York.